MOVERS AND MAKERS

T0347488

We live in times of extreme change. There could be no better time than now to interrogate the lives of new kinds of people – movers and makers – who navigate fragility and uncertainty to create with daring, often against great odds. Parminder Bhachu uses their dramatic life stories to uncover what makes for creativity and resilience in times of disequilibrium. What can be learnt from their creative moxie, as innovators outside establishment powers? Why has their creative reach grown exponentially in our globally connected twenty-first century? How have their abilities to innovate been catalyzed without subscription to knowledge hierarchies and monopolies? These culturally dexterous movers who possess movement capital, advanced with every migration, have translated ancient maker and craft skills into transforming modern technology, science, design, architecture and the arts. Generous, inclusive and deeply collaborative, they are at the heart of open-source sharing for collective intelligence, the common good and the maker movement. They invigorate the economies they reside in, greatly enhancing creative capacities and reach. Bhachu, herself a multiple-migrant maker, offers us a model for a hopeful way forward, bringing her unique ethnographic insights to illuminate what can be learnt about thriving in worlds of flux.

Parminder Bhachu is the author of *Twice Migrants* and *Dangerous Designs* and co-editor of *Enterprising Women* and *Immigration and Entrepreneurship*. She is a Professor in the Department of Sociology at Clark University, Massachusetts, USA. She has held a Henry R. Luce Professorship in Cultural Identities and Global Processes and has been a Director of Women's Studies. She has lived in multiple sites in East Africa, the United Kingdom and on both the east and west coasts of the United States.

"Sociologists have been known to spout rubbish about resilience. Don't let that put you off this unusual, stimulating and deeply thoughtful book. Parminder Bhachu has combined lucid analysis and reflection in truly unprecedented ways. The result is as creative as the itinerant mentalities it celebrates. She contributes artfully to the striking patterns that she has identified. The concept of culture emerges from this sparkling survey in enriched form, elaborated and restored from its ubiquitous trivialisation."

– *Paul Gilroy, University College London, UK*

"There are very few writers who understand the complex context of my body of work. I can always rely on Parminder Bhachu to 'Get' the significance of my creative choices like no other. For me, her precious voice from lived experience across four continents gives her analysis of the lives and work of 21st-century movers and makers a singular authenticity. She and I and others like us who have inherited a deep and complex history of movement across borders vibrantly assert our version of the world in defiance of the status quo, particularly in times of anxiety and ambivalence. We tell our stories in ways that only we can. It's the current anxious times that make *Movers and Makers* a 'must read' for today, a feisty riposte to anti-migration rhetoric illuminating a hopeful way for us to negotiate and inspire our collective uncertain future."

– *Gurinder Chadha OBE, Bend It Networks, UK*

"Another fascinating exploration of the creative aspects of migration from an author who is herself an expert on the subject and a living example of the process. *Movers and Makers* covers an exciting range of people and topics: artists, architects, designers, computer specialists and physicists. It concludes with an astute discussion of the immigrant imperative that only the author could explore with brilliant insight and an unparalleled knowledge of immigrant creativity."

– *John Stone, Boston University, USA*

"If, as W. E. B. Du Bois stated, the problem of the twentieth century is the problem of the color line, then the problem of the twenty-first is the problem of immigration redrawing every border we encounter. Or maybe it isn't a problem but a solution. As Lytton Strachey did in *Eminent Victorians*, Parminder Bhachu curates for us a portrait gallery of individuals whose odysseys are as admirable as they are emblematic. The cumulative effect is arresting: we are not only who we are but who we share our epoch with. There is much to learn from these characters, primarily that an itinerant life, yours and that of your ancestors, defines your DNA and the way you think of 'home'."

– *Ilan Stavans, Amherst College, USA*

MOVERS AND MAKERS

Uncertainty, Resilience and Migrant Creativity in Worlds of Flux

Parminder Bhachu

Routledge
Taylor & Francis Group

LONDON AND NEW YORK

First published 2021
by Routledge
2 Park Square, Milton Park, Abingdon, Oxon OX14 4RN

and by Routledge
52 Vanderbilt Avenue, New York, NY 10017

Routledge is an imprint of the Taylor & Francis Group, an informa business

© 2021 Parminder Bhachu

British Library Cataloguing-in-Publication Data
A catalogue record for this book is available from the British Library

Library of Congress Cataloging-in-Publication Data
Names: Bhachu, Parminder, author.
Title: Movers and makers : uncertainty, resilience, and migrant creativity in worlds of flux / Parminder Bhachu.
Description: Abingdon, Oxon ; New York, NY : Routledge, 2021. |
Includes bibliographical references and index.
Identifiers: LCCN 2020043941 (print) | LCCN 2020043942 (ebook) |
ISBN 9781472589224 (hardback) | ISBN 9781472589231 (paperback) |
ISBN 9781003086154 (ebook)
Subjects: LCSH: Immigrant business enterprises—Case studies. |
Artisans—Foreign countries—Social conditions—Case studies. |
Foreign workers—Case studies. | Immigrants—Economic conditions—
Case studies. | Emigration and immigration—Economic aspects—
Case studies. | Cultural industries—Case studies. |
Human capital. | Labor and globalization.
Classification: LCC HD2360 .B435 2021 (print) |
LCC HD2360 (ebook) | DDC 338.092/6912—dc23
LC record available at https://lccn.loc.gov/2020043941
LC ebook record available at https://lccn.loc.gov/2020043942

ISBN: 978-1-472-58922-4 (hbk)
ISBN: 978-1-472-58923-1 (pbk)
ISBN: 978-1-003-08615-4 (ebk)

Typeset in Bembo
by Newgen Publishing UK

I dedicate this book to my mother, Sartaj Kaur Bhachu, whose confidence and deep love for me have remained the central plinths of my life. My mother and father Kartar Singh Bhachu both died some years ago. I know they are with me at all times and sustain me in all my many journeys.

I have no interest in writing a sedated connoisseurial history of porcelain… I say come on in and come on this journey and discover… real human beings who have lived interesting and complicated lives, often with enormous difficulty but creatively.
Edmund de Waal, quoted in an article by Alistair Sooke, in *The Telegraph*, September 22, 2015[1]

As I grow older I become more and more interested in craftsmen – glass blowers, potters, makers of textiles.
A. S. Byatt, *Peacock & Vine: On William Morris and Mariano Fortuny*, 2016[2]

Migrations, with all the incidental collision, conflicts, and fusions of peoples and of cultures which they occasion, have been accounted among the most decisive forces in history.
Every advance in culture, it has been said, commences with a new period of migration and movement of populations… In both cases the "cake of custom" is broken and the individual is freed for new enterprises and new associations.
Robert Ezra Park, 'Human Migration and the Marginal Man', in *The American Journal of Sociology*, Vol. 33, No. 6 (May 1928)

Notes

1 With thanks to Alistair Sooke, Edmund de Waal and *The Telegraph*.
2 Excerpt(s) from *Peacock & Vine: On William Morris and Mariano Fortuny* by A. S. Byatt, copyright © 2016 by A. S. Byatt. Used by permission of Alfred A. Knopf, an imprint of the Knopf Doubleday Publishing Group, a division of Penguin Random House LLC. All rights reserved.
    The Agreed Upon 18 Words from *Peacock & Vine* by A.S. Byatt. Published by Penguin Random House, 2016. Copyright © A.S. Byatt. Reproduced by permission of the author c/o Rogers, Coleridge & White Ltd., 20 Powis Mews, London W111JN.

CONTENTS

FIGURES

ACKNOWLEDGEMENTS

This book has been a long time in the making. In between there was an extreme rupture in my life. My house burned down. I started all over again.

Many people helped me to reconstruct my life and this book.

Two utterly wonderful and thoughtful intellectual companions in particular have been with me throughout the thinking and writing process and have patiently and diligently helped me distill the book's ideas and themes. My simply brilliant and imaginative colleague at Clark, Professor Nancy Budwig in the Department of Psychology, gets at once to the significance of ideas and how they relate to analogous developments in many fields of intellect and practice which she commands expansively. She also kept me emotionally strong and made me believe in myself and my style of thinking and being in the world when I might have otherwise floundered. My second intellectual companion of old is Professor James Paul Gee, a former Clark colleague, and the current Mary Lou Fulton Presidential Professor of Literary Studies and a Regents' Professor at Arizona State University. Supremely generous in distributing his comprehensive knowledge of technology, media, popular culture and more, he allowed me to draw on his phenomenal intellectual prowess to give life to my own ideas. I am so lucky and grateful to have two such generous and munificent friends: I thank them both from the bottom-most cockles of my heart.

My former Clark colleagues, Professors Cynthia Enloe, Fern Johnson and Jody Emel, have all played such an important part in my life at Clark. They did not allow me to falter at critical times in my life, encouraging me and always believing in my work. There is no one like Cynthia Enloe in immediately grasping inchoate thoughts discussed with her and inculcating supreme confidence that one will succeed in presenting them powerfully.

Indeed, I thank all my colleagues at Clark University, so many of whom have been wonderful as friends in my thirty years here. Cathy Spingler is the most lovely, thoughtful and generous friend who took care of me within a few hours after my house fire till I found my feet. She welcomed me into her home and responded with supreme sensitivity to the traumatized person that I was at the time. Sarah Buie and Walter Wright are my thoughtful and kind friends who were especially generous towards me during the transition phase after my house fire when I lived in the same apartment complex as they do. My thanks, too, to colleagues Donna and Stephen Dirado for their exceptionally warm friendship and for inviting me to their home for weekly salons of creative people from all walks of life. These meetings of camaraderie and heterogenous conversations are a source of enormous stimulation and enrich my life in sumptuous ways. During this isolating lockdown period enforced by Covid-19, Stephen's in-person salons have mutated into trans-continental Zoom events. Each cyber-*adda* (to use the Indian word for a conversational gathering) now generates vivid, effortless and collaborative exchanges of ideas, knowledge and friendship across borders. Stephen's incomparable warmth, inclusiveness and conduit-generating prowess make him a splendid example of the sharism of makers and movers that I have described in this book.

I also want to thank my thoughtful and kind departmental colleagues for supporting me through some difficult times and in allowing me time to finish this book. I am especially grateful to Professor Patty Ewick for reading my initial book proposal finely and for saying some wonderfully encouraging things that made me want to get on with it and finish it.

What wonderful and generous colleagues, my pure good luck and joy to be with them and to have them in my life!

I owe many, many thanks to my siblings. My brother Binny Bhachu, who has lived in the realms of design and creativity all his life in East Africa, Europe, in particular Switzerland and Scandinavia, has been a determining influence on my life. To think and create through someone else's framework for him is a heinous crime. To imitate someone else is to lose one's style of thought and being in the world. After all, he said repeatedly, "They will always be better at it that you are. It is *their* frame of thinking and creating and not yours. Why give your power to someone else? You should fight for your own space and voice and fight hard". His deeply ingrained *modus vivendi* is one that his three sisters have all absorbed – that one must render one's creativity and be in the world according to one's own sensibilities, ethnicity and family history, and do so assertively. Such confidence-inspiring advice has been critical to me and for so many of us who are people of color and migrants outside the establishment status quo. It was Binny, too, who had observed our grandfather at work and educated me about our own making-and-moving family history, the complex peregrinations of earlier generations and their sophisticated, high-order maker skills.

My sister, Bindey Sehmi, is a *jugaadhan* par excellence and a true inheritor of my grandfather's master craftsman's skills that I describe in Chapter 1 of this book. She has a cutting-edge, much admired personal style which she operationalizes in a wide range of maker domains. When I could barely sew "Very Easy Vogue" patterns which required but basic skills, she could create designer garments requiring an exquisite level of execution, and similarly with the most complex knitting and crochet patterns, and embroidery designs. To boot, she constructed Bauhaus-y furniture for her first home after her marriage and executes all kinds of decoration projects, transforming existing objects into things of function and beauty. I am so grateful for her influence on me, one that undergirds my writing, thinking and sartorial styles.

My sister Baley and her husband Kanwarjeet Panesar came to look after me immediately after my house fire. They made sure my mind was orientated to an optimistic future and not the past. They found me a lovely house and did all the things that allowed me to restart my life and carry on my work with speed. My sister Baley's wonderful sense of humor and her ability to decode people finely, and mimic them with absolute precision, make for a mesmeric way of being in the world. My brother-in-law's help after the fire in negotiating with every interested agency, agent and institution – and there were many – made me so appreciative to have a hyper-efficient, assertive and humorous collaborator whom all those he came into contact with here in Worcester came to love and admire. I am truly grateful for both his and Baley's rapid and supremely effective interventions which got me going again post-fire: this book would not have been completed without them.

My closest and oldest of pals, Sasha Josephides, has made me finish all my books. She is wonderful at making me focus and write. I could not have done any of my writing without her sage advice.

A high-profile and rare cultural producer from the multiply migrant background shared both by the case studies in this book and myself, and a close friend with whom I have over the years discussed many of its ideas and themes, is film director Gurinder Chadha: I thank her for her insight, wit and wisdom. A chapter in this book, as originally intended, on her now considerable corpus and life was simply not enough to do justice to her incredibly prolific and successful career; a book-length project beckons.

My pal Jane Singh at Berkeley, California, has shared many journeys, conversations, happenings for more than four decades, and has given me her deep friendship in the most tolerant and wonderful ways in which only she could. Born and raised in California, a daughter of the first South Asian pioneers in the United States, like me she is the progeny of path-breaking migrants of the late nineteenth and early twentieth century, albeit in different continents. The profound connection I have with her through shared migration and cultural background is rare and matchless: thank you, Jane.

Bhajan Hunjan, the wonderful artist whose life and creativity I write about in Chapter 3 of this book, has designed the beautiful book cover. I thank her for doing this, a project that she had agreed to do many years ago. It has taken so much longer for me to take it to fruition. I am eternally grateful for her time over the years and her supreme patience for so long. Her generosity is in a class of her own. She is a rare and bountiful artistic priestess.

My precious London friends whom I have known for many decades, some of whom I have worked with at British universities, include Professors John Solomos at the University of Warwick, Michael Keith at the University of Oxford, Gargi

Bhattacharyya at the University of East London, Karim Murji at the University of West London and Les Back at Goldsmiths College, University of London. Professor Les Back has been critical to the making of this book: he suggested its title and helped frame its nascent themes at a time when I hardly knew what I wanted to focus on. I did not realize until the end of this enterprise how significant his earlier intervention was, which I cite in the penultimate paragraph of my concluding chapter.

I could not have finished this book without the insightful guidance of my writing goddess Susanne Morgan, who took me through this project from the time I got the book contract to the final submission of the manuscript to the publishers. She helped me develop the discipline to get on with the book despite tight teaching and campus schedules. She has been my writing therapist, a decoder of my moods, and someone who refused to brook any negative thoughts or excuses on my part.

What would I have done without my fabulous editor Judith Barrett, my long-term organizer of text and ruthless exciser of excess words? Thank you, Judith, for getting inside my mind and "getting it" with such unselfconscious ease, for your keen editorial skills and multifaceted expertise in many domains of publishing. You are a "maker" par excellence, an accomplished crafter of fine prose.

Many thanks are due, too, to those who facilitated my access to the individuals whose lives and work constitute the case studies in this book: Rishi Rich, who opened the path for me to interview Jay Sean; and Vina Bhogal who introduced me to Amarjit Kalsi; and Satwinder Sadhal, Professor of Aerospace and Mechanical Engineering and Ophthalmology at the University of Southern California, and his late older brother Kuldeep Sadhal who, together with Lakhbir Virdee – himself a distinguished scientist – put me in touch with Tejinder Virdee.

And, of course, my heartfelt thanks go to the individuals who allowed me to intrude on their lives and gave me permission to interrogate and to write about them. This book would not exist without their support and time. So many of them have allowed me to follow their careers for more than three decades and have given generously of their time and also intellect in multiple interviews I have conducted with them over the years. I have hung around their studios and viewed their creative work as it emerged and was then rendered fully. There are others whom I met in the later phases of my research, especially those in the worlds of technology and science, my interest in their lives from a cultural and migrant creativity perspective piqued by a persuasive conversation I had with Professor Sati Sadhal, who first suggested that I write about migrant makers in the realms of science and technology, viewed through my culturally and migration-orientated lens. This is an area I will pursue centrally in the next phase of my intellectual career, to investigate and explore the mechanisms and conduits through which ancient craft and technical capital has traveled and been translated into sophisticated modern science, engineering and technology, that is, all the building, construction and maker domains.

I have not mentioned many other generous people who have helped in making this book. Many on both sides of the Atlantic have been fellow travelers and co-collaborators: I thank them all, each and every one, for their contributions to my life and work.

A website to accompany the book can be found at: https://parminderbhachu55.wixsite.com/moversandmakers

The Movers and Makers channel develops the themes of *Movers and Makers: Uncertainty, Resilience, and Migrant Creativity in Worlds of Flux*. Parminder Bhachu interviews the creative people she writes about in the book, and others: www.youtube.com/channel/UCXdwTYasF3n3qmCCeQDCxLw/featured

INTRODUCTION

In March 2015, my house burned down completely within half an hour, with all my possessions. Also lost were the research materials I had collected for this book, along with draft chapters and many of my notes. I have since rebuilt my life, acquired new possessions and worked on reconstructing this book from what was left of a burnt computer and hard-drive. I did all this within a short period of a few months.

This experience of extreme disruption, which could potentially have had devastating consequences, has led me to dwell at length on issues of resilience, disruption, disequilibrium and uncertainty. They loom large in my life and have done so from childhood, and they take up a great deal of space in my mind and my thinking. These are also issues that are central to my long-term intellectual trajectory and my biography of multiple migrations across international and national borders. A generational history of movement, of making and remaking, has shaped my life and that of my grandparents and parents – all of us makers and movers.

These are the themes that govern this book. I interrogate what makes people who move remain resilient and vibrant in a world defined by conditions of flux, liquidity and dissonance. I explore the concept of movement capital which is accrued in the diaspora, a migrant and movement phenomenon, particularly among those with little or no orientation towards a homeland. I explore, too, the interplay between movement capital and maker capital, which involves technical skills and expertise.

Both movement and maker capital are built on skills, that is, social and cultural skills; they encode collaborative and distributive powers, an ability to improvise, and resilience. The latter, key to movement capital, emerges out of having to deal with a lifetime of disequilibrium. It is resilience that enables these movers and makers to negotiate dissonance – a taken-for-granted way of being in the world for them – the condition in which they make and create. These diasporic migrants do not represent the status quo, nor are they part of the power elite. They do not have the advantage of being national and local people of influence, with networks of social and cultural powers in the contexts of family, familiarity and kinship. Theirs is not the "decontextualized cultural capital" of Hannerz's transnational cosmopolitans – bureaucrats, diplomats, journalists and intellectuals.[1] However, the multiply migrant do have an important form of capital that works in different locations: an inherited expertise accrued directly as a result of their history of movement.

I write this book as a granddaughter of master craftsmen and women who moved multiple times across continents and countries, mostly in Asia and East Africa, with their origins in North India. My grandfather, before he settled in East Africa, had first migrated to Shanghai, and then to Japan, where he worked in the shipyards of Yokohama, learning Japanese woodworking techniques and absorbing the aesthetic of finessing tasks to perfection. He later worked in Malaysia, Burma and Basra, Iraq, before moving finally to employment in the British colonial steamship yards in Kisumu on Lake Victoria. There, he crafted the elaborate woodwork that was an essential component of early twentieth-century ships. He was known as a perfectionist and for his refined artisanal aesthetics in general. His toolbox was his most precious possession, and he had made many of his tools himself.

I am, thus, the progeny of makers and multiple movers. I, too, am a multiple-migrant who was born in Tanzania, raised in Uganda and Kenya, and, from the age of fourteen, London, UK. Twenty-one years later, I migrated to the West Coast, Los Angeles, USA, as a professional academic. I have now lived on the East Coast in Massachusetts for nearly three decades.

I am also a maker: a maker of academic discourse – which is my professional vocation; but additionally a proficient seamstress and a crafter in cloth and other materials, making my own clothes and much else besides. I have been a maker since I was a child inducted into the sensibilities and skills of pioneering migrant cultures in which everything had to be improvised and made using scarce materials in the early stages of settlement – a migrant-maker habitus that has developed and endured over more than a century of movement across borders, passed to all of us from childhood through everyday practices.

Some of the makers I write about in this book come from artisanal backgrounds and others have developed their own maker sensibilities and technical expertise. All of the people I write about are from multiply migrant families. They are experienced at the game of migration and possess a cultural dexterity, sophisticated skills to manage their minority status. With every migration into new lands, they have honed their ability to respond to new contexts, each time recontextualizing their skills and using their maker prowess and ability to put things together in new ways based on old knowledge.

Their movement capital is combined with maker capital – maker skills and sensibilities. Often this includes the ability to make things: technological, musical, artistic; a prowess with decoding how machines work or how they should work, and how to correct a glitch in a technological or musical device. But maker sensibilities are also simply a way of being in the world. The artisanal mindset of tinkering and working to perfection is a sensibility that you can bring to many tasks and translate into many domains of creativity – including the very construction of a life style and a *modus vivendi*. To be a maker, an artisan of objects and things, is akin to the social, cultural and technical expertise of dealing with the disruption of migration and settlement in new lands. In a sense, all movers are makers, crafting new lives for themselves in unfamiliar terrains.

This movement and maker capital, like other social and cultural capital, is durable and reproduces and builds itself in different contexts. It is uncodified knowledge acquired through observation, through practice, by osmosis. It encodes an ability to deal with the new, the uncertain and the unfamiliar, the contours of which cannot be known or navigated with established maps. The movers and makers I write about are comfortable with unknown cartographies which have yet to be discovered. In many cases, theirs is a capital which comes from generations of having to deal with dissonance, and through journeys traveled without the support of establishment power. Nothing in these contexts is easy. It is a hard struggle against many odds of newness, of racism, of dissonance, but it also produces inventiveness and the courage to think in ways that are not part of established systems of doing, living and making.

Movement capital combined with maker capital is growing and flourishing and rendering itself in powerful, innovative, courageous and inventive ways in the twenty-first century. It is supremely well placed to deal with the currents of our times. I explore the ability of those endowed with this capital to respond to change and remain vibrantly creative while at the same time sharing their skills and expertise with the world at large.

The creative people I write about in this book are rendering their movement and maker skills, as they are being formed and reformed anew, in the realms of technology, science, architecture, art, product design and music. They are drawing on their movement and maker capital, their generational inheritance, to discover and capture the new in powerful and courageous ways that remain largely invisible to the wider world. These are new kinds of people in emerging and dissonant global terrains whose maker and mover capabilities are defining the twenty-first-century landscape.

Migrant creativity: navigating uncertainty, embracing the new

I am writing this book at a time when migration and making, artisanship and resilience have a potent, high-profile valence. These are part of the zeitgeist of our globalized and hyper-connected century, acquiring influential currency in a world of disequilibrium, yet further unbalanced by a global pandemic.

The story of the diaspora and migrant creativity is *the* story of the global economy. Never able to take anything for granted, migrants are accustomed to living as artisans and improvisers of every aspect of life. Today, the knowledge and expertise they are generating, and sharing, increasingly define contemporary global landscapes across a great range of fields.

Some of the most creative people come from families who have moved and who use the mindset acquired from this movement in the locations in which they are settled. It's a fact often remarked on how many of the 'big names' in the new tech are first or second-generation migrants – for example: Jeff Bezos of Amazon, the child of Cuban immigrants; Sergey Brin of Google, born in Moscow, the child of Russian mathematics professors; the late Steve Jobs of Apple, the child of an Armenian mother and a Syrian father; Carlos Slim, cell phone titan, the son of Lebanese Maronite Catholic migrants from Lebanon to Mexico; Jerry Yang of Yahoo is Taiwanese as is his India-born partner, Sudhir Bhatia. And it's a trend that continues. Noubar Afeyan, the founder and CEO of Flagship Pioneering, the bio-tech incubator behind the Moderna coronavirus vaccine, is an Armenian multiple-migrant who was born in Lebanon, moved to Canada as a child and from there to the United States. Stuart Anderson notes in a 2018 policy brief from the National Foundation for American Policy that:

> Immigrants have started more than half (50 of 91, or 55%) of America's start-up companies valued at $1 billion or more and are key members of management or product development teams in more than 80% of these companies.[2]

There are many equivalent individuals in Britain and Europe, too – for example, Srichand Hinduja, owner of a London-based conglomerate of companies in fifty countries and a migrant from India to the UK; Anita Roddick of The Body Shop, a child of Italian immigrants; and Charles and Maurice Saatchi, former owners of one of the best-known advertising agencies based in Britain, Iraqi Jews born in Baghdad; and husband and wife team Dr Ugur Sahin and Dr Ozlem Tureci, the remarkable scientists whose inventive work and biotechnology company BioNTech underpins the Pfizer coronavirus vaccine, both children of Turkish immigrants to Germany.[3] Immigrants are crucial, too, to Britain's public sector employers, none more so than the National Health Service: in 2018, 12.7 per-cent of its staff held non-British nationality[4] and the NHS is stepping up its over-seas recruitment campaign, as numbers of workers from mainland Europe fall in the wake of the UK's 2016 referendum decision to leave the EU.[5] During the initial onslaught of Covid-19 in March and April 2020, it was immigrant NHS workers at all levels who were praised by the British public and politicians alike, whose contribution – and deaths – made the headlines throughout that time.[6]

It's perhaps less often remarked on how many of the high-profile migrant 'big names' in tech also come from a craft or maker background. Steve Jobs and Apple's one-time designer Jony Ives[7] are two cases in point. The Apple founder admired the craftsmanship of his adoptive father, Paul Jobs:

> … he knew how to build anything. If we needed a cabinet, he would build it. When he built our fence, he gave me a hammer so I could work with him … He loved doing things right. He even cared about the look of the parts you couldn't see.[8]

Sir Jony Ive, the design genius behind the iMac and iPhone, is also from a maker background: a British silversmith father, and a grandfather who was an engineer. Ive describes how he "'grew up understanding how things are made. That's something that's easy to take for granted, but everything that has been made has been thought about, designed, and I think that growing up with an appreciation of [that] was hugely influential on me…'"[9] His childhood memories of making things also remain vivid:

> Aged around 10 or 11… I remember making a box with a lid… making and remaking it… But it wasn't really about the object – it was about the process and seeing if I could make something perfectly.

This movement-craft trajectory applies in an earlier generation to Nikola Tesla, the founder of wireless power, after whom the Tesla batteries and cars are named. Tesla migrated from Croatia to Austria, from there to Hungary, and then onto Paris and finally New York, honing his skills with each migration. His father was a mechanically orientated craftsman, a craft expertise also shared by Nikola's mother, who was the main creative force behind his innovative technical skills.

There is certainly a resurgence of interest in 'maker skills' – for example, the 'maker spaces' which form the basis of some of Juliet Schor's work on the sharing economy,[10] Richard Sennett's trilogy examining the concept of 'craftsmanship' (about which I shall say more shortly), and anxieties expressed about the lack of maker expertise among young people who have spent their childhoods playing games on-screen rather than building Lego models or taking part in other hands-on activities. An apparent lack of maker dexterity in the current generation of medical students has been highlighted recently by leading medics on both sides of the Atlantic, for example.[11]

In terms of the wider economy, there is much talk about making in the context of "artisanship". Chris Anderson, author of *Makers: The New Industrial Revolution*[12] and co-founder of 3D Robotic, argues that "makers" are generating the Third Industrial Revolution – digital manufacturing. Makers are able to design and make things using digital technologies, open-source software and 3D printing – and so manufacture original designs with an ease previously unknown. Anderson himself was inducted into making by his grandfather who taught him "to work with my hands in his workshop…"; together, using a blueprint as a guide, they made a four-stroke gasoline engine:

> …we cut, drilled, ground and turned these blocks of metal extracting a crankshaft, piston and rod, bearings and valves out of solid brass and steel, much as sculpture from a block of marble… We were a mini-factory, and we could make anything.[13]

But for his grandfather, a watchmaker and inventor from Bern, Switzerland – another multi-talented immigrant – getting his inventions manufactured in the

1950s was a very different scenario from today. He succeeded in finding a manufacturer for his automatic sprinkler system, the Hydro-Rain, but not many of his other inventions. Now, however, an inventor is able also to be a manufacturer and entrepreneur, Anderson says. He enthuses:

> The great opportunity in the new Maker Movement is the ability to be both small and global. Both artisanal and innovative. Both high-tech and low-cost. Starting small but getting big… creating products that the world wants but doesn't know it yet…[14]

Lawrence Katz, Harvard-based labor economist, recommends an "artisanal economy" in which there is a rebirth and reimagining of craftsmanship in a service economy in order to meet the economic and political challenges facing the United States:

> 'Artisan' was the term used before the advent of mass manufacturing to describe people who made things or provided service with a distinctive touch and flair in which they took personal pride. Prior to the Industrial Revolution, this included just about everyone: the shoemaker, the doctor, the dressmaker, the saddler. Artisans gave a personal touch to whatever they did, and they often carved their initials into their work. It's a good mind-set to have for whatever job you are doing.[15]

This contemporary advocacy of an artisanal economy does in fact have historical roots: early migrants to the United States were often from practical artisanal backgrounds, as were those who arrived in the late nineteenth and early twentieth centuries – makers, who gave impetus to the US economy in its infancy. This older theme is the historical precedent for the current trend.

While Jeff Bezos, the late Steve Jobs and their ilk are hugely high profile, the achievements of many new creative immigrants in a broad range of fields largely remain unremarked upon. Indeed, they are often eclipsed by the rhetoric of anti-immigration movements. Brexit in the UK – the 2016 vote to leave the European Union – was largely fueled by talk of "the movement and flow of foreigners and migrants";[16] for many, "take back control" referred to borders to keep foreigners out, rather than any notion of political sovereignty. In the United States, President Donald Trump's central agenda was explicitly about fear of immigrants, making border walls and keeping people out, even when we know a very tiny percentage of the world's population moves from their place of birth.[17] It was reported that his plans for immigration may throw 4 million people off the immigrant waiting list.[18] In Canada, until now enjoying a reputation as a world leader in welcoming outsiders, the state of Quebec's Coalition Avenir Québec government which came to power in 2018 has pledged to reduce immigration by 20 percent[19] and views on immigration are thought to be polarizing.[20]

Others, meanwhile, urge governments to keep their borders open – for example, Robert Guest, business editor of *The Economist*, who extols the wealth-generating power of diaspora networks.[21] Similarly, urban studies theorist Richard Florida emphasizes the importance of harnessing the creative energies of immigrants for Europe and the United States to keep their innovative edge. In fact, Florida has suggested that all immigrants who come to study science at US universities should be given visas to stay once they graduate because they are and will be the most dynamic innovators of the future.[22] Harvard professor William R. Kerr takes a similar view, arguing that historically the United States has benefited hugely as the destination of choice for "exceptional inflows of human capital", in the tech sectors in particular, and that "America should cherish and protect its position at the center of global talent flows".[23] It is a view subscribed to by many others, including Kerr's Harvard colleague Ricardo Hausmann, who contends that "talent from outside" enables "communities of practice" in a particular place to advance;[24] and popularized by writers like Eric Weiner, whose book *The Geography of Genius* highlights the historical examples of ancient Athens and late nineteenth-century Vienna, among others, as rich, bustling, cosmopolitan cities that welcomed migrants and enjoyed phenomenal intellectual and artistic activity.[25]

Triple Pulitzer award winner and newspaper columnist Thomas Friedman, also recognizing immigrants' distinctive contribution, suggests that *everyone* should acquire an immigrant sensibility, as a solution to the problems that vex the United States and "Old Europe" in the global economy: "Approaching the world with the view that nothing is owed you, nothing is given… There is no 'legacy' slot waiting for you at Harvard or the family firm or anywhere else. You have to go and earn your place in the world…"[26]

But can an immigrant sensibility simply be willed? Is it possible to think like an immigrant and acquire the mindset needed to succeed in contemporary conditions of global hypermobility and uncertainty[27] without undergoing the migrant experience of movement and disruption? Migrants' openness to newness, their refusal to take things for granted, and their ability to respond to the moment is not something that is acquired overnight. It is developed through displacement and marginality, through having to fight for your space, your voice, in cultural, political and racial struggles, often over several generations.

Movement and maker capital: creativity catalyzed

Walter Gropius (1883–1969), the "man who built Bauhaus",[28] arrived in the United States in 1937 from Nazi Germany, via Italy and England. While Gropius and his colleague Mies van der Rohe were already esteemed creatives whose design aesthetics as rendered in the Bauhaus School were already well known and admired in European and US circles of design and architecture, their migration to the United States greatly increased their influence. Not least, Gropius taught at Harvard University for some fifteen years, so his students were many. Fiona MacCarthy,

Gropius' biographer tells us that Bauhaus, Gropius's creation, "affected generations to come… In fact, *the Bauhaus reshaped the world* [my emphasis]. Our cities and houses today, our furniture and typography, are unthinkable without the functional elegance pioneered by Gropius and the Bauhaus".[29]

Like the creatives I write about, Gropius was a multiple-migrant, although not with the same generational depth. In common with the maker sensibilities of the group of movers I discuss, he had a respect for and expertise in craftsmanship that defined the Bauhaus aesthetics. It not only defined a style of design but also a style of living and being in the world. According to MacCarthy, Gropius had:

> …a belief in the importance to designers of a knowledge of materials and techniques in evolving new forms of construction. *From the start Bauhaus teaching has its basis in the crafts* [my emphasis].[30]

Gropius benefited from movement and his design style gained prominence when practiced outside Germany, where it was considered degenerate by the Nazis. In the United States, his design vocabulary and influence multiplied in manifold ways; his preeminence as the "silver prince",[31] the master supreme of the Bauhaus, was possible precisely because he was an exile.

I will show a similar dynamic playing out in the lives of the creative people examined in this book. All are in some sense makers and all are movers, endowed with movement capital. This capital comes out of having to deal with difference and disruption at every stage of movement into new settings – and, in the case of all of the people I write about, settings in which they were, and remain, minorities. Like Gropius, they also carry with them their inheritance of maker capital, technical skills which are recontextualized by each act of movement.

Before turning to the case studies, I will look in more detail at what movement and maker capital entail, including the collaborative powers and ingenuity common to both.

Movement capital: resilience, antifragility and openness to the new

Disruption and disequilibrium are the defining characteristics of movement to new sites, where nothing can be taken for granted and nothing is given. Zygmunt Bauman suggests that in the contemporary period of hypermobility and liquidity, these are the conditions faced by all: society is fragmented, its citizens fragile and vulnerable in the face of the constant instability of our globalized capitalist world.[32] Those I write about possess a movement capital built out of the disruption of migration that is supremely amenable to such conditions, and so they can make use of opportunities in new settings in ways that people unused to disequilibrium cannot. This expertise, honed over several generations in difficult terrains, has important implications for how they are positioned in a liquid global world.

Their disadvantageous locations of the past have given them flexible and adaptable mindsets, which are in synch with the times.

So much of the literature that I have read describes the negative consequences of uncertainty, the virulent animosity against strangers and the fear that this state of affairs creates.[33] But times of dissonance and uncertainty also encode another story – a facet of the liquid times discourse – which is that migrant creativity has been catalyzed and has flourished precisely because of terrains of liquidity and disequilibrium. Being in conditions of flux is not necessarily a negative condition – it is in fact a source of creativity, of capturing the new based on the new, of discovering the future as it unfolds in the moment, and of responding to the moment with capital that is inherited but rendered in new ways in new terrains.

Resilience is the source code of this movement capital. It constitutes a movement skill honed by moving from one place to the next across national and international borders. The generational trajectory of movement and of having to operate in alien landscapes – where every intervention has to be negotiated with cultural dexterity and a sophisticated management of minority status almost entirely against the odds – is the story of all my creative agents and their parents and grandparents. This has led to the possession of resilience, a durable inheritance which has enormous generative powers. It is a way of being in the world, a disposition, a style of living and thinking, a frame of mind – a deep artisanal sensibility and an understanding that if things are not working one way, you can improvise and try another.

President Barack Obama is a high-profile example of someone who possesses this particular way of being. He "could live in the ocean",[34] with no need for routine or order, Michelle Obama tells us – and, indeed his background is one of repeated movement: Hawaii-born, raised in Indonesia and Hawaii, an undergrad at Pepperdine University in Los Angeles, then Columbia University in New York. After this, he went to Harvard to study law and to Chicago as a community organizer. At every stage of his life, Obama has flourished as a navigator of disrupted terrains, collaborating with diverse cosmopolitan populations with unselfconscious ease, without being anchored in a place of birth.

Resilience is explored fruitfully by Andrew Zolli and Ann Marie Healy in their book *Resilience and Why Things Bounce Back*. In the face of the current world's volatility, resilience, they suggest, is "imperative". They contend that our current circumstances (and they were writing before Covid-19) demand "resilience thinking" – an ability to adapt to constant change and turbulence, without returning to a previous state of stasis, and so thrive in times of "unforeseen disruptions".[35] This notion of "resilience thinking" captures neatly the experiences of migrants, and multiple movers in particular, who do not look for stasis after the disruption of movement and are not home-orientated as they settle in new sites. Unlike robustness, which is "typically achieved by hardening the assets of a system… Pyramids are remarkably robust structures but knock them down and they won't be able to put themselves back together",[36] resilience has elasticity and plasticity and the capacity to bend and adapt to circumstances without loss of identity or purpose.

Nassim Nicholas Taleb takes resilience one step further with his notion of "antifragility" which, he notes, is "the exact opposite of fragile" and "beyond resilience or robustness":

> Some things benefit from shocks; they thrive and grow when exposed to volatility, randomness, disorder, and stressors and love adventure, risk, and uncertainty… The resilient resists shocks and stays the same; the antifragile gets better.[37]

Whether characterized as resilience or antifragility, the tools of adaptation and an adaptive style of thinking are key to the movement capital of the multiply migrant. This resilience is a generational way of being in the world. There is no going back to what was before. There is, however, a memory and durable expertise of surviving and then thriving in a new setting that has nothing in common with an older site, the site of earlier migrations and settlement.[38] The adaptive style of thinking also predisposes the mover to be open to the new and creative. This capital is perceptive of and receptive to the new and includes a propensity to take risks, to experiment, to improvise and innovate with genuine unselfconscious command; thus, the volatility and disruption of migration catalyzes creativity, thinking through new frames while leaving older ones behind.

Maker capital: techne allied with episteme

My subjects' maker sensibilities are central to their *modus operandi* in the twenty-first century. Their socialization as makers plays a powerful part in their creative output.

Richard Sennett defines craftsmanship as "the skill of making things well".[39] I have already described my grandfather, the perfectionist artisan. I remember his interrogation of the woodwork in our train compartment as we prepared to travel from Kisumu to Nairobi: his fingers examined every detail of its workmanship. As a master craftsman, he demanded things be done just right. Alan Rusbridger, former editor-in-chief of *The Guardian* whose mother took up carpentry when he was a teenager, describes the exactitude it requires:

> I remember realizing as I watched her that the first lesson of carpentry is what a precise skill it is. It's no good measuring to approximately the nearest millimeter. It has to be exact. You have to choose the tenon rather than the bench saw, pick the small enough drill bit, and use the set square and the right grade sandpaper in order to end up with a table that works.[40]

My grandfather used to maintain that carpentry was the most demanding of the craft skills, as there was no room for error: if a mistake is made, the carpenter has to take a new piece of wood and start all over again. A bricklayer and builder can adjust with interstitial material – the cement or plaster in between. The ironmonger can smelt the material and rework it. But the carpenter has no such option: they have to work with exactitude. So these hand crafts – carpentry in particular, perhaps – also require mind skill, in the requirement for measuring and careful planning.

Richard Sennett further develops this notion; for him, "making is thinking": "The good craftsman… uses solutions to uncover new territory; problem solving and problem finding are intimately related to the mind… Every good craftsman conducts a dialogue between the concrete practices and thinking…"[41]

Sennett's definition of craftsmanship as "the skill of making things well" also allows him to extend it in other directions, too, beyond the notion of hand-work. For him, craft has not vanished from the world but has shifted into the realms of science, technology and life skills:

> Craftsmanship is alive in so many domains of life as an enduring, basic human impulse, the desire to do a job well for its own sake. Craftsmanship cuts a far wider swath than skilled manual labor; it serves a computer programmer, the doctor, and the artist, parenting improves when it is practiced as a skilled craft, as does citizenship.[42]

Sennett seeks to break down the opposition between Aristotle's techne – the lower-status hand skills of the artisan; and episteme – the higher-status theoretical, mind knowledge of the university-educated. For the creative people I am writing about, movement catalyzes their technical abilities by formally combining hand and mind knowledge – in an alliance similar to that which underpins the development of science in the Renaissance.[43] A scientific revolution was made possible then by the exchange of ideas between the theorizers – the scholars – and the craftsman/artisans, as described by Pamela Long, historian of science and technology in the late Medieval and Renaissance period. After their collaboration, science could be measured and experiments could be done with precision because the artisans made the instruments to allow this; the two groups shared their knowledge and this produced the new science.[44] Hand and mind knowledge collided, coalesced and mingled to produce new and world-changing kinds of understanding. Many revolutionary inventors and thinkers of the past embodied this hand and mind combination within themselves: Baruch Spinoza was both lens grinder and philosopher; Isaac Newton made his own scientific instruments: telescopes, sundials and more. The same techne-episteme alliance was also present in many of the scientific advances of the Industrial Revolution. For example, the "Lunar men", a group of eighteenth-century thinkers/inventors in the British Midlands who built canals and named plants, gases and minerals, were happy to undertake practical, physical work as well as being intellectually engaged. They too had a hand-mind sensibility, and were all thinker-makers who combined art, commerce, science, making and manufacturing.[45]

But there is a wider, moral dimension to maker capital, too – an aspect of craft and craftsmanship that interests contemporary thinker-makers such as Sennett, and also Peter Korn, master craftsman and the author of *Why We Make Things and Why It Matters: The Education of a Craftsman*.[46] For Korn, the creative practice that a craftsman engages in encodes how he or she lives and contributes to society, and making things well is much more than the physical work of crafting an object: "Every man-made thing, be it a chair, a text, or a school of thought made substance. It is the expression of someone's (or some group's) ideas and beliefs".[47] Crafting an object well is about the creation of a caring society, the good life.

In the second book of his craftsmanship trilogy, Sennett extends the notion of craft yet further to include the "craft of cooperation". Cooperation can be defined, he says, "as an exchange in which the participants benefit from the encounter... Instantly recognizable, because mutual support is built into the genes of all social animals; they cooperate to accomplish what they can't do alone".[48]

Sennett describes being struck by just how crucial the social skill of cooperation is to doing practical work: "Cooperation oils the machinery of getting things done and sharing with others can make up for what we may individually lack".[49] It is an activity, he says, that requires a high level of skill and, although embedded in our genes, "needs to be developed and deepened... particularly... when we are dealing with people unlike ourselves".[50]

The ability to cooperate and collaborate in a deep way is a key aspect of both movement and maker capital as lived by the creative people I am writing about, as I explore below.

Collaborative powers and sharism

Theodore Waitz, the nineteenth-century German anthropologist, understood how important it is for people(s) to live and work together in order to exchange ideas, and how we deteriorate mentally when we live in isolation from one another:

> Whenever we see a people, of whatever degree of civilization, not living in contact and reciprocal actions with others, we shall generally find a certain stagnation, a mental inertness, and want of activity, which render any change of social and political condition next to impossible. These are, in times of peace, transmitted like an everlasting disease...[51]

And in the present moment, writer Walter Isaacson reminds us, too, that "creativity is a collaborative process". He explains how the technological revolution driven by the internet and computer was led by hackers, geeks, technologically minded people who were, crucially, collaborators whose "ability to work as a team made them even *more* creative".[52] He says that there are many talented people but, especially in the digital age, the ability to collaborate and share is crucial to succeed, and to be a good leader.

But, even more than our desire to be as creative as possible, our central challenge today is to find a way of engaging and making a life of cooperation and collaboration with people who are different in terms of religion, ethnicity, economic class, migration trajectories and political views. How can we learn to cooperate and dialogue in a super-diverse world which is fluid, which is uncertain, in which nothing can be taken for granted and in which disruption and disequilibrium are the norm and are likely to be so for the foreseeable future?

Dialogic skills are key to bridging these differences between us – the art of collaboration and cooperation – and such collaborative powers are integral to the movement and maker capital of the people I am writing about. Distributing the knowledge and skills they possess is intrinsic to their style of living – a sort of bridge-building or bridging capital common to both movement and maker capital. As I will show in more detail in the next chapter, the milieu that has produced my subjects is defined by a kind of diasporic crowd-sourcing, in which skills and resources are shared and passed on vigilantly. Their hand and mind artisanship is open and inviting; they are democratizers of knowledge in an open-source way.

Their style of living is thus an eloquent riposte to the negativism of our contemporary world, which sees only instability, a failure to communicate and a deterioration in contemporary civic life: a "cosmic fear" of strangers;[53] a loss of "a sense of our connectedness to each other and to our ideals";[54] disengagement and disconnection from family, friends and social organizations, and a diminishing of social capital, the conduits and mechanisms through which our lives are made more productive.[55] Yet the people I write about are engaged in reaching out to others, sharing what they know, building bridges between groups and strengthening social bonds.

These cultures of generosity, which do not hoard their capital but distribute it, have deep roots in the migration and movement cultures of the creative agents I describe and constitute a sort of "radical openness".[56] In early migrant cultures – pioneers in new settings – innovation is accelerated precisely because it is governed by a sensibility of collaborating and passing on skills to a wide range of people regardless of class and ethnicity. This style of being in the world undergirds the formation of movement capital.

This ethos is very much in tune with twenty-first-century notions of "sharism", venture capitalist Isaac Mao's philosophy of a "mind revolution"[57] and open-source knowledge: the creative people in this book are thus in synch with the ethos of the times. Generosity and sharing of information lead to prosperity, we are told[58] – most notably, when Tim Berners-Lee and colleagues opened the internet up equally to everyone. Huge benefit has also accrued both to individuals and businesses from the distribution of open-source software such as Linux and Drupal, collective projects that may in fact represent the next stage of human organization and economic production.[59] There's also the democratizing impact of the open licensing system of Creative Commons, which in part makes Wikipedia possible.[60] As well as prosperity, the definitive ethos of communities of people who share is a respect and "a mind switch called Sharism"; those who share in this way accumulate enormous social capital.[61]

Jugaad *and ingenuity: improvisational skills*

An ability to collaborate and a propensity to share cut across both maker and movement capital, and so too does the ability to improvise and the notion of *jugaad*.

Pioneers, in any context, have to work with unfamiliar materials and require skill to craft them as they wish. In the United States we talk about Yankee ingenuity, and *jugaad*, a Punjabi and Hindi word, captures a similar notion. The term was originally coined for the inventive use of tractor diesel engines by enterprising Punjabis to drive carts or wagons or to run water pumps, when it meant a form of "frugal engineering".[62] Today it has come to mean more generally a "flexible mindset" and is defined as:

> an innovative fix... quite simply a unique way of thinking and acting in response to challenges; it is a gutsy art of spotting opportunities in the most adverse circumstances and resourcefully improvising solutions using simple means... about *doing more with less* [the authors' emphasis].[63]

It has striking similarities to the notion of *bricolage* in the writings of Lévi-Strauss.[64] Sherry Turkle, MIT professor of the social studies of science and technology, uses *bricolage* to discuss the "the triumph of tinkering" she observed among computer programmers, the notion of problem-solving through a "soft style" of flexible, non-hierarchical, bottom-up improvisation that is open to experience, in which nego-tiation, relationship and attachment rather than distance and objectivity are seen as "cognitive virtues":

> A bricoleur scientist does not move abstractly and hierarchically from axiom to theorem to corollary. Bricoleurs construct theories by arranging and rearranging, by negotiating with a set of well-known materials... The brico-leur resembles the painter who stands back between brush strokes, looks at the canvas and then decides what to do next...[65]

Jugaad, *bricolage* and ingenuity are the *modus operandi* of the artisanal diaspora. They are an aesthetic that has been transmitted to the contemporary generations of diasporic creative agents for whom it is second nature. As we shall see in my case studies, they have taken these creative sensibilities in new directions to build twenty-first-century machines, buildings, technology, architectural art and much more.

The case studies

In this book, I will interrogate the life experiences and creative impact, in the domains of technology, art, architecture and architectural art, theater, science and music, of eleven diasporic agents, all movers and makers. I have followed their work and lives over many years, in the context of ethnographic study conducted over more than four decades; and for the purposes of this book I have also interviewed each of them at length and in depth.

The stories I narrate are not just of triumph and achievement. They constitute spaces of improvisational and innovative creativity hard won through courage and pain, from which have emerged some significant successes in the contemporary world. These are not easy struggles, though they animate creative interventions across the world today in ways not possible for earlier generations. In many of the cases described, I highlight creativity that is incredibly visible, though often not named as diasporic. All this creative activity is a manifestation of accumulated diasporic expertise that is now defining the world in yet larger ways through shared networks, extensive interconnected creative fields and enduring inheritances.

I write about the eleven individuals in nine chapters as follows:

Kuljit Bhamra – tabla player and sound engineer, he transformed bhangra, Punjabi harvest music, into globally popular dance tracks and has designed an electronic tabla, as well as devising a notation system to enable anyone to read music and play it on the tabla – thus democratizing musical knowledge traditionally monopolized and hoarded by guild-like musical domains (Chapter 2).

Bhajan Hunjan – a versatile artist fearless in working with a huge range of materials and in different mediums. She demonstrates supreme comfort also in collaborating with people of disparate backgrounds and experiences to create beautiful, community-enhancing works of art in public spaces – from floorscapes to gates to bridges (Chapter 3).

Amarjit Kalsi – the late former partner of Rogers Stirk Harbour + Partners, and one-time protégé of the practice's founder, eminent architect Richard Rogers. Amarjit's work includes iconic European buildings such as the European Court of Human Rights, Strasbourg; the Law Courts, Bordeaux; Terminal 5, Heathrow Airport; Barajas Airport Hub in Madrid, having cut his architectural teeth on the Lloyd's Building, London (Chapter 4).

Jasleen Kaur – an artist initially trained as a goldsmith whose dialogic works catalyze connections and conversations, often inspired by the movement and maker experience of her grandfather who migrated from the Punjab, India, to Glasgow, Scotland, in the 1950s. She is a latter-day situationist, creating happenings and works of art designed to challenge the status quo and contest capitalist consumption (Chapter 5).

Rishi Rich (Rishapal Rekhi) and **Jay Sean (Kamaljit Jhooti)** – they found early musical fame and enormous popularity together in the Rishi Rich Project (with another singer, Juggy D) and now both successfully pursue their separate global careers, Rishi as composer and sound engineer based in Mumbai, London and Los Angeles and Jay as New York-based, globe-trotting R&B singer-songwriter (Chapter 6).

The Singh Twins, Rabindra and Amrit – defiant and daring identical twin sisters who work as one artist, The Singh Twins. Based in the Wirral, near Liverpool, and acclaimed as "the artistic face of modern Britain",[66] they have revolutionized the traditions of Mughal miniature painting to capture and comment on contemporary issues as well as their own lives. They were the first British artist after Henry Moore to be exhibited at the National Gallery of Modern Art, Delhi (Chapter 7)

Suneet Singh Tuli – "classroom revolutionary"[67] and serial technological entrepreneur determined to eradicate the digital divide and lift billions out of poverty, who together with his brother has been responsible for the design and marketing of a handheld computer giving digital access to vast numbers of people until now unable to afford it (Chapter 8).

Jatinder Verma – artistic director and co-founder of Tara Arts, the first Asian theater group in Britain, in 1989 he was the first person of color to direct a play at the Royal National Theatre, London. In 2016, he secured a permanent base for the theater company, Tara Theatre, an exquisitely designed and vibrant performance space in south-west London (Chapter 9).

Professor Sir Tejinder Singh Virdee – he represents the zenith of migrant technical capital as professor of physics and a lead scientist at CERN (Conseil Européen pour la Recherche Nucléaire – the European Council for Nuclear Research) – who sourced the materials for and co-designed one of the key instruments to test the theoretical underpinnings of contemporary physics and push the boundaries of current scientific understanding. He has been at the center of experiments carried out over the past three decades, which in 2012 confirmed the physical reality of the hitherto merely theoretical Higgs boson particle (Chapter 10).

But first, in Chapter 1, I will set out the origins of my case studies' creativity: I describe the sophistication of their ancient maker skills during the Sikh and British empires and the experiences of their parents and grandparents, the pioneering generations who moved from North India to East Africa during the nineteenth and twentieth centuries – so showing how the movement and maker capital expressed in the current generations' creativity was accrued.

My conclusion, in Chapter 11, draws together common threads from the case studies and explores how they relate to current debates about migration.

Notes

1 "Cosmopolitans… are 'the new class', people with credentials, decontextualized cultural capital… they share a 'culture of critical discourse'… Their decontextualized knowledge can be quickly and shiftingly recontextualized in a series of different meanings." Ulf Hannerz, 'Cosmopolitans and Locals in World Culture', in *Global Culture: Nationalism, Globalization and Modernity*', ed. Mike Featherstone (London, Thousand Oaks, CA and Delhi: Sage Publications, 1990), 246.

2 Stuart Anderson, *Immigrants and Billion Dollar Companies*, National Foundation for American Policy, Policy Brief October 2018, https://nfap.com/wp-content/uploads/2018/10/2018-BILLION-DOLLAR-STARTUPS.NFAP-Policy-Brief.2018.pdf (accessed August 6, 2019). Anderson's 'startup companies' are those valued at over $1 billion (as of October 1, 2018) that are not publicly traded on the stock market and are tracked by Dow Jones VentureSource and *The Wall Street Journal. See also, 'Immigrant entrepreneurs prove it doesn't matter where you were born'*, www.forbes.com/sites/stuartanderson/2019/05/06/immigrant-entrepreneurs-prove-it-doesnt-matter-where-you-were-born/#1aed050749b7 (accessed August 6, 2019).

3 'The husband-and-wife team behind the leading vaccine to solve Covid-19', *The New York Times*, November 10, 2020; www.nytimes.com/2020/11/10/business/biontech-covid-vaccine.html (accessed December 2, 2020).

4 House of Commons Library, 'NHS staff from overseas: statistics', October 10, 2018; https://researchbriefings.parliament.uk/ResearchBriefing/Summary/CBP-7783 (accessed August 6, 2019).

5 BBC News Reality Check, 'NHS staff shortage: how many doctors and nurses come from abroad?', May 12, 2019; www.bbc.co.uk/news/world-48205445 (accessed August 6, 2019).

6 See, for example: 'Coronavirus: Remembering 100 NHS and healthcare workers who have died', *BBC News*, April 20, 2020, www.bbc.co.uk/news/health-52242856; 'Bojo's angels: Hero NHS nurses who saved Boris Johnson's life pictured as PM hails ICU medics who 'stood by bedside for 24 hours', Mark Hodge, Tom Newton Dunn and Gerard Couzens, *The Sun*, April 12, 2020; 'Coronavirus: First working NHS surgeon dies in UK from Covid-19', Thomas Mackintosh, *BBC News*, March 28, 2020; Public support for immigrant NHS workers also forced the Conservative government to drop plans to include them in the NHS-levy paid by other non British citizens – see 'Boris backs down on NHS charge for foreign health workers', James Tapsfield, *Daily Mail*, May 21, 2020.

7 Jony Ives left Apple in June 2019 to set up a new creative company, see: www.theguardian.com/technology/2019/jun/27/jony-ive-apple-designer-leaves-imac-iphone?CMP=share_btn_link, www.nytimes.com/2019/06/27/technology/jony-ive-apple.html (accessed August 6, 2019).

8 Walter Isaacson, *Steve Jobs* (New York, London and Toronto: Simon & Schuster, 2013), 6.

9 Naomi Campbell, 'Quiet by design: Naomi Campbell interviews Joni Ive', *Vogue*, April 2, 2018, www.vogue.co.uk/article/naomi-campbell-jonathan-ive-interview (accessed August 6, 2019).

10 See, for example, Juliet B. Schor, Connor Fitzmaurice, Lindsey B. Carfagna, Will Attwood-Charles and Emilie Dubois Potea, 'Paradoxes of Openness and Distinction in the Sharing Economy', *Poetics*, Vol. 54 (February 2016): 66–81.

11 Matthew Weaver, 'Medical students "raised on screens lack skills of surgery"', *The Guardian*, October 13, 2018, www.theguardian.com/society/2018/oct/30/medical-students-raised-on-screens-lack-skills-for-surgery; Kate Murphy, 'Your surgeon's childhood hobbies may affect your health', *The New York Times*, May 30, 2019, www.nytimes.com/2019/05/30/well/live/surgeons-hobbies-dexterity.html (both accessed August 6, 2019).

12 Chris Anderson, *Makers: The New Industrial Revolution* (New York: Crown Business, 2012).

13 Anderson, *Makers: The New Industrial Revolution*, 10.

14 Anderson, *Makers: The New Industrial Revolution*, 16

15 Lawrence Katz, 'Get a liberal arts B.A., not a business B.A., for the coming artisan economy', *PBS Newshour Making Sen$e*, July 15, 2014, www.pbs.org/newshour/nation/get-a-liberal-arts-b-a-not-a-business-b-a-for-the-coming-artisan-economy (accessed August 8, 2019).

16 See, for example, Matthew d'Ancona, 'Let's be honest about what's really driving Brexit: Bigotry', *The Guardian*, December 2, 2018; www.theguardian.com/commentisfree/2018/dec/02/honest-brexit-bigotry-ugly-chapter-history (accessed August 8, 2019).

17 Phillip Connor, 'International migration: Key findings from the U.S., Europe and the world', *Pew Research Center*, December 15, 2016: "If all of the world's international migrants (people living in a country that is different from their country or territory or birth) lived in a single country, it would be the world's fifth largest, with around 244 million people. Overall, international migrants make up to 3.3% of the world's population today. However, international migrants do not live in one country. Instead, they are

dispersed across the world, with most having moved from middle income to high income countries. Top origins of international migrants include India (15.6 million), Mexico (12.3 million), Russia (10.6 million), China (9.5 million) and Bangladesh (7.2 million)." www.pewresearch.org/fact-tank/2016/12/15/international-migration-key-findings-from-the-u-s-europe-and-the-world/ (accessed August 8, 2019).

18 Stuart Anderson, 'Trump immigration plan may throw 4 Million people off immigrant waiting lists', *Forbes*, May 16, 2019; www.forbes.com/sites/stuartanderson/2019/05/16/trump-immigration-plan-may-throw-4-million-people-off-immigrant-waiting-lists/#7537db8b6943 (accessed August 6, 2019).

19 Terry Glavin, 'Why race and immigration are a gathering storm in Canadian politics', *Macleans*, April 23, 2019; www.macleans.ca/news/canada/why-race-and-immigration-are-a-gathering-storm-in-canadian-politics/ (accessed August 6, 2019).

20 Ekos Politics, 'Increased polarization on attitudes to immigration reshaping the political landscape in Canada', April 15, 2019; www.ekospolitics.com/index.php/2019/04/increased-polarization-on-attitudes-to-immigration-reshaping-the-political-landscape-in-canada/ (accessed August 6, 2019).

21 Robert Guest, *Borderless Economics: Chinese Sea Turtles, Indian Fridges and the New Fruits of Global Capitalism* (New York: Palgrave Macmillan, 2013).

22 Richard Florida, 'America's Looming Creativity Crisis', *Harvard Business Review*, October 1, 2004.

23 William R. Kerr, *The Gift of Global Talent: How Migration Shapes Business, Economy and Society* (Stanford, CA: Stanford Business Books, 2018).

24 Ricardo Hausmann, in discussion with Paul Solman and Eric Weiner, January 2016, www.pbs.org/newshour/show/hotbeds-of-genius-and-innovation-depend-on-these-key-ingredients#transcript (accessed August 6, 2019).

25 Eric Weiner, *The Geography of Genius* (New York: Simon & Schuster, 2016).

26 Thomas Friedman and Michael Mandelbaum, *That Used To Be Us: What Went Wrong with America* (New York: Picador, 2012), 148.

27 Zygmunt Bauman, *Liquid Modernity* (Cambridge, UK: Polity, 2000).

28 Fiona MacCarthy, *Gropius: The Man who Built the Bauhaus* (Cambridge, MA: The Belknap Press, 2019).

29 MacCarthy, *Gropius*, 484.

30 MacCarthy, *Gropius*, 6.

31 MacCarthy, *Gropius*, 4.

32 Bauman, *Liquid Modernity*, 4.

33 Zygmunt Bauman, *A Chronicle of Crisis: 2011–2016* (Falkensee, Germany: Social Europe Edition, 2017), *Liquid Times: Living in an Age of Uncertainty* (Cambridge, UK: Polity, 2007); *Liquid Modernity* (Cambridge, UK: Polity, 2000); Andrew Zolli and Ann Marie Healy, *Resilience: Why Things Bounce Back* (New York: Free Press, 2012); Arlie Russell Hochschild, *Strangers in Their Own Land* (New York: The New Press, 2016).

34 Michelle Obama, *Becoming* (Penguin UK, 2018), 211.

35 Andrew Zolli and Ann Marie Healy, *Resilience: Why Things Bounce Back* (New York: Free Press, 2012), 8.

36 Zolli and Healy, *Resilience*, 13.

37 Nassim Nicholas Taleb, *Antifragile: Things That Gain from Disorder* (New York: Random House, 2012), 3.

38 See Parminder Bhachu, 'Twice Migrants and Multiple Migrants', in *The Wiley Blackwell Encyclopedia on Race, Ethnicity and Nationalism*, ed. Professor John Stone, Dennis Rutledge, Anthony Smith and Polly Rizova (Hoboken, NJ: Wiley Smith Publishers,

2015); 'The Invisibility of Diasporic Cultural and Multiple Migrant Creativity', in *Mutuality: Anthropology's Changing Engagement*, ed. Roger Sanjek (Philadelphia, PA: Penn University Press, 2014); *Dangerous Designs: Asian Women Fashion the Diaspora Economies* (London: Routledge, 2004); 'Identities Constructed & Reconstructed: Representations of Asian Women in Britain', in *Migrant Women: Crossing Boundaries and Changing Identities*, ed. Gina Buijs (Oxford, UK and New York: Berg Publishers Limited, 1993); 'East African Sikh Settlers in Britain: Twice versus Direct Migrants', in *The Modern Western Diaspora*, ed. Ceri Peach, Steve Vertovec and Colin Clarke (Delhi: Oxford University Press, 1991); *Twice Migrants: East African Sikh Settlers in Britain* (London: Tavistock Publications, 1984); Ivan Light and Parminder Bhachu, 'California Immigrants in World Perspective', in *Immigration and Entrepreneurship: Culture, Capital and Ethnic Networks*, ed. Ivan Light and Parminder Bhachu (Piscataway, NJ: Rutgers University, Transactions Press, 1993).

39 Richard Sennett, *The Craftsman* (New York, 2008).

40 Alan Rusbridger, *Play It Again: An Amateur Against the Impossible* (Farrar, Strauss and Giroux, 2013), 227.

41 Sennett, *The Craftsman*, 9.

42 Sennett, *The Craftsman*, 9.

43 This is in contrast to elites who start out with mind rather than hand knowledge – for example the Brahmins, who only entered the field of engineering once it was professionalized and reclassified as a mind skill, a scientific enterprise divorced from the physical hand-skills domain. As Subramaniam explains: "The professionalization of engineering in the colonial period – associated with state and scientific enterprise – elevated public works to imperial scale and invested engineering with an aspiration to mastery over nature, land, and people alike." Ajantha Subramaniam, 'Making Merit: The Indian Institutes of Technology and the Social Life of Caste', in *Comparative Study of Society and History*, Vol. 57, No. 2 (April 2015): 293.

44 See, for example: Pamela Long, *Artisan/Practitioners and the Rise of New Sciences 1400–1600* (Corvallis, OR: Oregon State University Press, 2011 and 2014).

45 Jenny Uglow, *Lunar Men: The Friends Who Made the Future 1730–1810* (London: Faber & Faber, 2002). The men included: James Watt who made the steam-engine; the pioneer toy manufacturer Matthew Boulton; the potter Josiah Wedgwood; the physician, inventor, poet and botanist Erasmus Darwin (Charles Darwin's grandfather); and Joseph Priestley, the preacher and chemist.

46 Peter Korn, *Why We Make Things and Why It Matters: The Education of a Craftsman* (Dorking, UK: Square Peg, 2013), 159–160.

47 Peter Korn, *Why We Make Things*, 159–160.

48 Richard Sennett, *Together: The Rituals, Pleasures and Politics of Cooperation* (New Haven and London: Yale University Press, 2012), 6.

49 Sennett, *Together*, 6.

50 Sennett, *Together*, 6.

51 Theodore Waitz, *Introduction to Anthropology* (1863) quoted in Robert Ezra Park, 'Human Migration and the Marginal Man', *The American Journal of Sociology*, Vol. 33, No. 6 (May 1928): 881–893. We might not go as far as Waitz did, in recommending war as a means of removing the mental inertia that results from lack of contact! "These are, in times of peace, transmitted like an everlasting disease and war appears then, in spite of what the apostles of peace may say, as a saving angel, who rouses the national spirit, and renders all forces more elastic".

52 Walter Isaacson, *The Innovators: How a Group of Hackers, Geniuses, and Geeks Created the Digital Revolution* (New York, London and Toronto: Simon & Schuster, 2014), 479.

53 Zygmunt Bauman, *Strangers at Our Door* (Cambridge, UK: Polity, 2016), 1.

54 Robert Reich, *The Common Good* (New York: Alfred A. Knopf, 2018), 4.

55 Robert D. Putnam, *Bowling Alone: The Collapse and Revival of American Community* (New York: Simon & Schuster, 2000), 19.

56 Chris Anderson, 'How web video powers global innovation', TED Talk, 2010, www. ted.com/talks/chris_anderson_how_web_video_powers_global_innovation?languag (accessed August 6, 2019). Anderson draws attention to the phenomenon of crowd-accelerated innovation by means of YouTube clips and calls it "a self-fueling cycle of learning that could be as significant as the invention of print. But to tap into its power, organizations will need to embrace *radical openness* [my emphasis]."

57 Isaac Mao, 'Sharism: A Mind Revolution, Freesouls Essays', https://freesouls.cc/essays/07-isaac-mao-sharism.html (accessed August 6, 2019).

58 Tim O'Reilly, *WTF: What's The Future and Why It's Up to Us* (London: Random House Business, 2017).

59 Yochai Benkler, 'The Wealth of Networks: How Social Production Transforms Markets and Freedom', in *Journal of Media Economics*, Vol. 20, No. 2 (May 2007): 161–165; 'The New Open Source Economies', TED Global, July 2005, www.ted.com/talks/yochai_benkler_on_the_new_open_source_economics? (accessed August 6, 2019).

60 Lawrence Lessig, *Free Culture: The Nature and Future of Creativity* (New York, Penguin Books, 2005). See also, 'Laws that Choke Creativity', TED Talk, March 2007, www.ted.com/talks/larry_lessig_says_the_law_is_strangling_creativity (accessed August 6, 2019). With Creative Commons he has created a license-free terrain in which individuals can create content in an engaged 'read-write' environment instead of one that is controlled and restricted, 'read-only'; in Lessig's terms, Facebook, blog posts and YouTube videos are all read-write and remix interventions in which their creators are active agents, as well as consumers of others' creative content.

61 Mao, 'Sharism'. See also Rutger Bregman, *Humankind: A Hopeful History* (New York, Boston and London: Little Brown and Company, 2020) who argues for "a radical idea" – the goodness of human beings: "to stand up for human goodness is to take a stand against the powers that be (p. 19); "the time has come for a new view of human nature. It's time for a new view of humankind" (p. 20).

62 Swaminathan Anklesaria Aiyar, 'Jugaad is our most precious resource', | *The Economic Times*, August 15, 2010: "Many years ago, innovative Punjabis mounted a diesel irri-gation pump on a steel frame with wheels creating a vehicle they called *jugaad*. It was ultra-cheap but did not conform to vehicular regulations."

63 Navi Radjou, Jaideep Prabhu and Simone Ajuja, *Jugaad Innovation: Think Frugal, Be Flexible, Generate Breakthrough Through Growth* (San Francisco, CA: Jossey-Bass, 2012), 4.

64 Claude Lévi-Strauss, *The Savage Mind* (Chicago, IL: University of Chicago Press, 1968).

65 Sherry Turkle, *Life on the Screen: Identity in the Age of the Internet* (New York: Simon & Schuster, 1997), 7.

66 Simon Schama, *The Face of Britain: The Nation Through Its Portraits* (New York: Viking, 2015); *Simon Schama's Face of Britain*, five-part series broadcast on BBC Two, 2015.

67 Caroline Howard, 'Impact 15 – Classroom Revolutionaries', *Forbes*, 2012; www.forbes.com/pictures/emii45fhhe/suneet-tuli/?sh=2eba6b9a772e (accessed December 1, 2020).

1

MAKER ORIGINS AND MIGRANT CREATIVITY

The past is alive and kicking in the current period. As the author William Faulkner almost said, "The past is never dead. It's not even the past".[1]

This chapter on the roots and routes of diasporic creativity examines the skill sets that were developed and honed in earlier phases of migration. The migrant creativity I describe in this book emerged from the needs-based economies of the nineteenth and twentieth centuries and was transmitted to the generations that followed. I narrate the experiences of the pioneering generations, the parents and the grandparents, in earlier sites of migration, to demonstrate how the movement and maker capital that manifests itself in twenty-first-century creativity was first accrued in unfamiliar environs. I am taking the particular example of Punjabi makers, but their experience has much in common with other migrant groups living in a needs-based economy – I will draw comparisons with the pioneers who settled the Northwest Territory, for example, whose story was recently told by David McCullough.[2]

This narrative of generational struggle, hard work and skills established by earlier generations of craftsmen has been elided from the analysis of migrant creativity. Migrants improvised technologies and materials to constitute their lives anew in hostile lands. Working against the odds, these pioneers developed a generous spirit of sharing newly learnt skills and passing on established ones, together with an aesthetic of creative improvisation.

Zygmunt Bauman and other commentators on globalization contend that the knowledge of the past is outdated and irrelevant to the requirements of twenty-first-century employment. They argue that there are new rules and you have to respond to the changing times that require flexible responses to new job markets.[3] Indeed, this is the case. Skills and expertise do need to be updated and to move with the times. But moving with the times and flourishing despite the odds is something the migrants I write about can do with ease, thanks to the convertibility of their ancient mover and maker capital, reimagined and re-articulated in new ways.

Theirs is not the only ancient capital leveraged to good effect in the modern world. Inherited capital – of many different kinds – is generative and has enormous powers of reproduction in the contemporary world.[4] Knowledge and expertise developed in the past is significant in many domains. For example, Ajantha Subramanian has demonstrated how the members of an elite intellectual group, the Tamil Brahmins, are also able to leverage their ancient capital within cutting-edge financial and technological domains central to the modern world.[5] Through education in the prestigious IITs (Indian Institutes of Technology), today's elites can find spectacular jobs in a global market, where they represent India at its technological and scientific best.[6] The priestly Brahmin caste – with its literacy and dominance in law, science, and mathematics and its recent ascendance in technical and management sciences – has been consistently associated with the most coveted forms of knowledge. The cumulative effect of this history has been their production of a highly educated, urbanized, mobile elite, 'Brand India'.

But the story I am telling is one of movement and maker capital. It is not unique: it is an old story in a new era and has clear parallels with that of other artisanal groups. Indeed, in the nineteenth and twentieth centuries, regions around the world have been settled by artisans whose energies and expertise gave impetus to expanding economies. Just taking one example from the United States, notable numbers of Jewish migrant makers arrived in the late nineteenth and early twentieth centuries, mostly from central and Eastern Europe. Often young, unmarried men free of family responsibilities, once arrived in the United States, many were well positioned to apply their handicraft skills in the enterprises of the growing urban centers.[7] Seventy percent of Eastern European Jews who came through New York's Ellis Island in the thirty years or so before the First World War had some kind of occupational skill.[8] In Europe, they had been bookbinders, watchmakers, tailors and dressmakers, hat and cap makers, furriers and tanners. Many had experience in *Schnittwaren Handlung*, the handling of cloth and fabrics, or "piece-goods", as they were known. Putting these skills to use, Jewish immigrants had, by 1900, come to dominate the garment industry both in New York and London. Writer Malcolm Gladwell likens their arrival to "showing up in Silicon Valley in 1986 with ten thousand hours of computer programming already under your belt".[9] Sociologist Stephen Steinberg notes the timing of their arrival, on the cusp of the mass production of clothing.[10] Most of the leading US fashion designers are also from this background – from Levi Strauss, who founded Levi Strauss & Co. in 1853 – the first company to manufacture blue jeans – to contemporary big names like Kenneth Cole, Donna Karan, Anne Klein, Calvin Klein, Michael Kors, Ralph Lauren, Isaac Mizrahi, Zac Posen and Diane Von Furstenberg, among many others. All the leading Hollywood costume designers in the film world's heyday were Eastern European immigrants. They created the quintessential "American glamour look" known all over the world thanks to actresses and other leading ladies of the day, including presidential wives. Many of the movie moguls also came from a Jewish artisanal migrant background: Harry Cohn, Columbia Pictures, was a cobbler and a vaudevillian; Jesse Louis Lasky, founder of Paramount Pictures, was in the shoemaking business and his co-founder, Adolph Zukor, was an upholsterer and later an accomplished designer of fur garments; Carl Laemmle of Universal Studios worked for a clothing company, where he also built window displays; the Warner brothers were cobblers and bicycle repairers; Samuel Goldwyn was a glove maker and Louis Mayer, co-owner with Marcus Loew of MGM (Metro Goldwyn Mayer), previously owned theaters and nickelodeon stores but had started out as an ironmonger in the scrap metal business, a gatherer of industrial detritus and things on the edge.[11]

There are equivalent examples from the garment and fashion industries in the UK – Cecil Gee and Lee Cooper, for example, and also in the world of theater and film. The eminent Oscar-winning actor Daniel Day-Lewis is the grandson of film producer Sir Michael Balcon, legendary head of Ealing Studios, which was the most famous and innovative British film studio for much of the twentieth century, allied with MGM in the United States. Like his US contemporaries, the innovators of Hollywood studios, Sir Michael also came from a migrant East European Jewish family. Before entering the world of film, he began his career as an artisan, a jewelry apprentice. Daniel Day-Lewis, as well as being one of the most admired actors of his generation, is also an expert carpenter and a cobbler, an artisanal expertise he acquired during a five-year apprenticeship with a master shoemaker, the legendary Stefano Berner in Florence, whose handmade bespoke shoes are world renowned and sell for many hundreds of dollars. Thus, Day-Lewis reproduces his maker inheritance from the world of film and an artisanal legacy.

The demand for their skills in the burgeoning cities of the late nineteenth and early twentieth centuries was the migrant advantage of Eastern European/Jewish artisan immigrants. Some moved into the creative fields of theater and film, at a time when mainstream professions were not open to them. Others, successful in accumulating financial capital through small-scale peddling and shopkeeping, set up their own larger-scale businesses, for example in mining (Meyer Guggenheim) and banking (Joseph Seligman) – but these were businesses created from the edges, not by working with exclusive, dominant players in the economy.[12] Within three decades in the United States, Jewish immigrants and their progeny were upwardly mobile, "from proletariats to middle class", and taking advantage of the opportunities for formal education open to them.[13]

Such upward educational mobility of American Jews is not so different from the British Asians I describe (children of parents who migrated in the mid to late 1960s). They are "making it" within a period of thirty-five years or so in the UK despite inequalities and enormous racism faced.

Like the Jews who went to North America and the UK, the earlier migrant craftsmen of North India also responded to the social and political conditions of their time and place. They were readily mobile, migrating with their skills and equipment to wherever there was a demand. Not all of the people I write about come from an explicitly artisanal background, however. My story is about movement as it is encoded in creativity where the capital is generationally transmitted and absorbed by artisanal groups, and it is also about the creativity of people who do not have artisanal inheritances but have lived among pioneering migrants and whose creative capital comes from this pioneering sensibility.

The Punjabi maker background[14]

Sennett's conceptions of the relationship between hand and head – his notion that "making is thinking" and the use of hands to do a job well – resonate with powerful Punjabi sayings about the hands:

> *hath kul javay*: the hand becomes fluent through practice
> *hath taang hai*: the hand is tight and not generous
> *hath saaf*: a clean hand that can work with finesse and clarity
> *hath waylay nah rahan*: hands should not be idle doing nothing
> *pakka hath*: a strong hand (refers to doing a job well)
> *kaccha hath*: a weak hand (a job handled badly, without care)

From the earliest phases of consciousness and socialization, these metaphors are drilled into all of us who are the progeny of Punjabi artisans, and we are reminded of them on a daily basis. We learn that work done in the past is encoded in hands and gives them the facility to move with fluidity and skills, almost without thought, making appropriate gestures to get things right, to create work of quality and finesse. These bodily practices of the hand produce skill sets and habits of work embodied in the "making of things" with precision and perfection. The development of craft skills dates back to the Indus civilization which flourished in the fertile river valleys, 2600 BCE.

By the nineteenth century, carpenters, blacksmiths and masons were employed in rural villages by landowning patrons as woodworkers and furniture makers; makers of technical equipment, farm implements, armaments and machinery; and builders of houses and bridges.

Their skills also included the production of the Persian water wheel used for irrigation. In Punjab, it seems to have been in extensive use by the twelfth century, while south of Delhi it remained infrequent even in the twentieth century.[15] In 1872, Baden Henry Baden-Powell, a civil servant in Bengal, observed:

> The Persian wheel [is] used in most wells in the Bari Doab [an area of the Punjab]… and but little used in those parts of the Punjab bordering on Hindustan [Hindi-speaking North India]… Every peg and bit of iron or other material used in making up these implements has its appropriate and distinctive name.[16]

Most Punjabi migrants in the diaspora are from the Doab, or Doaba region. Their ancestors were subjects of the Sikh kingdom of Maharaja Ranjit Singh (1780–1839), which included the Doab and was the last independent area of India annexed by the British:

> Ranjit Singh's kingdom [earlier had] achieved self-sufficiency as regards the production of weapons and munitions... In 1810, the *mistries* [master craftsmen] in Punjab were capable of manufacturing flints [for guns]. The government established cannon foundries, gunpowder magazines and manufactories of arms in Lahore and Amritsar... The equipment (matchlock cannons, mortars, howitzers, shots, shells, ammunition, spears, daggers, boots, belts, saddles, tents, etc.) required by the *Dal Khalsa* [Sikh army] was manufactured in the foundries and workshops maintained by the state as well as by various private individuals.[17]

Ranjit Singh rewarded the metalworkers highly for their contribution to armaments, and also the marble workers for their decorative effort at the Darbar Sahib (Golden Temple).[18] In 1831, the British presented the Maharaja with a pair of cannons as a diplomatic gift. The cannons were cloned by the blacksmiths and other artisans with great skill in the king's foundries and later "inflicted extremely heavy losses on the British forces in the first Anglo-Sikh war in 1846".[19] The kingdom's technological base matched that of the British East India Company, which did not defeat it until the second Sikh war of 1848–49 – and then not because of the technology, but because of the Maharaja's defective command structure.[20]

Unsurprisingly, then, the British colonial administration in the later nineteenth century thought highly of the skilled craftsmen of the Punjab, viewing them as enterprising, industrious and innovative. They were brought to build the colonial infrastructure of the British summer capital in Shimla and the main capital, Delhi; their skills were also adapted to new purposes such as making British-style furniture and cutlery. They worked in every domain of high-level craft and building. Punjabi craftsmen were recruited for the Indian railways, to lay track and build rolling stock, and as engineers and skilled artisans (rather than laborers), to build and operate the extensive canal irrigation system of North India, in which the British Empire invested heavily in order to develop large tracts of semi-arid land.[21] The quality and efficiency of Punjabi craftsmen's work also recommended them for migration to build the railways in Assam in eastern India,[22] and in East Africa. Baden-Powell, in his report of 1872, had commented in particular on the "remarkable... skill and minute carefulness in execution" of "the native artisans of the Punjab" and the high esteem in which they were held by the officers of the railway.[23]

So, many moved first within the subcontinent, from agricultural settings to urban areas including Delhi, Shimla, Calcutta, and elsewhere. This pattern of early migration within India may well have increased willingness to consider opportunities in more distant lands subsequently: Punjabi artisans were among the first to move when opportunities opened outside India. Traditionally, such artisans would have invested any surplus money that they earned in agricultural land. However, between 1900 and 1947 the Punjab Land Alienation Act made this impossible in areas under British control – possibly this even further increased the impetus to travel afield for work. Some switched to investing in land in urban areas instead (my own family, for example, were thus able to develop an iron foundry in Jalandhar, Punjab, using money remitted by my grandfather who was plying his carpentry skills overseas). Late nineteenth and early twentieth-century industrial development created significant demand for their skills in the cities, as well as overseas in British colonies. Migration removed them from oppressive village caste hierarchies, in which upward mobility was restricted. They benefited from the status dissonance that movement to Indian cities and overseas produced, as their artisanal and craft skills flourished in new urban and global diaspora sites.[24] In addition, kin in Punjab gained from remittances sent home in the early days of diasporic success, when the myth of return was still strong.

The craft workers' skills flourished, first because deployed in new and challenging environments and also, in some cases, because of the opportunity of formal training.

In 1885, Mayo College of Industrial Art in Lahore, named for Viceroy Mayo of India, was established to harness and professionalize the expertise of Punjabi artisans. Its first principal was John Lockwood Kipling – an Englishman who promoted indigenous craftsmanship, himself a craftsman who had been apprenticed in the Staffordshire Potteries as a painter and designer; he was also father to Rudyard Kipling.[25] His star student at Mayo College was Ram Singh Sohal, later its vice principal. He was the architect of the elite Aitchison College in Lahore and Khalsa College in Amritsar, and in 1891 Queen Victoria invited him to the UK. There he designed the Durbar room at Osborne House, her summer palace on the Isle of Wight off Britain's south coast, where he built intricately carved wooden fireplaces, ceilings and cornices, drawing on traditional Indian motifs.[26]

With growing prosperity, the technical skills of a number of Punjabis of artisan background were further enhanced through university education. The possibility of such an education arose from the remittances of successful migrants. Nand Singh Sehra, a son of artisan parents, obtained a mechanical engineering degree from the University of California in 1910 and later taught at US universities before returning to India to represent the Ford Motor Company in the 1930s. Together with Sohan Singh Thekadar, who struck it rich in the oil fields of Assam, and Mohan Singh Hadiabadi, a wealthy building contractor, he was subsequently a driving force in establishing an engineering and technical college in Phagwara, Punjab, where students from artisanal families found educational opportunities unavailable to them elsewhere. Members of my family who became architects and engineers were educated at this college in the 1940s and 1950s before they migrated to Kenya and Britain; my two great-grandmothers, who owned the foundry business in Jalandhar, Punjab, were among the top donors to this institution. Dalip Singh Saund, the first Asian US Congress member, who served from 1967 through 1973, was from a similar artisanal background; he earlier had earned a PhD in mathematics from the University of California, Berkeley in 1924. His brother Karnail Singh, a prominent engineer whose legendary technical skills were featured in the Indian press, became the chairman of Indian railways.

All these eighteenth, nineteenth and twentieth-century activities catalyzed and also honed the Punjabi artisans' technical and craft skills, combined as they were with their enterprise and industry. The artisanal groups benefited greatly from movement within India, from migration overseas which catalyzed their artisanal skills further, and from industrialization which made their skills much in demand and took them away from the oppressive caste restrictions placed on them in landed feudal hierarchies, in which they were accorded inferior status. They also benefited from being at the heart of a technically savvy and technology-orientated Sikh kingdom, especially as related to the construction of armaments, having studied British techniques in the East India company workshop and having employed French experts for their technical and military knowledge.[27] They also had access to earlier European and Persian designs which they studied, and were expert at inventing their own designs. A wide knowledge base acquired from Europe and Asia undergirded their sophisticated and ancient technical expertise. Additionally, the Punjabis benefited from being the last to be annexed and brought under British rule as by that time the British Empire was into building and developing its infrastructure, rather than simply extracting resources as in earlier phases of colonization.

Diaspora maker expertise in East Africa: *jugaad* and generosity

In *Out of Africa* (1937), her memoir of life in Kenya, the Danish Baroness Karen Blixen, aka Isak Dinesen, evoked with admiration the artisanal skills of Punjabi migrant Pooran Singh, the *fundee* on her coffee plantation in the Ngong hills outside Nairobi, the British colony's capital. *Fundee*, or *fundi*, is Swahili for the skilled artisans and mechanics employed in the workshops, railways, British government-owned institutions and private enterprises of East Africa. The term derives from the Swahili *kufunda* – to pass on knowledge, to teach; a form of pedagogy. Punjabi artisans were well known for transmitting their skills to Asians and Africans alike, a reflection of the diasporic sensibility of collaboration and co-construction. This generosity, in contrast to Asian mercantile groups, held them in good stead, and they were not seen as exploitative capitalists. (In fact, it was a Punjabi Sikh artisan, Makhan Singh, born in India and raised in East Africa, who in 1935 co-founded and led the region's first trade union: the East African Trade Union, which was inclusive of African workers, and fought for the rights of all workers . As well as better working conditions, in 1950, he demanded the right to vote and independence of the East African territories from British rule; his eleven-and-a-half-year prison sentence was longer than that of any other freedom fighter or political activist.[28])

As Blixen portrays him, Pooran Singh could make or repair anything needed, an expertise not uncommon at that time among artisanal migrants who arrived in East Africa with technological skills attained in the Punjab or previous sites of sojourn:

> Pooran Singh worked at a superhuman pace, as if his life depended upon getting the particular job of work finished within the next five minutes...
>
> He was our Fundee of the farm, which means an artisan of all work, carpenter, saddler and cabinet-maker, as well as a blacksmith; he constructed and built more than one wagon for the farm, all on his own. But he liked the work of the forge best, and it was a very fine, proud sight, to watch him tiring a wheel...
>
> He had taken much pride in our machinery, such as it was... When he went away [after she sold the farm]), he carried no luggage with him but a small box of tools and soldering outfit.[29]

During fieldwork concerning early Punjabi migrant families in Kenya, I interviewed the daughter-in-law and grandson of engineer and master craftsman Jivan Singh, who, like his sister's son Arjun Singh, was part of my grandfather's circle in Kisumu on the shores of Lake Victoria. The daughter-in-law, Gursharan Kaur Nagi, now in her eighties, related the story of Jivan Singh's repair in the 1920s of the airplane of Lord Maurice Egerton, a colonial landholder in Kenya's White Highlands, and the grandson, Surinder Singh Nagi, provided the following details and family history:

> My father tells us the story when Lord Egerton's water plane engine failed. One of the pistons had cracked and getting parts during the World War would have taken a very long time, and he asked around if there was anyone who could do the job locally. The word passed that a competent Indian engineer could have a look. My grandfather Jivan Singh was summoned, and he said he will [sic] give it a go. So, in short, he took measurements, made a die-cast, and molded a new piston, piston rings, etc., and accurately machined the piston to the right size. He put the engine back together and there was a sigh of relief when the engine fired and got going.

Jivan Singh was a pioneer who brought as many as eighty to one hundred people over from Punjab to Kenya whom he also trained and found jobs for. Jivan Singh's nephew, Arjun Singh, was one of those he taught. Arjun Singh had his workshop in Kisumu, where they made grinding crank shafts for cars and lorries to keep them moving, and also did welding and made car body parts. He also repaired farm machinery of all kinds, especially in Kibos where a number of Asians owned farms and saw mills, and grinding machines for sugar cane, flour and wood mills. He himself owned flour mills to grind *posho* [maize] flour that the local Africans and also Asians used for making *ugali* [stiff maize porridge, like Italian *polenta*]. There was a cinema called Silver Cinema whose owner came to see him because a projector part broke. This was an urgent task and if he had sent for the part from Europe it would have taken months to get it, and the cinema had to go on showing films. Arjun Singh examined the broken part and was able to not only copy it, but also make a spare part for the cinema owner in case there was future breakage. The description of his activities resonates strongly with David McCullough's account of the role of the blacksmith in the pioneering community in nineteenth-century North America:

> The blacksmith was gunsmith, farrier, coppersmith, millwright, machinist and surgeon general to all broken tools and implements. His forge was a center of social as well as industrial activity… Chains, reaping hooks, bullet molds, yoke springs, axes, bear and wolf traps, hoes, augers, bells, saws, and the metal parts of looms, spinning wheels, sausage grinders, presses and agricultural implements were a few of the items either manufactured or repaired in his shop.[30]

Another East African master craftsman, Jaswant Singh Bharij, could make guns as part of his repertoire of artisanal skills. He taught Mau Mau fighters to make basic guns using pipes and other locally accessible materials in the early 1950s in the Nairobi area, to help the Africans in their struggle to overthrow British rule. He thus reproduced the earlier armament-making skills that artisans demonstrated in the eighteenth and nineteenth-century technologically sophisticated Punjab and Sikh kingdom.[31] In May 1954, he was arrested by the Kenya Police Reserves and detained at Takwa Camp with other Indian "hard cores" for four and a half years.[32] He was initially given the death penalty, but this was transmuted at the last stage. Like many of the pioneering artisanal settlers, he was someone who generously shared his technical knowledge; he distributed his resources and skills to others who needed them.

The artisans of my grandparents' and parents' generation had an intuitive feeling for how things worked, and could "make, repair, improvise" machinery and parts – as demonstrated in the accounts above of Jivan Singh's skills in repairing the plane and Jaswant Singh's ability to use the scant materials available to make guns and ammunition. Such improvisation – "making-do with material at hand", the notion of *jugaad* (also Swahili *jua kali*, literally 'fierce sun', because the artisans work outside in the sun – now also meaning more generally 'the informal sector') was a highly developed creative aesthetic of the Punjabi diaspora. In the same way, early settlers in North America relied on Yankee ingenuity: a grassroots, bottom-up, pioneering sensibility of innovative improvisations where materials are scarce.

Shortly before he died in 1990, Gurdial Singh Pandhal told the story of having to use stone tools to cultivate his father's 105 acres of marshy land in Kibos, outside Kisumu in Kenya's Nyanza province in the early 1900s. This demonstrates the powerful aesthetic of making do with what was available:

> It was all forest, you couldn't see your neighbours. The settlers cleared the trees from the land with just *pangas* [machetes]. My father and the others had

to make their own implements out of wood, there wasn't even iron for hoes or ploughs. They'd do the final shaping using sharp stones.[33]

This demonstrates the material daring which existed in these earlier generations – making tools from stones to dig third-rate soil. Third-rate land was given to Asians by the colonial government after the railway building was completed at Kisumu. (The best, most fertile land went to the white colonials in the Kenyan Highlands around the Rift Valley.) Asians successfully cultivated and used this inferior land, for growing sugar cane, maize and finger millet – and for industrial mills to process grain and wood. The making of simple tools using material at hand, in this case just the local stones (like Neolithic stone tools), was reproduced into making sophisticated instruments and technology of work.

The women settlers shared the same innovative skills and culture of inventiveness as their husbands, brothers, uncles and fathers, deployed in different domains. During the 1950s, for example, the polythene liners of Tetra Pak milk cartons were used to make tea cozies and cushions, and fishing net string was used for crocheting bed sheets and table cloths, thus demonstrating the aesthetic of recycling everyday objects and making do with materials at hand. This form of women's *jugaad*, or improvisation, utilized ingenuity acquired in village and small-town India, where dowries displayed the craft skills of brides and their kinswomen, and many things were made at home. Again, there are strong resonances with the culture of nineteenth-century settler America, where similarly demanding circumstances required a high level of domestic expertise. David McCullough details the tasks required of the women:

> Making good butter was a skill in which women took particular pride… Then there was the yarn to spin, wool to weave, clothes to make for large families, clothes to wash, mend and patch. And just as the man of the house had his ax, plowshare, long rifle, and those tools necessary for the work to be faced, so, too, did the woman of the house – knives, needles, spoons, paddles, hickory brooms, spinning wheels, and, most important, the heavy, bulbous iron pots to be seen in nearly every cabin that were used more for cooking than any other item and led to countless aching backs by the end of the day.[34]

Women had to be expert in the skills that in a more developed economy would be done by professionals, so, not just cooking, but catering for large numbers of people at a wedding, for example; not just sewing, but tailoring – designing, cutting and stitching blazers, coats and trousers, in addition to simpler *salwar kameez* or dresses. Skill in embroidery was particularly highly prized, a *de rigueur* competitive domestic skill, its products shown off by parents of daughters. The girls in this domestic economy were hyper-observant for design information and interrogated technique and stitch craft with alert eyes as to how other people did things so that they could acquire expertise. Many practiced embroidery and stitching style espionage to learn skills even when some people did not want to pass it on – for example, an imbricated lace that one contemporary reports that she watched surreptitiously, then came home and sat till midnight until she was able to reproduce the pattern. There was enormous emphasis on the *hath khulay* or *khul jaway* – that you should have practiced hands that could do and make things with ease and fluency. You did not leave hands free and idle: you made. You worked on a craft, like knitting, embroidery, crocheting, hemming stitched garments or you did a bit of the craft preparation to get on with the actual job when you gossiped, conversed, listened to the radio or television. You had to be "fortilli" (sharp, smart), pick new skills up fast and be attentive to your job. And you did your work neatly, quickly and with care, not with "shoosti" (laziness). You could not sit around doing nothing.

Work had to be finely executed, whether in making objects or organizing the kitchen shelves with domestic produce and products or putting clothes properly folded in drawers. Shoddy work was frowned upon and disapproved of publicly as the work of hands that were not skilled at fine work. We were all raised with this sensibility that hands had to be busy and work rendered with finesse even when sitting around watching television or when listening to the radio or chatting with pals who were visiting. People visited all the time and chats were constant, a facet of the conviviality that defined life in pioneering settings in Africa.

But there was also a more flexible division of labor, on many fronts. People shared tasks and taught each other, carrying out all kinds of tasks that in the Punjab were performed on the basis of caste or gender where the boundaries could be maintained with greater ease. For example, a particular woman in Gulu, Uganda, used lathe machines to meet a deadline in her father's workshop: this use of tools and machinery was highly developed among women. One of my male relatives told me he saw Punjabi women all over East Africa during the 1950s and 1960s using saws to cut wood and doing carpentry jobs traditionally reserved for men in India. These diasporic women did not hang around for their men to do a "masculine job". They just did it. In pioneering settings, the conventional social boundaries were less stringently policed. Men cooked as they were often on their own without families in the early days; women performed traditionally defined masculine tasks because there were fewer men around to do them.

The ability to succeed in such a needs-based economy depended hugely on collaborating with others and on a spirit of generosity, from participating in preparing meals for large public functions to the sharing of embroidery designs and recipes. When the *choost* pajama – the tight trousers with folds near the ankle worn by Indian Prime Minister Nehru – became fashionable during the 1960s, few women knew how to cut and make it. An expert seamstress taught my mother, who in turn taught my sisters and so the making of this more complex, bias-cut garment was taught, learnt and passed on: participatory pedagogy in the domestic domain. The communities were also characterized by a tradition of open hospitality: *jayra dhar tay ayah ohnu jee ayaan aakhidha* (whoever comes to your door, welcome them with open arms and warm, unstinting hospitality). Traveling as an Asian family in East Africa during the 1950s and 1960s, it was usual to arrive in a town not knowing anyone and to knock on the door of an Asian household and be welcomed and asked to stay. The mother would go into the kitchen and help prepare the food with the woman of the house and feel completely at home. This openness and contributive generosity is deeply embedded and undergirds the diasporic creativity I describe.

Having to start afresh in pioneering communities in which a new infrastructure has to be formed makes people more collaborative and co-operative, generous and open to the new in ways not possible if residence is in one stable and bounded site. Having to settle in new places in which none of the old is familiar or present, one has to improvise at very high level together with whomever is around: kin, kith, friend or foe. Gurdial Singh Pandhal reminisced:

> In those early days we were all like brothers, Europeans, Indians and Africans. When the railway reached Kisumu Muslims had their mosque and the Hindus their temple both in one temporary building in the *landhies*. That building was made of mud and poles with a *mabati* [corrugated iron] roof. There was no trouble, there was lots of good feeling between everyone.[35]

Corrugated iron sheets, *mabati* as they are called in Swahili, were a commonly used and cheap, easily available building material. It is waterproof and durable and is still the building material much used in construction of buildings in many parts of Africa. The pioneering settlers who worked and built in material-scarce environments used *mabati* to construct shops and houses, and also temples. The construction of the gurdwara was a statement of community and an affirmation that 'this is our collective home, this is where we plan to stay'. Those built by my

FIGURE 1.1 Gurdwara Bazaar, Nairobi, June 7, 1939 by Gopal Singh Chandan

Source: Amarjit Chandhan and Gurinder Mann

grandfather's pioneering generation were made entirely of corrugated iron sheets. The *mabati*-built gurdwara in his home town of Kisumu stood until the mid-1950s when a stone building took its place. The original corrugated iron structure of the first temple built in Nairobi, in 1903, has been preserved as a heritage site to remind people of the huge contribution of the pioneering generation in building the earliest settlements and establishing their religious and cultural institutions (see Figure 1.1).

The construction of a frontier community's infrastructure, when everything had to be built from scratch with few materials and few tools, was hard work. However, their deep collaborative community ethos undergirded this process, a sharing and contributive sensibility which persists in the diasporas of today.

Notes

1 William Faulkner's exact words, from his 1950 book *Requiem for a Nun*, omit the second "the".

2 David McCullough, *The Pioneers: The Heroic Story of the Settlers Who Brought the American Ideal West* (New York: Simon & Schuster, 2019).

3 See, for example, Zygmunt Bauman, *Liquid Times: Living in an Age of Uncertainty* (Cambridge, UK: Polity, 2007), 2–3: "…the collapse of long-term thinking, planning and acting… leads to a splicing of both political history and individual lives into a series of short-term episodes and projects… Past successes do not necessarily increase the probability of future victories, let alone guarantee them… A swift and thorough *forgetting* of outdated information and fast ageing habits can be more important for the next success than the memorization of past moves and the building of strategies on the foundation laid by previous *learning*."

4 Pierre Bourdieu, 'The Forms of Capital', in ed. John G. Richardson, *Handbook of Theory of Research for the Sociology of Education* (Westport, CT: Greenwood, 1986), 241–258.

5 Ajantha Subramanian, 'Making Merit: The Indian Institutes of Technology and the Social Life of Caste', in *Comparative Study of Society and History*, Vol. 57, No. 52 (2015), 291–322 and 'Recovering Caste Privilege: The Politics of Meritocracy at the Indian Institutes of Technology in New Subaltern Politics' in *New Subaltern Politics: Reconceptualizing Hegemony and Resistance in Contemporary India*, ed. Alf Gunvald Nilsen and Srila Roy (Oxford Scholarship Online, 2015); Vikram Chandra, *Geek Sublime: The Beauty of Code and the Code of Beauty* (Minneapolis, MN: Graywolf Press, 2014).

6 Subramaniam argues that the avowedly meritocratic IITs, with their highly competitive exam entry, confer upon their graduates a gloss of high-status deservedly held because of ability, but are in fact merely consolidating millennia-old privilege: "the IITian has become an exemplar of intellectual merit, someone seen as naturally gifted in the technical sciences. What such assessments occlude are the forms of accumulated social and cultural capital that have enabled admissions to IITs. The majority of IITians come from upper-caste families of bureaucrats, school teachers, and academics where capital had long been held in education." Ajantha Subramaniam 'Recovering Caste Privilege: The Politics of Meritocracy at the Indian Institutes of Technology in New Subaltern Politics', in *New Subaltern Politics: Reconceptualizing Hegemony and Resistance in Contemporary India*, ed. Alf Gunvald Nilsen and Srila Roy (Oxford Scholarship Online, 2015), 77.

7 Barry Supple, 'A Business Elite: German-Jewish Financiers in Nineteenth Century New York', in *The Business History Review*, Vol. 31, No. 2 (Summer 1957): 143–178.

8 Malcolm Gladwell, *The Outliers: The Story of Success* (New York: Little, Brown and Company, 2008).

9 Gladwell, *The Outliers*, 158.

10 Stephen Steinberg, *The Ethnic Myth: Race, Ethnicity and Class in America* (New York: Atheneum, 1981), 99.

11 Henry Feingold, 'Investing in Themselves: The Harvard Case and the Origins of the Third American-Jewish Commercial Elite' in *American Journal of Jewish History*, Vol. 77, No. 4 (June 1988): 530–553.

12 Supple, 'A Business Elite'; Feingold, 'Investing in Themselves'.

13 Feingold, 'Investing in Themselves'.

14 Much of the text in this and the following sections of this chapter first appeared in Bhachu, 'The Invisibility of Diasporic Cultural and Multiple Migrant Creativity', in *Mutuality: Anthropology's Changing Engagement*, ed. Roger Sanjek (Philadelphia, PA: Penn University Press, 2014).

15 Satish Saberwal, *Mobile Men: Limits to Social Change in Urban Punjab* (New Delhi: Institute of Advanced Study, Shimla, in association with Manohar Publications, 1976, revised 1990), 97.

16 1872, quoted in Saberwal, 1990: 97. (Baden Henry Baden-Powell was the older brother of Robert Baden-Powell, founder of the Scout Movement.)

17 Kaushik Roy, *War, Culture and Society in Early Modern South Asia 1740–1849* (London: Routledge, 2011), 143.

18 Saberwal, *Mobile Men*, 89–91.

19 Roy, *War, Culture and Society*, 143.

20 Roy, *War, Culture and Society*, 164.

21 Saberwal, *Mobile Men*, 89–91

22 Harish C. Sharma, *Artisans of the Punjab: A Study of Social Change in Historical Perspective 1849–1947* (New Delhi: Manohar Publishers and Distributors, 1996). Sharma says that crafts workers "were the first ones to avail of opportunities available outside the Punjab. They went as far as to Assam to work on the laying down of the railway track under difficult conditions."

23 Saberwal, *Mobile Men*, 10.

24 Saberwal, *Mobile Men*, 89–91.

25 Deborah Swallow, 'John Lockwood Kipling: A Post-Postcolonial Perspective', in *John Lockwood Kipling: Arts and Crafts of the Punjab and London*, ed. Julius Bryant and Susan Weber (New Haven, CT and London: Yale University Press, 2017).

26 Naazish Ata-Ullah, 'Stylistic Hybridity and Colonial Art and Design Education: A Wooden Carved Screen by Ram Singh', in *Colonialism and the Object: Empire, Material Culture and the Museum*, ed. Tim Barringer and Tom Flynn (London: Routledge, 1998), 68–81.

27 Sana Aiyar, *Indians in Kenya – The Politics of the Diaspora* (Cambridge, MA: Harvard University Press, 2015), 190.

28 Sana Aiyar, *Indians in Kenya – The Politics of the Diaspora* (Cambridge, MA: Harvard University Press, 2015), 127.

29 Karen Blixen, *Out of Africa* (Middlesex: Penguin Modern Classics, International edition, 1985), pp. 219, 256.

30 McCullough, *The Pioneers*, 71.

31 Nazmi Durrani, *Liberating Minds, Restoring Kenyan History: Anti-Imperialist Resistance by Progressive South Asian Kenyans 1884–1965* (Nairobi: Vita Books, 2017).

32 Aiyar, *Indians in Kenya*, 197.

33 'Farming with stone tools', www.sikh-heritage.co.uk/heritage/sikhhert%20EAfrica/sikhsEAfrica.htm (accessed August 6, 2019).

34 McCullough, *The Pioneers*, 72.

35 www.sikh-heritage.co.uk/heritage/sikhhert%20EAfrica/sikhsEAfrica.htm (accessed August 6, 2019).

2

KULJIT BHAMRA

Artisanal music maker and democratizer of musical knowledge

The measure of my success… will be that I become redundant…[1]

Kuljit Bhamra is a tabla player and composer best known now for his many collaborations with musicians from different genres and continents, and as one of the record producers who pioneered the British bhangra sound.[2] His musical interests are wide-ranging, inclusive and involve radical hybridization; his talents and interests reflect the geographical context in which he lives now and also his migration trajectory.

But Kuljit is multifaceted in the skills he possesses. He is a qualified civil engineer, a technically sophisticated music producer and arranger, an inventor, a maker and repairer of musical instruments and an expert carpenter and electrician who built his own recording studio, as well as a composer and performer of music in many genres. In addition, he is a sharer par excellence in the most cutting-edge way. In the open, distributive, contributive tradition of pioneering migrants, he seeks to pass on the expertise that he possesses by making the skills of tabla playing accessible to all, by both traditional and digital means. He is thus also an exemplar of contemporary sharism and knowledge democratization. His style of working is that of the community which has produced him and is very much in synch with the currents of our times.

A self-taught musician, he deployed his deep musical understanding and technical know-how to engineer the bhangra sounds of the 1980s and 1990s.[3] From there, his career moved into film scores and West End musicals both as performer and composer,[4] as well as collaborations with musicians from classical and wide-ranging folk traditions.[5] His musicianship and influence has received establishment recognition with the award of an MBE in 2009 "for services to Bhangra and British Asian Music" and an honorary doctorate from the University of Exeter in 2010; he was the first person of color ever to hold the position of artistic director of the

FIGURE 2.1 Kuljit Bhamra with the world's first electronic tabla, The Tabla Touch, 2019

Source: © Ammy Phull

Society for New Music (now Sound and Music[6]). He says his mission now is to ensure that his instrument, the tabla, is accessible to all musicians, both composers and performers, whatever their musical tradition.

A matrilineal musical inheritance

Born in Nairobi in 1959, where his parents and grandparents had lived for decades, Kuljit came to the UK aged two with his mother, to join his father who was already in London studying civil engineering. In 1968, the family settled in Southall, an area of west London which came to be known as "Little Punjab". A skilled maker of all kinds of things, Kuljit's father later insisted that his son, too, should become an engineer. "My father always thought music should be a hobby", says Kuljit, "[but] I… eventually pursued my dream". His professional achievements as a musician have by now softened his father's objections: "he's a lovely dad", says Kuljit.

Like Rishi Rich, Kuljit's musical inheritance is from his mother. Mohinder Kaur[7] is an extremely talented musician and a lovely, warm-hearted woman who has had a singular influence on her son. Kuljit has played tabla with her since he was a child. She was brought up in Kenya and Uganda, where she was exposed to the complex musical landscape of East Africa, including many forms of African music, Hollywood and Bollywood musical styles, the pop scene of the day and the jazz and rock 'n' roll scene of earlier times. She has enormous command of both Punjabi folk and popular music as well religious hymns and music. The milieu she was raised in and its music were reproduced in Britain by the early pioneers and further honed by the second generation – those such as Kuljit – who have reinvented the music and put it into global landscapes. I interviewed Mohinder when she was in her late seventies and still much in demand with her vast network of friends and relatives to sing at the frequent *sangeets*, the lively pre-wedding celebrations. While once-popular bhangra bands like Alaap and Heera are now out of fashion, she remains "as busy as ever", Kuljit told me.

In early-1960s London, she was rare in carrying an expertise in *kirtan*, the devotional songs, and also the religious rituals, when newly arrived immigrant populations were conducting their life with little religious or cultural infrastructure. Secular singers and musicians were scarce, too. So Mohinder conducted religious rituals as well as performing wedding songs and other popular music outside the religious domains. She was a recording artist with EMI, traveling to India each year to make her records, as well as a pioneer in initiating a mixed-gender dance floor, encouraging women who used to stay in the peripheries to enter the dance floor on equal terms.[8] As a child, Kuljit would play the tabla with her when she performed at functions and this honed his musical skills from an early age.

At nine years old, Kuljit was taken to a master musician to extend his playing skills. However, he was frustrated by this experience, he told me, because of the expectation that he would adopt his teacher's particular style of playing: this is the way Indian musical education is executed traditionally, with a single master player who inducts young novices into their brand and style of playing:

> …although the people who were trying to teach me were very good players themselves, they couldn't explain things in a way that I could understand… asking me to memorize long complicated phrases that would have no use to me. I just wanted to play the tabla and enjoy myself playing simple grooves.

Growing up in 1960s and 1970s Britain wasn't always easy. Before leaving Kenya, Kuljit had contracted polio, which left him with a weakened leg. Today, as an adult, Kuljit wears a brace and sometimes walks with a stick – his disability is obvious. As a child, he was teased in school, but his tabla playing accompanying his mother's public performances made him "feel unique", he notes. His disability, which marginalized him in school, also in a sense encouraged him to take the path of playing percussion instruments, which later led him into the path of being a professional musician, composer and music producer. Now renowned, he is a role model for people with disabilities and inspiring to many.

Kuljit and his family also suffered from the explicit racism of the time, experiences shared with the other creative agents in this book who grew up during this period, when racism was rife and virulently expressed in public, resulting in many humiliating and denigrating incidents daily. Kuljit's father cut his hair and stopped wearing a turban, as did many other Sikh men who otherwise could not get a job.

The marginality that Kuljit experienced due to racism and his disability gives him courage to stand up and assert his point of view, and, more importantly, to work with the new in creative innovative ways. He overcame his disability and the racism of his youth to become a successful man and has deep empathy with a vast range of people on the margins, with new immigrants like the Somalis more recently arrived in Southall, with children and old and young people at the temples – and in secular spheres, too.

Kuljit the maker

Kuljit has vast technical prowess and an ability to decode how things work and how they can be rejigged and translated for other purposes.

Kuljit has high-level maker skills and a technical curiosity that undergird his innovative, inventive capabilities; he often tweets about new items of musical equipment and other machines or "how things work".[9] While he says he is not obsessed with gadgetry – "My gadgetry is to get my creativity out", he told me – his interest is deep-rooted, inherited from his father and his grandparents' generation, and developed since he was child figuring out how machines worked. He can take things apart and put them together, all kinds of equipment from sampler machines and recording equipment to restringing tablas and all kinds of wood work and carpentry. As a teenager, he learnt how to restring the table, which involves pulling and tightening a ten-meter-long leather strap around the drum to make its skin tight, a process which leaves blistered skin and painful fingers. He used to rejig his own tabla because he wanted his instrument "to sound amazing". He said he would go to the instrument shop and they would not have the right-size string because there was no standardization. He had to improvise and teach himself this critical task without local professionals in London. His tablas are now made to his specification in Mumbai; he insists on the *syahi* (the black spot, which gives a deeper sound) always being exactly in the center because he found it better for playing the tabla from his perspective – a technical innovation or adjustment on his part.

His recording studio – Red Fort Studios, in Southall – looks like a nondescript factory or warehouse from the outside but inside is a house and professional studio and work space. It is a rendering of his multiple talents and skills. He did all the carpentry and building work, demolishing walls and remaking the space to his own specification. He installed the state-of-the-art recording equipment, and all the complex sound technology needed for a professional recording studio.

Engineering a musical revolution

Kuljit is entirely self-taught, which is what gives him the freedom to work and perform in different genres of music and his openness to many musical styles. He is a remixer par excellence. He has played with many different musicians and provided music for a huge range of events. He says that if you are taught in a particular style that is ingrained into your musical training, it is difficult to leave that. For example, if you are an orchestral musician and you are good at reading music, it can be difficult to improvise. Conversely, if you are a traditional Indian musician who is accustomed solely to the improvisational style, it will be difficult to follow a pre-composed musical score. "Because I have straddled those two worlds", he notes, "I enjoy collaborating and working with different artists from different cultures and backgrounds".

He likes to innovate – for example, playing with seven tabla drums rather than two:

> The tabla is always a two-piece drum – one tuned to a high note and one to a low note and you play them together. I have started to play to a seven-piece tabla drum. Each small drum is tuned to a different note. I can play [them] like a xylophone.

And of course he was one of the pioneers of bhangra. It entered the global sonic landscape via the interpretation of two music producers in particular – Kuljit, and Deepak Khazanchi,[10] both from a multiply migrant East African background.

The first record Kuljit produced was one of his mother's when he was still a teen-ager. He persuaded her to let him produce a record for her, rather than EMI in India – "and she trusted me",[11] he says. It was the late 1970s, the Bee Gees' disco movie *Saturday Night Fever* was a huge hit, and "the whole world was dancing at that time… and then suddenly I started to mix bass drums and funky rhythms with Indian rhythms and then it began to take off and that's how bhangra, in my world, came of age".[12]

Talking to me about its development, Kuljit notes:

> People like myself and Deepak Kazanchi took Punjabi folk music and transformed it into dance floor music produced in such a way that it became more acceptable in the West and more "dancy". We applied Western production techniques to it. And it really is now accepted as a dance phenomenon worldwide… Bhangra is a UK creation alongside fish and chips and chicken tikka masala.

Kuljit, Deepak and others used multi-track recording techniques, Indian percussion instruments and Western orchestral sounds to produce a huge range of albums in an act of combinational daring. The debut albums for the bhangra groups Heera and Premi were played on the local Asian pirate radio *Sina* twenty-four hours a day, one after the other (*Sina* later became the fully fledged legitimate *Sunrise* radio listened to by Asians all over Britain). But the new genre that Kuljit and Deepak created also had a massive effect in India. Bollywood incorporated strong bhangra elements, often unacknowledged. According to Kuljit, "I really believe that Bollywood would not be Bollywood today if it wasn't for bhangra",.

In common with other British Asian diasporic interventions, British Punjabis remixed and recontextualized bhangra in innovative ways, which created powerful local and international conduits for this music to travel in beyond ethnic domains. Thirty years on, bhangra may be less fashionable as a music genre in its own right but there are bhangra dance and exercise classes in gyms right across Europe and North America, and its influence in Bollywood and India endures. These migrant/diasporic developments have much in common with the popularity of Irish step dancing among American Irish dancers who have given it a new vibrancy, made it transnational and also supremely revived it in Ireland itself; New York-based Afro-Caribbean diasporics developed hip hop influenced by reggae and sent the new musical form to the Caribbean; raï music, the music of the bordellos of Oran in Algeria, Algerian music banned in Algeria, was similarly given new impetus through the re-mixings by French Algerians exposed to a range of music in urban France. In the same manner, bhangra as interpreted in the diaspora has been reborn in the diaspora and traveled back to its country of origin.

Kuljit is in this way a crafter of sound – a high-level mechanic of sound whose powerful engineering skills created a new musical genre. He says he "does the thinking, the creating and crafting and engineering of sound" in ways that the performers themselves may not understand. They sing, but the producer creates the song through the engineering and arrangement of the music. Kuljit's musicality was important, his understanding of melody, rhythm and beats, but his technical skills are what allowed him to transform traditional Punjabi bhangra into twentieth-century dance music with a global reach.

Kuljit points out what he calls "a delineation between the Midlands Punjabi music and London". The London-based migrants who formed the earlier bands were multiply migrant, from East Africa, and were predominantly middle class with higher incomes, technologically sophisticated in many domains of life, an expertise they translated into their music. In contrast, the migrants in Birmingham and elsewhere in the Midlands had arrived directly from rural areas of the Punjab in India, and were less well-off. "[The Londoners] could afford accordions, congas, and guitars etc. The Punjabi music that developed in London was broader musically, whereas in the Midlands it was always *dholki* and *toombi*, very simple rural things", Kuljit told me. "That is why I had no hesitation in adding drum kits and bass guitar. In Birmingham, they would never do that – they could not afford these instruments". In addition, the London-based musicians had already developed an aesthetic of remixing in East Africa, an aspect of their durable inheritance from earlier migrations which they were able to reproduce rapidly on arrival in UK; they reproduced an earlier expertise in the London context. Kuljit has in fact written his own account of the development of bhangra, as part of a project funded by the University of Exeter celebrating the contribution of Southall to arts, music, poetry and literature.[13]

Performer and composer for film and theater

As a tabla player, Kuljit has worked on Hollywood films (e.g. *Charlie and the Chocolate Factory*, 2005 and *The Guru*, 2002) and also on musicals like *Bombay Dreams* and *The*

Far Pavilions – mainstream West End theater experiences which professionalized and honed his skills in these theatrical domains; expertise he then brought to Gurinder Chadha's *Bend It Like Beckham: The Musical* for which he was co-composer with eminent English musician Howard Goodall.

Kuljit told me the biggest challenge for the producers of *Bombay Dreams* and *The Far Pavilions* "was to find a tabla player that could do the same thing twice, because most Indian musicians can't do that because they are improvising and playing in the moment. You never would hear a recital that was exactly the same that it was before – it is impossible". So, as Andrew Lloyd Webber's percussionist on stage every night in *Bombay Dreams*, Kuljit had to adapt his improvisational style of playing and instead perform in the same precise way every time, for every performance, day in day out. As a result, he became proficient at following a musical score and from then on was confident about playing with a Western-style orchestra. It was a brilliant opportunity in another way, too, he says: "to actually somehow notate what I was playing so if I was not able to do a show one evening someone else could step in and take my position". No such notation system for the tabla existed, so Kuljit was on his own – but he succeeded in developing a system not just for the tabla but for other Indian drums, too. "That was one of the most challenging things I have ever done and also one of the most rewarding things I ever did."

Then, Kuljit was both percussionist and co-composer along with Howard Goodall for Gurinder Chadha's musical, the first Asian musical to be performed in the West End: *Bend It Like Beckham*, adapted from her earlier film success. Gurinder

FIGURE 2.2 Kuljit Bhamra playing many tablas on stage at the Queen Elizabeth Hall, in the Bollywood to Hollywood concert, which was part of the Alchemy Festival 2013

Source: © Ammy Phull

Chadha's ambition for the new work "was to create a totally new British musical. That is what I wanted to do, something that spoke to us today – of the last thirty to forty years of Britain". Kuljit and Goodall collaborated and created their very own British Punjabi music in the moment. Gurinder witnessed the discovery, the fusion, happening in the moment: "We started with one thing, [Howard] started on the piano, a drum came in, a voice came in, [Howard] said, 'Can you do it like that?' and before you knew it, it was fusion happening in front of our eyes".[14] And so they created something new. They were discovering the contours of the new while navigating landscapes that are not known in advance. Diasporic musicians like Kuljit have combinational daring in engaging and creating remixed musical forms, and this constitutes his musical leitmotif and core sensibility. Howard Goodall notes that the process of creating something new took time: "By the time we came into the final workshop, in the final stages of creating a piece, we were actually creating our own Punjabi music... we couldn't have done this at the beginning of the process. We needed... three to four years to get it so in our skin so that... it wouldn't feel fake".[15] This is the real *modus operandi* of the diasporics who work on the new on the basis of the new – the daring combinations that are discovered and recovered in the making of the music – capturing the moment as it unfolds and so creating the new licenses of participation. The composition of the music was organic, complex and dynamic. It did not sound fake, as it was something new that had emerged from complex mixings and re-mixings and a call and response in the moment. For Howard Goodall, the process of composition was also an opportunity to discover "all the wonderful sounds and the possibility of instruments that come from the Indian tradition... I love the idea that the tabla becomes one of those instruments that you can use around the world".[16]

Beyond 'East meets West'

"One of the things that really inspires me are cutting-edge and cross-cultural projects", Kuljit told me. However, he complains that East is always just "meeting" West and suggests that it is time to move beyond that and do something "more exciting".[17] He gives a reason for this dynamic:

> Indian music is shrouded in a cloak of magic and mystery and that is a cloak left over from the Victorian times, when India was represented as a land of silk and spice – magic rope tricks, flying carpets and people sleeping on a bed of nails... The Victorians, I imagine, felt that they knew the answers to most things. But my theory is that people don't want answers to everything. People want to believe in magic. In my opinion, the West is still mesmerized by the magic of the East. And us Indians are very good at selling that magic to the West.[18]

But he dislikes this "East meets West" dichotomy and he does not like the duet formula that it usually encourages – in which one genre of music is played by a musician and then another one plays from another region, ethnicity and genre – they take turns to play. His desire is to create and compose in a more radical way. "I think the most satisfying projects I have been involved in are ones that are collaborative. I find a way of expanding my own horizons is actually in work with other people", he told me. His path-breaking stint as director of the Society for New Music gave him many such opportunities to develop his expertise in new directions. He has played with many groups on so many platforms, from Scottish bag pipes, to punk, to Trinidadian Chutney music, to all kinds of orchestras, big and small. He has also worked with Somali musicians in Southall, and with them produced a song which became a transnational hit in Somalia and across the Somali diaspora.[19] He also co-organized a Punjabi and Somali music event in Southall which combined bhangra and Somali music.[20] In this way, he helped the Somali community in Southall – new underprivileged immigrants into this hyper-Punjabi area which disdains them as the Punjabis themselves were disdained when they came into white Southall. Kuljit has empathy and enormous openness to the new and using the supreme powers of remix, generously sharing his expertise. Kuljit's ability to collaborate with this exceptional range of people and musicians is a testament to the diasporic sensibility that governs his creativity – that of generosity, an openness, sharing knowledge and being able to work with people whose skills and talents are different from his own. In this he resembles physicist Tejinder Virdee, architectural artist Bhajan Hunjan and architect Amarjit Kalsi, in particular: each has significant bridge-building capital.

Making the tabla accessible to all

Kuljit is a democratizer and distributor of knowledge who breaks down hierarchies. He tweeted an eBay ad to show how tabla can be made accessible using straightforward language. He said: "If all tabla teachers could learn to speak like this eBay seller we would have more people playing the tabla". The seller's ad was as follows: "A used tabla drum, the smaller one of the two, in good working order, goes bong when you bang it. From a pet and smoke free home".

Kuljit's desire is to encourage composers based outside India "to use Indian instruments in their works as a way to break down the barriers between Indian and Western styles of music". He wants the tabla to be ubiquitously played and for knowledge of how to play it to be commonly available to people who are both familiar with Indian music and for people who are new to it and would like to learn it:

> I really would like to see music being taught in colleges and schools, I would like to see more people playing Indian instruments. I would like to see it being taught in a way that is simple and easy to understand without the magic and the mystery and no complications. That is my dream…[21]

In part, he attributes the absence of Indian instruments in the wider musical landscapes to the learning and teaching techniques which are closed to the wider public and potential learners. The traditional way of learning within Indian classical music – the one he rejected as a child – is from a maestro, a guru or an *ustad*, a teacher or practitioner whose clan or *gharana* has a distinctive musical tradition and ideology; a novice would serve an apprenticeship and become part of the entourage of the maestro, expected to adhere to that one style of playing for a lifetime, eventually becoming a virtuosic soloist in their own right. Traditionally, these music houses were geographically specific, like the Delhi *gharana*, or the Patiala *gharana* in the Punjab, or the Benares *gharana* of Uttar Pradesh, Gwalior in Rajasthan. Kuljit views these lineages of knowledge as reproducing creativity that is timid and panders to the sacred pasts. He is ambivalent about the stunning and exquisite performances by maestros which display their exceptional expertise and seduce the public through beautiful performances – yet play no pedagogic function in terms of inviting the public into learning the instrument, or encouraging others to make the music part of their everyday repertoires. Such performances are narcissistic interventions – self-centered grandiosity, self-absorbed and arrogant – and an expression of knowledge exclusivity, a demonstration of knowledge transmitted from one master to one talented pupil, a boundary marker of exclusivity that restricts entry. He likens this type of performance and the *gharana* system itself with its exclusive master–student relationship to "a blood clot which stays in one place", that is to say, it blocks access to knowledge, restricting its expertise to a tiny exclusive few and closed to the new – and thus ultimately fatal to the creative health of tabla playing.

Kuljit told me that since he is completely self-taught and had no teacher, when people ask him about his training and musical style, he says that his *gharana* is the west London area of Southall where he was raised. He does not want to "hug the skill [of playing the tabla] to myself with the guru but give it away". His outlook resonates powerfully with what Harvard law professor and originator of Creative Commons, Lawrence Lessig, says about "Read Only" and "Read-Write" cultures. In a Read Only culture, argues Lessig, you listen to or view or read a controlled, already-created product and of course clap and show admiration – "a culture in which creators get to create only with the permission of the powerful, or of creators from the past"[22] – much like the tabla performance in the *gharana* system. In contrast, in the "Read-Write" culture, there is an invitation to participate in and learn from and change what has been offered by making your own input, an open, boundary-less concept that invites remix,[23] which is the fundamental sensibility of Kuljit.

The standardized notation system for the tabla that Kuljit developed while working on *Bombay Dreams* and *The Far Pavilions* is a key element in Kuljit's project to enable anyone and everyone to participate in learning the tabla. Called 'Universal Indian Drum Notation', the four-symbol system works for all Indian drums and can be used by anyone with a basic knowledge of Western notation:

> As part of a project with students from the Royal Academy of Music, I wrote a four-part work for the tabla… During the performance, you could see the looks of confusion coming from the Indian musicians in the audience. They

couldn't understand how the students could possibly learn to play the tabla in such a short time![24]

The notation system is supported by a series of course books available at Keda Music, Kuljit's company and website, as well as a series of video tutorials – *Demystifying Indian Music* – available free on YouTube. As it says on the website:

> The exciting and revolutionary Universal Indian Drum Notation used in this course allows students, teachers, composers and musicians to play the tabla and enjoy its rich, beautiful sounds. This breakthrough in tabla-education makes the instrument more accessible to musicians from differing backgrounds and cultures.[25]

Kuljit's dream to take the tabla to a wider audience is now being realized, as reflected in Portsmouth schools that include tabla lessons as part of the school curriculum, in which both students and teachers learn how to play and teach the tabla. In addition, for anyone wishing to compose using the notation system, it is also available as software produced by a cutting-edge German company, Dorico, which specializes in music notation and composing software.[26]

Kuljit has invented the world's first electronic tabla, named The Tabla Touch, officially released in December 2020, in collaboration with CLR (Central Research Laboratory), a west London-based company whose agenda is "to bring new hardware products to the market and to encourage designers and entrepreneurs to work with industry in creating innovative products".[27] The patented device combines the traditional instrument with modern electronics and enables whoever is playing it to digitally record what is played.

Kuljit is thus extending his diverse expertise both pedagogically and technically. His ultimate ambition, he told me, is to make himself redundant, having ensured that tabla playing can thrive without him:

> The measure of my success in what I am doing will be that I become redundant in those things. This sounds really weird, that is my thing. I can find something else to do. Let other people do it – that is my success.

Kuljit: inheritor and reproducer of movement and maker capital

Kuljit's style of music and way of being is fundamentally part of a new form which is not a duet. His agenda is a much more radical shift in the pedagogic frame and the sonic landscapes of the world. His life mission is to break closed systems and knowledge monopolies to "create new possibilities and behold a new future", he told me – the vocabulary of openness which he uses to invite people to learn the tabla.

Kuljit has built on both his mother's cultural capital, her inheritance of Punjabi music amplified and complicated by its exposure to new musical forms in East

Africa, and his father's technical maker capital, formalized and sophisticated by his university degree. Migration has catalyzed their skills and Kuljit's, who like his father is also formally qualified as an engineer. In the same way that the artisans from the Punjab honed their skills in new arenas both within India and abroad, so Kuljit has extended his inheritance and early expertise, using the recording engineering of the twentieth century and the electronic and digital technologies of the twenty-first century to create a new genre of dance music and share his expertise with a maximum number of people. Kuljit is using the open landscapes of the digital media to do a complicated thing, creating and participating in online social networks to amplify the collective act of music learning and making.[28] The use of digital media as distributor also applies to Bhajan, to Jatinder Verma, and to Suneet – again, that impetus to share resources, *kaam sikho tay kaam sikhayo* (learn a skill and teach it to others).

Kuljit's democratizing musical sensibilities render him open to new publics. He responds to and collaborates with an incredibly wide range of music and musicians and uses his extensive technical expertise and knowledge to remix and create new forms of music. He jives with the currents of our times in terms of his open pedagogic practice, freeing knowledge for the benefit of the most in the world; his style of engagement with the digital world; and his technical ability to invent new electronic hardware. He is a creative-commons creature and a remixer par excellence who has set the ground for further, more complex and sophisticated re-mixings in times to come through his democratizing interventions and impulses. Kuljit has disrupted the established and traditional restrictive systems of knowledge transmission and invited people to engage in open platforms in synch with knowledge production and engagement, which invites participation through collaborative pedagogic learning platforms that digital media facilitates.

Notes

1 Kuljit Bhamra, interview with the author, January 13, 2015.
2 The genre of music developed by Kuljit and others in the UK during the 1980s and 1990s, as a fusion of Punjabi folk rhythms and Western pop styles. The musical genre became a thriving and vibrant transnational musical industry, adopted by the Bollywood film industry and many musicians within the diaspora.
3 For example, Mohinder Kaur Bhamra featuring C Bawa – *Kuri Southall Di* (1981), Azaad Group – *Nachdi Jawani* (1986), Sangeeta – *A Breath of Fresh Bhangra Air* (1991), Reshma & Mangal – *Gentle Touch* (1993).
4 For example, films he both composed and played for: *Bhaji on the Beach* (1993), *Bend It Like Beckham* (2003); musicals: he was the percussionist for *Bombay Dreams* (2002–4) and both composed and played for *Far Pavilions* (2005); theater: he played the tabla for Birmingham Repertory Company's production of *The Ramayana* both in Birmingham (2000) and at the National Theatre (2001). With Howard Goodall, he wrote the score for the West End musical version of *Bend It Like Beckham* (2015).
5 For example: a jazz collective, Cascade (2006), mixing bhangra and Latin American rhythms, *Bhangra Latina* (2008), with the BBC Concert Orchestra, *Raga Mela* (2009).
6 'The national charity for new music': www.soundandmusic.org/ (accessed August 6, 2019).

7 For a detailed biography and her innovative musical and cultural interventions in transforming the dance floor and introducing gender equality, and her pioneering and iconic role in the establishment of Punjabi folk music in Britain, see: Navtej Purewal, 'The Sound of Memory: Interview with Singer, Mohinder Kaur Bhamra', *Feminist Review* 2012, Number 100: 142–153.

8 See, for example: 'Giddha Pao Haan Deo', Mohinder Kaur Bhamra, Original Classic, www.youtube.com/watch?v=jQvynqKuSR8 (accessed August 6, 2019).

9 March 12, 2019: Singing tablas – hypnotic beats and audio-triggered disco lights (which were bought from a car boot sale for £3!); December 2, 2018: Brocket Parsons playing on his piano arc – a new piano designed for canons and fugues – swivel stool extra; https://twitter.com/kuljitbhamra?lang=en (accessed August 6, 2019).

10 Deepak Khazanchi was born in Srinagar, Kashmir, and raised in Uganda. He was interested in music from a young age and took up guitar playing, inspired by British bands The Beatles and The Shadows. He moved to Britain to study as an undergraduate at the London College of Music. Later as an adult he set up a professional recording studio and produced some early bhangra hits through his own label, Arishma Records.

11 Brave New You, 'Audience with Kuljit Bhamra', June 6, 2019; www.youtube.com/watch?v=7H4vzHRsmUY&t=22s&app=desktop (accessed August 6, 2019).

12 Brave New You, 'Audience with Kuljit Bhamra'.

13 Kuljit Bhamra, Shakila Maan and Ammy Phull, *The Southall Story*, 2010. A project, including an exhibition and website, telling the cultural history of Southall, www.thesouthallstory.com/decades-of-music/ (accessed August 6, 2019).

14 Bend It Like Beckham The Musical, 'Bend It Like Beckham The Musical – Gurinder Chada and Howard Goodall', January 8, 2015; www.youtube.com/watch?v=USh85Lg2MEM (accessed August 6, 2019).

15 Bend It Like Beckham The Musical, 'Gurinder Chada and Howard Goodall'.

16 Keda Music Ltd., 'Tabla and universal drum notation', May 6, 2017; www.youtube.com/watch?v=RCWlD6oZFUg (accessed August 6, 2019).

17 Keda Music Ltd., 'Demystifying Indian Music – Episode 1 – Why Demystify?', March 24, 2017; www.youtube.com/watch?v=ipn_s8HnC28&list=PLwToDf6zj4qY-9wV0JOCgy-U-4tWLVXnQ&index=1 (on August 6, 2019).

18 Keda Music Ltd., 'Demystifying Indian Music – Episode 1'.

19 Abdulkarim Raas/Kuljit Bhamra [CD and MP3], *Somali Party Southall* (Keda Records, 2012).

20 BBC World Service, 'Somali Party Southall bridging the India and Somali gap in London', 2015; www.bbc.co.uk/programmes/p03d4cp3/p03d4dj2 (accessed August 6, 2019).

21 Keda Music Ltd., 'Demystifying Indian Music – Episode 1'.

22 Lawrence Lessig, *Free Culture: How Big Media Uses Technology and the Law to Lock Down Culture and Control Creativity* (New York: Penguin Press, 2004), xiv; 'Laws that Choke Creativity', TED2007, www.ted.com/talks/larry_lessig_says_the_law_is_strangling_creativity?language=en (accessed August 6, 2019).

23 Lawrence Lessig, *Free Culture*; 'Laws that Choke Creativity'.

24 Kuljit Bhamra, 'Tabla notation – Kuljit Bhamra – Keda Music Ltd.', March 7, 2019; www.youtube.com/watch?v=1iaZRMD6z4s (accessed August 6, 2019).

25 http://keda.co.uk (accessed August 6, 2019).

26 'Universal drum notation', https://steinberg.help/dorico/v2/en/dorico/topics/notation_reference/notation_reference_unpitched_percussion_universal_indian_drum_notation_c.html (accessed August 6, 2019).

27 www.centralresearchlaboratory.com/ (accessed August 6, 2019).

28 Howard Rheingold, *Smart Mobs: The Next Social Revolution* (New York: Basic Books, 2003), 101: "The essence of homo sapiens is that they do complicated things together. Online social networks can be powerful amplifiers of collective action precisely because they augment and extend the power of ever-complexifying human sociality. The web is an existence proof that these capabilities can be amplified – our species social inventiveness is central to what it is to be human."

3

BHAJAN HUNJAN

Architectural artist – expansive collaboration and material daring

Two sisters are abandoned by their father in the forest. Their mother has died and he has a new wife. The girls are lost and do not know which way to go or what to do. The more adventurous sister climbs up a tree and spies a hut with smoke coming out of it. The girls walk toward it and there find a holy man, a mendicant who relies on people giving him what he needs for his daily meal. Usually this is flour sufficient for two rotis but today he has been given enough for six, and he is wondering why. Indeed, the answer reveals itself when the two sisters arrive at his door. The universe, knowing that visitors were coming to eat with the holy man, provided him with the extra flour.[1]

Artist Bhajan Hunjan cites this story as a key influence on her way of being in the world: you know that you will be delivered safely, even in a world in which you are abandoned by the very people whose duty it is to care for you. She can take risks and be bold with techniques because the largesse of the universe will provide and acknowledge the pathway you took the risk to tread.

Bhajan is an artist of public spaces where she creates work that responds to the site and connects to its local community. Her art is characterized by a material daring that ranges across silk-screen printed glass, laser-cut acrylic, sandblasted granite, water jet-cut sandstone, and laser-cut metal and poured concrete.[2] She admires the work of Antonio Gaudi, like herself the proud descendant of generations of craftsmen;[3] though not an architect, she is an architectural artist. Like Gaudi, she has designed streetlights and gates; inspired by his *trencadis*, she embeds ceramics, jewelry and coins in concrete: she incorporates his techniques and styles in her own art which defies categorization. She is a British East African Asian and also a product of influences from Europe. But while Gaudi was a firmly rooted man of Catalonia supported by his family and church, Bhajan is a woman of color, unmarried and an artist in an immigrant community which valorizes the security of high-prestige professions, not art. Her art is diasporic – a product of multiple movements which are not undergirded by a national entity nor by a powerful territorial location nor by a transnational elite. Instead, she is endowed with movement capital and has a propensity to try out the new on the basis of the new without patronage or powerful interlocutors negotiating for her. Bhajan also has deep-rooted powers of collaborating with a wide range of people and improvising to discover the new – the fundamental *modus operandi* of the diaspora. And she is fearless about using different materials and has done so in her artwork, which has moved from painting, working with print on paper and fabric, from lithographs and etching into surfaces, to colored cement on walls and floors and shaping the cement into shells, to large works of public art rendered in concrete and metal by industrial engineers.

Bhajan's earliest work was figurative, often including self-portraits. Next, inspired by the crocheted squares and cross-stitched sheets of her Kenyan childhood, she arranged individual paper mono-printed tiles in oils and acrylics in a grid pattern and made ethereal abstract works incorporating Devanagari and Gurmukhi script. The tiles became larger: she created her first floor – for a dance studio, working with the Academy of Indian dance students and Richmond College students AKADEMI; it was inspired by the Chipko trees of India and represents the gifts that trees give us. Then, under the influence of Gaudi, she discovered concrete as a medium in which to create wall art (e.g. Priestley Road Bridge, 1996; a particularly gorgeous tree at Great Holland Primary School, Bracknell), and also floors (Peepul Centre, Leicester, 2005). She has also created beautiful floorscapes in granite and marble (e.g. Words in Stone, St Paul's Way, London, 2012; The Town Square, Slough, 2008; St Matthew's Housing Scheme, Leicester, 2003). Other work includes multilingual electronic display boards (the Sacred Spaces, Leicester, and the Welcome lightbox at the Royal Berkshire Hospital, both 2002) and she now also works in metal, in steel (e.g. White Hart Gates, Thurmaston; the Three Mills Pontoon, River Lea, 2012; streetlights on St Paul's Way, London, E3, 2012). For herself, Bhajan continues to work with paper, experimenting and creating in the solitude of the studio, as she describes it, "without a brief, giving chance to creative expression... each time hoping to arrive at a place which feels right in the moment".[4] The white embossed image shown in Figure 3.1 represents the multifaceted skills Bhajan experiments with, in this case, a creative expression rendered in paper, a facet of her material dexterity and experimental audacity. She translates her printmaking technical expertise and complex cutting techniques into creating a visual object of elegant beauty made from an everyday material.

In the absence of interest in her work by the white consecrators of the mainstream art galleries, and a natural reticence on her own part to promote herself as an individual – she holds the key Sikh belief in living without *homay* (arrogance, ego) – Bhajan has worked successfully on the margins, devising collaborative projects, publicly funded, within which she can practice her art to the benefit of the wider community.

FIGURE 3.1 *Emerging 1*, 2019. Embossed cut-out relief in paper. Size: 30 square centimeters.

Source: Courtesy of the artist

A Kenyan childhood: stackable beds and golden threads

Bhajan was born in 1956 in Nanyuki, in the Kenyan Highlands close to Mount Kenya. She was raised both there and some 200 miles away in the capital, Nairobi. It was in Juja Road, Nairobi, that Bhajan went to school: first at the Race Course Primary and then Ngara Secondary School where she developed her love of art and had a wonderful teacher, Harjit Sandhu. Bhajan and her siblings stayed with their mother's older sister in the Vehra, a rectangular grid of rooms with kitchens and communal bathrooms arranged around the compound. There children could play freely and safely with many adults to supervise them; if her aunt was not at home when Bhajan returned from school, she would just go to a neighbor. Juja Road was a self-contained South Asian area with temples and mosque, shops, schools, doctors and a hospital; a predominantly working-class and lower-middle-class area, it had a strong sense of community, and those who became wealthy, eschewing a move to more exclusive neighborhoods, built bigger houses where they were, and stayed.

The sense of community was strong, too, in Nanyuki. Bhajan's family owned a hardware store called ModSan, the only one in the town, set up by her father the year before Bhajan was born and fronted by a German woman because he didn't like the idea of shop keeping. Bhajan sometimes helped with the stock taking and served behind the counter. Her father also owned a quarry which supplied stone to local builders, and was himself a building contractor and skilled craftsman possessing a wide range of expertise, not least in carpentry and plumbing. All these were skills he transferred into the domestic sphere in a gamut of tasks that needed to be done.

Bhajan particularly admired the way he made stackable bed frames out of plumbing pipes and corner brackets (see Figure 3.2). The bedframes were like a nest of tables, one bigger than the other, each fitting into the next, to save space when they were not being slept in. The frames were strung with *nawar*: bands of cotton two to three inches wide woven in and out of each other across the frame to form a webbed base for the bed, but which could be removed at any time. When guests visited, the frames could be put together easily, strung with *nawar*, and then dismantled again afterwards – hugely practical and a good example of *jugaad*, made out of the materials easily to hand and adapted to the particular purpose. "These were perfect beds because [the webbed base] is best for your back", Bhajan told me. Her mother removed the *nawar* once a year from the beds that were in everyday use, to string it anew to the frames, so it remained tight. The *nawar* was sold at the family's hardware shop.

Her father played a central role in her life and encouraged her artwork. He was and remains the force behind her artistic work and is the man who believed in educating his daughters. He paid for her to move to the UK in 1975 to study Fine Art as an undergraduate at the University of Reading, and later financed her graduate work at the Slade School of Art in London. But Bhajan also grew up surrounded by strong women who were socially powerful and technically skilled, their skills honed through migration and the experience of living in pioneering communities. In particular, there were the two women she considers as mothers – her Bibiji, the

FIGURE 3.2 A dismantlable and stackable bed made by Bhajan's father with plumbing pipes. The webbed nawar-band base was strung by her mother

Source: Reproduced with permission from the photographer, Bhajan Hunjan

aunt who she lived with while at school in Nairobi, and her birth mother who was in Nanyuki, both equally creative and hard-working.

As I have described in Chapter 1, the culture of the East African diaspora was one in which there was enormous emphasis on the notion of *hath khul jaway* – the hands become fluent with practice: in the needs-based economy, expert hand skills were essential to ensure everyone was clothed and fed, and to make the home beautiful. In Bhajan's eyes, many of the products of the domestic craft that was done by the women in her family were and are art of the highest quality. She cites the example of Sonia Delaunay, whose work for much of the twentieth century was classified as merely "decorative, applied art" as compared to the "pure art" of Robert Delaunay, her husband, and argues that creative work undertaken in the domestic domain merits equal status with art created for its own sake outside the home. She includes within this the weaving of cloth using the back of the bed frame, the *disooti* (cross-stitched) sheets, crochet *tikkis* (squares), and the weaving of the bed base with *nawar* bands. But Bhajan particularly remembers the vast range of decorative embroideries using many types of thread, and gold coiled wire – *zardozi* (literally, gold work), dazzlers called *sippis*, beads of all kinds, *tilla*, which is gold or silver flat thread used for clothes and *dupattas* (headscarf), and *gota* (appliqué) and many other types of gold and silver thread among the silk and cotton ones.

She says that her work as an artist has been very influenced by her mothers: "They made everything they needed... They were very skilled and they made sure you learnt these skills". Embroidery, especially *disooti*, and crochet *tikkis* were centrally inspirational in Bhajan's early grid art style, transferring the stitched patterns via metal plates onto acrylic tiles and using them in repetition, in part because she wanted to demonstrate that they were art.[5]

However, her mother and her aunt weren't the only women she admired. Another woman who particularly impressed her as a child was Pardhanani – not her actual name, but rather a title, a moniker for a charismatic and commanding presence, a woman of good authority, not an authoritarian or oppressive one. Pardhanani had the expertise of religious rituals and performed them at the public temple events as well as organizing the *sangat* (congregation) – hence her title. In addition, she was mother to six daughters and one son and could make doors and beautiful wooden toys. She was an equal partner in her husband's building contracting enterprise and carpenter's shop that manufactured small and large wood products, and helped him out in many ways. She wasn't the only woman to perform tasks traditionally done by men. Another woman considered to be the most stylish and stunning beauty who was supremely socially skilled also drove trucks to deliver building materials to the various building sites. As noted in Chapter 1, the boundaries of the traditional sexual division of labor were far less keenly observed in small-town pioneering communities. As Bhajan says of her father's brother, *sara kuch kar landa si* (he could do everything), from cooking to cleaning to doing the building work and many other technical tasks – because when both brothers lived together in their early days in Nanyuki there were few other community members around, so they simply had to get on with whatever task needed to be done.

Bhajan imbibed the values of the women she was brought up among and by. They taught her the skills they had in generous and sharing ways – the notion of *kaam sikho tay kaam sikhayo* (learn yourself and teach to others what you do) – the deeply embedded sensibility and ethos of the diaspora. And, in addition to their practical skills, Bhajan learnt from these superbly competent pioneering women the sensibility of being your own person regardless of the terrain and in defiance of traditional gender roles and the status quo division of labor. Bhajan therefore carries a legacy of command of complex domestic skills and also of a technical expertise in carpentry and stone masonry, which women in an earlier generation had in pioneering settings.

Material daring and versatility

Bhajan is enormously courageous and daring with materials of all kinds. She told me that even when she was in art school she never stuck to one medium. She worked with a variety of materials and always wanted to move on to others: "I kept breaking through. I work with many materials. When I was supposed to be doing print making, I was working with clay and so on". In order for her to develop, she went on to work with different materials. She did not want to be compartmentalized but kept breaking through; she went across borders. Consequently, she has supreme comfort with many different mediums – more than twenty-one materials[6] – and can swap between them with absolute ease. She has an intuitive understanding of how different materials weld and meld and coalesce or repel and works with them without feeling intimidated.

We discussed this boldness, as well as her instinctive feel for their adaptability of use. She has an ease with the material world, being observant of it and so able to figure out how a particular material might react, whether touched and manipulated and molded and melded and formed or transformed by an energy source, by lasers, heat or cold. Where does her fearlessness with materials and the courage to use them in inventive ways come from and why does she feel she can cross borders with such ease? Some of the answers are to be found in her deep-rooted and long-term familiarity with how materials have been used in the past. She has been socialized to materials of all kinds since she was a child: raised among the building materials and equipment that her father used and that were around the house and in the family's builders' yard, the sand and stone from their quarry; all the equipment and hardware objects that were sold in her family's hardware stores, which was used for what purpose and why – knowledge she acquired vicariously and remains part of her internal database that she draws on still.

More importantly, she is skilled at the domestic tasks in which diasporic women in East Africa and many other pioneering contexts had to be proficient across the many domains of domestic life. Bhajan comes out of the needs-based economy in which you had to know to how to sew, for members of the family to have clothes, bed sheets and table cloths; as well as all the sweet-making and complex cooking – expertise that women needed to command to run an efficient household with no professional service providers. These were tasks that were universally expected of the women, including those with paid jobs outside the home. Since Bhajan was raised in such a milieu, where proficiency in domesticity was expected, learnt, performed and practiced, it is a command that she herself possesses. It is this understanding of making and doing and improvising that she translates into her artwork and it is there in her daring use of materials and in moving in and out of different mediums.

Concrete: embroidered and colored

The Priestley Road canal bridge in Coventry[7] in 1996 was a breakthrough project for Bhajan. "It is done in concrete. Gaudi inspired me to do it", she told me. Working together with local Muslim women of the Al-Nisa Centre and local artists from the Coventry Art Exchange, she decorated the eight-meter-long bridge wall with five "embroidered" concrete panels. It was the first time that she worked with concrete in this way. She learnt how to mold it using glue, adhesives, sand and other reinforcing agents as builders do to translate it into a material she could work with on her own terms. She used pigments designed for coloring plaster and mixed the concrete "to a dough-like consistency, ideal for molding shapes and for embedding small hard objects".[8] She used these small hard objects to embellish the concrete with shards of ceramic and glass, beads and coins, in the style of Gaudi's *trencadis*. This is a technique that she has returned to regularly throughout her career – for example, in 'Our Tree of Knowledge' with Great Holland School, Bracknell (1999); to celebrate Marion Richardson Primary School's centenary (2007); creating 'A Welcome Tree' at Woolmore Primary School with Year 5 pupils, teachers and parents, and looking at the life of the River Thames at St Paul's with St Luke's (both with Bow Arts Trust[9] in London). These works demonstrate her diasporic legacy of *jugaad* in their materials, in adapting concrete to a new artistic purpose, and using the ceramic and glass shards discarded by others. The works also display the influences of her multiple visits to Barcelona to work with artists there and absorb the Catalan techniques of trencadis. She describes her use of these as resembling "embroidery, the embroidery of the building in the best possible way". She thus renders her mothers' aesthetics in her architectural art and translates the highly developed heritage of domestic craft into the public artistic domain.

She also took all of this experience back into the domestic sphere at her childhood home in Nanyuki. Inspired by the fish pond in Gaudi-designed Güell Park in Barcelona, Bhajan decided to create a similar pond for her father. As well as embellishing it *trencadis*-style, she also colored the concrete:

> [My father] did not think I would be able to do it, though he did give me one of his building assistants. I persisted and... when I finished, he was really

impressed by my persistence despite opposition and told me 'you have done *bauhat alla kaam*' – very fine work.

She was pleased with her father's reaction to the pond, which she made developing an aspect of the skills he possessed and the material he used in his own work. Bhajan told me, after her father's death, that although clearly influenced by her mother and aunt: "As an artist, I am closest to what my father did" – thinking in terms of the materials she has used as her career has developed, a process that began with her use of concrete. She likes working with concrete in part because it is considered "masculine": "For me, it's been wonderful… tackling a material with which women don't work. What I have done is to push myself in terms of what material I am using… Cement is a builder's material, Women don't use it".

But Bhajan crosses and breaks down the sexual division of labor in the way in which she uses the material, not just by using it, but also in the way she describes its use. She domesticates and feminizes the process by likening it to the traditionally female activity of baking biscuits, as well as ceramics: "You can work it like making biscuits", she told me. "You bake ceramic and you bake clay but cement dries naturally and builders put it on pavements and much else." Here we also see the legacy of her pioneering inheritance in which the gender division of labor was often much more fluid than in countries of origin.

With concrete, Bhajan has discovered a new material for herself and the art produced in it is durable: it does not disintegrate easily. She says she has enough knowledge about how to tackle this material in innovative ways and the confidence that allows her to take risks and be comfortable with molding new forms. Indeed, it is a material that she has been familiar with since childhood and one central to the development of the technical skills of her maker forebears, an addition to their traditional materials of wood, iron, and bricks and mortar.

Floor art in concrete: the Peepul Centre, Leicester (2005)

Bhajan notes that she has always been observant of floors and interested in the history of their design, inspired in part by the wonderful floor designs at the Golden Temple in Amritsar and at the Taj Mahal. In Kenya, when she was growing up, many older Indian migrant homes in Nairobi had red and green floors. These were made by adding color to the plaster and, when it was dry, polishing and burnishing the floors with coconut husks – a technique developed in India which flourished in East Africa in the late nineteenth and early twentieth centuries but which had fallen out of vogue by the 1950s when floors were plain concrete or terrazzo.

It was these polished red and green surfaces that she had in mind when she was asked to design a floor for the Peepul Arts Centre[10] in Leicester for a South Asian women's organization called the Belgrave Behno. (The peepul is an Indian fig tree that symbolizes knowledge and enlightenment, sacred to Hindus, Buddhists and Jains.) The money for this multi-purpose center – 15 million pounds sterling – was raised from the National Lottery Fund and other sources by Belgrave

Behno's dynamic, politically savvy and entrepreneurial women. This was Bhajan's first big public project in which she was the lead artist. By this stage of her career, she had confidence in her design vision and was able to negotiate assertively with the builders and others implementing it, while responding to their suggestions and modifying the design to take account of the limitations of the materials presented by the builders and structural engineers and also their own frames of thinking. She says she can combine art, architectural and engineering work in part because she is used to dealing with building materials and familiar with builders from her experience at home in Kenya in her father's storage yards.

Bhajan, as lead artist, worked on the initial masterplan for the center, together with the women and the architects, which was then presented to the community. The process involved workshops with women's groups and the elderly and children in the schools. She was then also in charge of the design for the floor of the center's main atrium and chose colored concrete as her material:

> I wanted earthy colors… I worked on lots of different designs and how you can embed [peepul] leaves… I was trying to see how the designs looked on glass and each time I came back I felt like crying… You had to prove constantly that you have something to offer. I was saying I would like to see transparent things in the floor.

The contractor called her design "calligraphy from your culture". She was taken aback and frustrated by his reductive reading of her work because to her the pattern was not calligraphy but an "organic pattern and organic leaves". Bhajan experienced what many ethnic writers and creative people from marginal communities face, which is that their frame of conceptualization is reduced to their ethnicity and "your cultures and its calligraphy".

Meanwhile, she was also working on a textile project with local women. She wanted their embroidery to be preserved in resin and put on one of the walls, but the men looked at the embroidery and said it meant nothing to them. Instead, Bhajan took the color schemes of these samples of embroidery, and the *phulkari* (shawl with flower embroidery) that her birth mother had given her − originally stitched as a wedding present by Bhajan's aunt − to use as the color scheme for the center.

Bhajan notes that this was "a very challenging project", especially when it came to the process of casting the concrete floor which was "quite radical". Usually, concrete is cast in individual square blocks: "They will cordon off and put a piece of wood there and they will concrete and let it cure and then do another bit". However, Bhajan's design had a six-meter oval at its center which required the concrete to be poured in one go:

> …the contractor who did it said, 'I have never done this before' and he is very well known in this country. He said 'it's too large an area' but the architect said it should be fine because it had under floor heating. They had to cast it in one go. It took three days with three different layers…

The colors – paler than Bhajan had originally intended – were troweled into the freshly poured concrete as it was being smoothed, and then the stenciled patterns, based on the peepul leaves, were etched into the set concrete.[11] It turned out beautifully even though, as Bhajan recalls, "people had to be persuaded to sandblast the white concrete… They put a chemical silicon carbide, like mica [in the concrete]… When the light shines on it, it glitters like jewels in the floor. The only bits that glitter are sandblasted ones".

Bhajan subsequently designed a further eight floorscapes in Leicester in 2008 – street entrances to the Cultural Quarter development where the Curve, the performance arts center, was built.

Floor art in granite and glass: the Town Square (2008) and Lightbox (2009), Slough

The skills and experience that Bhajan had acquired in Leicester stood her in good stead for the five years that she subsequently worked in the town of Slough, on projects including two further floorspaces: the Town Square[12] and the Lightbox.[13] Both were commissioned by Slough Borough Council in order to bring new life to the town's high street.

The Town Square was constructed out of granite, with a colorful mosaic at its center in shades of green, cream and brown (again, more muted than she had originally envisaged). The design consists of a circle, with curved lines cutting across and from it, inspired both by the work Bhajan had done with Fusion, a local dance company, and her research into the history of the town, which included horticulture (the commercialization of the Cox apple and the development of various types of carnation) and astronomy (Frederick Herschel was living in Slough when he identified the planet Uranus). The cross-cutting curves evoke both the loose petals of a carnation and the trail of a comet, as well as movement across the square: "I started thinking about the way people cross the square", she told the local newspaper, "following desire lines". The square's larger design incorporates text from a poem by fellow Kenyan Asian Amarjit Chandan, carved by sculptor and lettering artist, Alec Peever. This was an opportunity for Bhajan to return to the use of text, as in her earlier work, a feature of her work that has become stronger in subsequent floorscapes – for example, at St Paul's Way, east London[14] – in part, as a means of making visible the voices of the community whose space her artwork occupies.

Some aspects of these large projects she finds straightforward in a way that someone of a different background may not. For instance, she knows by instinct how to scale up her initial A4 drawing in the same way that she had watched women in her household scale up a blouse design from a basic template. (Interestingly, one of Gaudi's technical innovations was the use of a scale model to calculate structures.[15]) Bhajan translated the process by which a new garment is cut in cloth without a pattern – purely by placing the older worn garment on the cloth to be cut and by so doing figuring out the dimensions for the new garment on the basis

FIGURE 3.3 The Town Square, Slough, 2008

Source: Courtesy of the artist

of the original one – into the medium of concrete and the creation of an extended floorscape. She told me:

> When I think of size and dimension I think like a tailor. People ask me how I can make a small drawing into a full size one. People measure everything, I don't do that – I just fold the paper… and enlarge the design. It was never a problem. It is like you put the *kameez* on cloth and cut another garment in many sizes.

Bhajan thus uses the techniques of tailoring and dressmaking that she was inducted into within the domestic domain and transfers them into her contemporary creativity.

The Lightbox she created in Slough consists of a concrete and glass floor underlit with LED lighting and surrounded by granite seating. The lights change at night and "its colors are of shimmering water", Bhajan says. Its artwork was inspired by the children's game of hopscotch, which is played all over the world. In Kenya, we drew the squares on the ground on the soil with a wooden stick and used a flat stone to throw in the appropriate square.

These projects again required Bhajan's deep powers of collaboration and her bridge-building capital. There were a number of contractors and subcontractors, cach dealing with a different element of the project, all of them men. A lot of work went into finding engineers who could implement the glass element of her Lightbox design:

> ...it took us a long time because they were worried about the slippery quality of the glass... It is a block, and this goes on the paving. It's so thick and it is lit from underneath... In the final drawing, the design changed a little bit more as they wanted me to bring the rougher part in to reduce the total amount of clear glass. So I amended the design and came up with the design they liked.

This constant editing and amending and clarifying is part of the process of negotiating with a wide range of personnel as designs get rendered and modifications are requested and negotiated and made – determined both by the limitations of the materials or the demands made by a monitoring official who requires a floorscape in glass to be non-slip and safe for people to walk and play on. Such struggles to instantiate her creative vision are a recurring theme of all Bhajan's public work. This is not to suggest that they do not exist for everyone who works on public projects in which obstacles emerge regardless of ethnicity, gender and class. But it is definitely the case that when you are an Asian women and dealing with mainly white builders, structural engineers, architects and fabricators – a mainly male preserve of builders and makers – then there is a struggle to hold your own ground and not be stifled.

Although sometimes companies are known to each other and have collaborated on previous building projects, at other times Bhajan is the one who creates the team and innovates anew with them and takes their skills in new directions. In Slough, the team leader complimented her and commented admiringly on her supreme skills of patience and negotiation and co-construction with a comprehensive range of people from many walks of life. Her collaborative and improvisational and patient listening skills are an expertise vital to undertaking public art that seeks to incorporate the voices of those who will use the new space. Bhajan's ability to listen and collaborate and negotiate is a deep-rooted and highly developed diasporic sensibility. "I always try to work on it", Bhajan says, "...you can work on your listening and your not-talking skills". She notes that listening deeply with all one's physical and mental faculties with patience and quietude is what she does well and all the time. It is the deep-seated sensibility of the diaspora that has produced her, underpinned by her egalitarian and democratic Sikh values of sharing skills and resources, and including and heeding people.

There is a generosity always present in Bhajan's work, evident in the projects above and also in a trip to India to restore the museum[16] in which are housed the paintings of eminent Sikh painter Sobha Singh (which are found in every Sikh home and Sikh temples all over the world and which he gave freely to the community). Together with museum expert Ian Burrand, she made the necessary repairs both to the building and display, having organized the trip with British museum experts and raised the funds.

Metal work: through gates to a bridge and streetlights

Like Gaudi, whose father was a coppersmith, Bhajan too is impacted by her father's craft. His expertise was in metal pipes and plumbing and through him Bhajan was familiar with how metal was used and made into all kinds of objects. Whereas Gaudi worked in wrought iron, Bhajan works in mild steel.

> It was the first time, I got an opportunity to do a little gate. I had never done a gate before. Someone said they had money to design a gate. Although I had never done one… I could try. After this I did a number of gates.

This is what led in the end to the making of the Three Mill Pontoon in London's Olympic Park, because Bhajan had acquired the expertise and experience of making gates and working with steel.

The first "little gate" was in Leicester,[17] in fact two, the White Hart gates at Thurmaston, commissioned by Leicester Housing Association as part of a new housing scheme. Bhajan's design was inspired by the site – next to a park and near a canal – and also by research she carried out with the local heritage group and workshops with pupils from the nearby school. Regarding the gate's construction, she says, "[it] was a sandwich. It was two layers of metal stenciling which was set together".

Then, when she was artist in residence at a school in Reading, she was asked to design another: "They said, 'you have done a gate, it would be nice if you could do one for us'". She worked with A level students and they entered their design for a competition to make a gate for a garden entry for the Hampton Court Flower Show – and they won. The gate was made and used for the show and has since been installed permanently at Birmingham Botanical Gardens.

These projects inducted her to new techniques and also new materials. Bhajan's story is not only about her fearlessness and adventurousness with materials but also that she is always open to the new, interrogating techniques and finding innovative craftsmen to render her art. This is something she enjoys doing and is good at: "the exciting thing is when you start researching you find a firm that does it. You actually find people who do it. It is wonderful".

Her experience in creating gates and working in metal opened up the opportunity for Bhajan to design the Three Mills Pontoon[18] on the River Lea for British Waterworks, a project associated with the Olympic Park for the London Olympics in 2012, on the traffic route to the park itself. To this, she applied her inheritance of metal to frieze work, elaborate designs cut into steel sheets, to build the walls of the pontoon, "to catch the shadows and the sunshine", she told me.

Bhajan prepares herself well when she does these projects and is open to suggestions about how materials can be applied, the strengths and shortcomings and also the ways in which a particular material can be manipulated and repurposed and applied in new ways. She is open to the design and technical suggestions of others – as in the case of the streetlights in St Paul's Way, London (2012).[19] These are distinctive because they have spotlights in the column of each light, as well as at its top, in addition to Bhajan's curved-line motif. The spotlights were the idea of the lighting company:

> They told me, 'there are certain possibilities that we haven't put into practice yet'. I told them, 'let's go for it'. That is where these lights [the blue spotlights in the column] are coming from the side as well as the light at the top. They are beautiful. I was surprised when I saw them because they turned out so well.

As well as the streetlights, Bhajan worked both on the floorscape (Words in Stone) and the bollards for the St Paul's Way project. The designs and the text emerged from workshops with young Bengali women. Bhajan gathered two hundred sentences on the theme of health and wellbeing from which ten were selected. She cut the words of the text in rubber to make a stencil and then had the text sandblasted onto the stone; a contrast was created using monumental paint. The designs for the granite bollards were transferred in a similar way.

Conclusion

Bhajan's architectural-based art is a product of her diasporic journeys and the legacies of artisanal skills she has inherited, which she has reworked anew in her art. Bhajan says that her mother drew her to her roots and her father facilitated her routes. Her father, she recalls, was more future orientated and innovative in a different way from her mother, who was more orientated towards India.

While Bhajan's early work drew heavily on the domestic craft/art of the women in the household, as a more experienced and more mature artist, she has turned to her father's building materials – concrete, stone and metal – to create her architectural art. However, its decoration and artwork still recall the motifs and patterns of her mothers' creations: she has thus translated her two mothers' skills into public art using her father's materials.

Bhajan has had to overcome many obstacles in her career. When sculptor Rasheed Araeen curated 'The Other Story: Afro-Asian Artists in Post-War Britain' at the Hayward Gallery in 1989, he did not include work by *any* Asian woman artist. Regional galleries have been more receptive to her work, such as in Bradford, Birmingham and Leicester, but Bhajan has received little interest in her work from mainstream galleries in London whose white consecrators want an Indian from India, not a British Asian. Bhajan tells the story of a day spent with a powerful interlocutor who wanted to exploit Bhajan's connections to gain access to a particular Indian artist but was unprepared to offer space or time to Bhajan's own work. It is absolutely about, "Give me your connections and time, but I will not reward you with gallery space to show your art, because in my classificatory frame, you are not Indian and there is no category of British Asian art that I am interested in as I do not even recognize this as a legitimate category which I am willing to validate."

When the consecrators of mainstream creative spaces do not want to acknow-ledge you, the risk that creative agents like Bhajan take is to do their own thing in the way in which they are inspired. They tinker, they improvise, they experiment, they collaborate, and try out ways of making and doing which are drawn from their own experiences. In so doing, the new emerges on the basis of the new from mar-ginal spaces unconsecrated by mainstream power brokers.

Bhajan's aesthetic is no longer that of the gallery: "go and look and interrogate in an art space controlled by gate keepers and where you have to buy a ticket at the entrance or buy the art" – she is into a free, more egalitarian, public art. Her art innovates through different materials to generate the new in landscapes that encode her unique design signatures.

The list of the people and agencies she has worked with and for and collaborated and improvised with is long: communities of students, working-class Bangladeshi women from London's East End, entrepreneurial middle-class Gujarati women who secure a Lottery grant and employ an architectural teams and artist, school children and teachers of all kinds, and also engineers, architects, stone masons and carvers, granite and metal specialists, public sign makers, and electronic and lighting specialists.

Bhajan has a similar ability to that of physicist Tejinder Singh Virdee, artist and product designer Jasleen Kaur and music producer Kuljit Bhamra in being able to work with a vast range of people from diverse backgrounds in egalitarian and collaborative ways.

She has a genuine unselfconscious command of working with people of different ethnicities, ages, skills, professions, temperaments and languages in a way few people can if they have not emerged from multiply migrant contexts in which living with new groups of people and in new sites is usual. She herself is a speaker of Swahili, English, Punjabi, Spanish and Hindi, and can converse in Urdu. This ability to work with people in new projects and new settings has been part of her diasporic inher-itance now for three generations and gives her an edge in this style of working.

Bhajan's ease and comfort in working with different materials and the ability to translate the small-scale, private personal drawing and design to the large-scale public artwork are skills drawn from the largesse of her movement capital. These skills have a great deal of connection with the past, with her cultural inheritance, undergirded by deep-rooted and high-level improvisational collaboration and co-construction. Such capital – cultural, social and technical – was acquired impli-citly and vicariously as well as taught and learnt explicitly at home and in the environs of the hardware store and builders' yard, and acquired also through pro-fessional training and art school pedagogy. These are the sources of the expertise she plays out in her public art using a vast range of materials, moving between them with unselfconscious courage and inventiveness, which can only come from her particular biography of multiple movement. Bhajan holds cultural, social and technical capital durably accrued and transmitted via a sophisticated cultural appar-atus developed by earlier migrants settled in pioneering diasporic locations, capital that has been further honed and catalyzed, gestated, through multiple movements across borders, and now expressed in new ways in her daring, border-crossing art, that takes courage to produce, created despite resistance, despite scarcity and despite establishment art norms. Bhajan's art is innovated in a process of melding and bending, melting and reforming and reconstituting materials, designing on the basis of the new to generate the new to create public spaces of singular authenticity. This is a supreme comfort with being in new domains and discovering the new on its own terms, capturing the contours of new discoveries as they unfold in the moment, emerging through a fusion, a combining and recombining of materials, crafted by methods that draw from both older expertise and developing expertise, as new forms of art rendered by new kinds of people who are making a mark in the fluid, liquid globalized world.

Notes

1 As recounted to me during my interview with Bhajan, January 8, 2015.

2 An overview of her work is available at https://slideplayer.com/slide/14861996/, also showing her earlier figurative work (accessed August 6, 2019).

3 Gijs Van Hensbergen, *Gaudi: A Biography* (New York: Perennial, 2001), 3. "I have that quality of spatial apprehension because I am the son, grandson, and the great-grandson of coppersmiths. My father was a smith; my grandfather also. On my mother's side of the family there also smiths; her grandfather was a copper; my maternal grandfather was a sailor, who also are people of space and circumstance. All these generations of people give a preparation".

4 For an overview of Bhajan's work, see https://bhajanhunjan.com/ (accessed August 6, 2019).

5 "I wanted to take the patterns that I saw on my mother's sheets with embroidery – *phulkari* [embroidered sheets and shawls using green, orange, yellow, and red silk thread], and tablecloths of crochet and also those that were embroidered and… to show that this was art. They were art forms by any standards found in our homes. It is thinking of these that I started to make prints from these sheets with *disooti* (cross-stitch embroidery), using technical processes of creating form of embroidery on metal plates which I could reproduce endlessly". See, for example: 'Open Space', 'She Sowed the Seeds', and 'My Mother's Embroidery'; https://slideplayer.com/slide/14861996/ (accessed August 6, 2019).

6 Bhajan's materials: acrylic, anodized metal, beads, canvas, ceramics and clay, concrete, fabric, glass, granite, ink, LED lights, lithographs and etching, marble, neon signs, paint of all kinds, paper, pigments, printing materials and printing press which she owns, resin, stencils, steel, terrazzo.

7 Priestley's Bridge and Reflections mural by Bhajan Hunjan and Naida Hussein, Coventry Canal, 1996.

8 Frimley & Camberley Society of Arts, 'Bhajan Hunjan: Architectural Art, 5/9/2008', www.fcsaonline.org.uk/HISTORY/Hunjan/Hunjan.htm (accessed August 6, 2019).

9 Bow Arts Trust Poplar, Tower Hamlets, is a social enterprise organization for artists and communities who collaborate with a social landlord, a housing association, the Poplar Housing and Regeneration Association HARCA. It offers "artists and creative practitioner's access to affordable live/work spaces" and helps to foster both a deeper understanding and exposure to the work of visual artists but also helps to regenerate an impoverished area; https://bowarts.org/ (accessed August 6, 2019).

10 "Commissioned by Belgrave Behano, this floor design was inspired by the name of the project 'Peepul', a well-known Indian tree symbolizing knowledge and enlightenment.

Dispersing from the middle, a cluster of abstracted symbolic leaves float as seedlings to different parts of the building covering over 200 square meters". Technique – poured concrete. Architect: Andrej Blonski. Contractor: Lazenby Contracts.

11 Frimley & Camberley Society of Arts, 'Bhajan Hunjan'.

12 The Town Square, Slough, 2008. Designed as part of the *Art at the Centre* scheme for Slough Borough Council. The inspiration for the design was derived from Slough's horticultural past, its rich canvas of diverse communities and a place which is ever-changing in the face of new challenges. Initial workshops were carried out with Fusion Dance Company at Slough Young People's Centre. Incorporated text from a poem by Amarjit Chandan; Lettering carved by sculptor Alec Peever; Landscape architects: Allen Scott; Sub-Contractor: Pomery Natural Stone with Incoveca – Granitos (Portugal); Material: Granite and stainless steel; Size: over 200 square meters.

13 Lightbox, Slough, 2009. Commissioned by Slough Borough Council for the High Street, this artwork was inspired by children's games like hopscotch, which is played all over the world. This under-lit piece surrounded by granite seating is made of recycled glass and stainless steel. Comprising symbols and numbers, it is a playful piece for children to interact with and for adults to reflect on games they played as children. Coming on in the evening, the LED lights are programmed to a set sequence, changing from individually lit glass tiles to uniting colours, lighting up the whole piece. Landscape architects: Allen Scott Ltd. Structural engineers: Packman Lucas Structural Designers. Materials: Eluna recycled and toughened glass, stainless steel and LED lighting: Architainment Lighting Ltd.

14 Words in Stone, St Paul's Way, London, 2012. Ten sentences selected from 220 sentences put forward by members of the community. Fabrication: Pomery natural stone. Installation: J B Rineys & Co Ltd. Material: Granite.

15 Van Hensbergen, *Gaudi*.

16 Vikas Kahol, 'Sobha Singh's portraits have been left to rot', *India Today*, April 23, 2012: "The artist's fans who live abroad, recently sponsored the visit of Ian Barrand, Yorkshire Museum's art restorer, to Andretta. Barrand, along with a noted artist from London, Bhajan Hunjan, critically accessed, restored and rearranged the paintings preserved by the family according to the standards followed by international museums." www.indiatoday.in/opinion/vikas-kahol/story/artist-sobha-singh-vicky-donor-lalu-prasad-pgimer-99938-2012-04-23 (accessed August 6, 2019).

17 White Hart Gates, Thurmaston. Situated on the site of the historic White Hart Public House, two gates were commissioned by Leicester Housing Association (ASRA) as part of a new housing scheme. A collaboration with Spirit Projects, the design was inspired by the site (adjacent to Watermead Park and canal side), and research with Thursmaston Heritage Group and workshops with pupils from the Church Hill Church of England School, Thursmaston. Fabrication and installation by Chris Campbell Designs; Material: double-layered laser-cut and painted mild steel.

18 The Three Mills Pontoon, River Lea, 2011. Commissioned by British Waterways with London Thames Gateway Development Corporation. Laser-cut stainless steel. Installation: Intermarine Ltd. Fabrication: Premier Laser. Lights: Rolec Services Ltd. Material: Stainless steel.

19 St Paul's Way, London, E3, 2012. Commissioned by Tower Hamlets Council Highways Team, as part of St Paul's Way Transformation project, with Bow Arts. Design for Street Lamp Column was developed with Tower Hamlets Council and Mark Bailey Associates. Installation: J. B. Rineys & Co Ltd.

4

AMARJIT KALSI

Lyrical architect and virtuoso draughtsman

His draughtsmanship was extraordinary, elevating technical drawing to an art form…
The result was a thing of beauty.[1]

We created a roof of dancing arches.[2]

Architect Amarjit Kalsi, who sadly died in 2014 while I was researching this book, was for most of his career co-director of Rogers Stirk Harbour + Partners (RSHP), a globally influential architectural firm created and led by multiple-award-winning architect Richard Rogers.[3] During that time, Amarjit – Amo as he was known to his colleagues – played an influential role in the making of some of the most iconic buildings in Europe. His last major project was the design of two remarkable subway stations in Naples: Capodichino, at the airport, and Santa Maria Del Pianto, both designed as major transport hubs. Other work included Terminal 5 at Heathrow Airport and, as a raw recruit, the Lloyd's building in London; the European Court of Human Rights in Strasbourg and the law courts in Bordeaux, France; and the Madrid–Barajas Airport, Spain. But his design interests ranged widely, including a series of bus shelters and street furniture and also a lighting system. His body of work constitutes a powerful expression of migrant creativity and movement capital, the flow of his life rendered in the flow of his designs. A product of deep-rooted cultures of movement, his multiply migrant British East African Asian background ensured he was an architect peculiarly in tune with his times – when the steel that features so prominently in his Sikh heritage was a defining building material, and construction to facilitate mass global movement yielded many of the late twentieth and early twenty-first centuries' key architectural projects. There was a happy synergy between his personal biography and background, and the nature and purpose of the buildings he built, the design problems he had to solve for them – the flow of people, air, light – and, often, their defining aesthetic, their smooth forms and undulating, fluid lines.

Amarjit Kalsi: the carpenters' grandson

Amo was born in Kenya in 1957, where both his maternal and paternal grandfathers had migrated as carpenters, working initially for East African Railways and then setting up their own workshops and enterprises. His paternal grandfather later had a joinery shop in the Asian section of Nairobi where Amarjit would hang around as a young boy to help out and play, all the while absorbing craftsman values. "As a kid, at my grandfather's workshop in River Road, Nairobi, outside the Ramgarhia Sikh temple, I used to play with wood after school. I remember the smell of Scotch glue used for carpentry and the wood pieces that we were given. You got used to dealing with wood – you had an affinity to it", he told me – a sensibility that was subsequently to play out in his professional work as an architect.

Amarjit's father, Asa Ram Singh, had gained a college degree in India and worked as a civil servant in the administrative sectors of the Post Office in Kenya. He was posted to a remote town, Garissa, on the Kenya–Somalia border, far from the metropolitan and cosmopolitan centers of Nairobi and other major towns of East Africa. Amarjit wondered how his parents survived there with "the snakes and bandits". There was little exposure to manufactured entertainment from outside. "You did not have games and you had to create your own fun", Amarjit told me. "You made things and played cricket".

But there were also "fabulous" family holidays in Malindi on the coast, with its beautiful tropical white sand beaches and palm trees – Kalsi learnt to fix his father's truck when it broke down while traveling there – and his parents took him regularly to visit his grandparents in the capital city, Nairobi. This, Amarjit remembered as "a smart place, and the times were optimistic. We used to go to the annual agricultural show which was a major attraction for all of us. I also went to see Elvis Presley playing and there was of course American television and… the drive-in cinema, Bellevue, in Nairobi South C".

He migrated to Britain in 1970 with his parents, staying first with relatives from India living in Slough, close to Heathrow Airport, and then settling in Forest Gate, in East London. Racist attitudes among local white British people were powerfully virulent at that time and both immigrant children and their parents suffered as newcomers in many aspects of settlement in Britain from education to housing to employment. His father worked in the Mars chocolate factory. Amarjit talked about how "the *goras* [whites] were arrogant and told you that you smelt of curry. Many educated men in senior positions in East Africa could not find jobs". He and his father both gave up the turbans that they had always worn in Kenya. The racism of the times was also apparent in teachers' low expectations of immigrant students in school. Amarjit and his peer group at Little Ilford Comprehensive mostly played football and tennis, he said.

However, his imagination was engaged by two landmark television programs. The first was art historian Kenneth Clark's thirteen-part BBC series *Civilisation*,[4] which traced the history of European art, architecture and philosophy from the so-called Dark Ages to the present. He loved the descriptions of "the Renaissance period, the height of human creativity" and also Sir Kenneth's accessible and engaging way of conveying information. Later, in 1973, he watched Jacob Bronowski's television series, *The Ascent of Man*,[5] designed to complement *Civilisation* by focusing on the development of society from the point of view of science. Both these programs were watched avidly by Amarjit, more powerful than anything he was learning at school, and determined his choice of architecture as a career, a field that he felt would enable him to combine mathematics, science and art. His father consulted with an engineer neighbor who advised Amarjit to change, but he stuck to his choice. In particular, he demonstrated great passion and skill for technical drawing, a skill nurtured at technical college. He enrolled at the prestigious Architectural Association School of Architecture in 1975, funded by a local authority grant that was the norm for all higher education students at that time.

According to his obituary in *The Times*, Amarjit struggled with the modernist aesthetic then dominant at the Architectural Association, to the extent that his tutors doubted he would gain his Part One qualification.[6] Happily, in the third year of Amarjit's course, Richard Rogers was an external examiner for his class, noticed his prodigious talent and offered him a year's placement at his practice. Looking back, Amarjit modestly described this encounter as "a miracle". The placement enabled Amarjit to learn, as he said, "lots of different jobs", which gave him "a feel for working in an office, learning how to answer the phone and deal with clients and consultants". He returned to the Architectural Association to complete his studies, though said of that time that he was "[i]nfluenced more by two unpopular students in the unit than by tutors".[7] On qualifying in 1981, he joined RRP as a full-time employee, at once becoming a member of the team then working on the Lloyd's building - a crucial period of apprenticeship:

> You learnt to be part of the design, about organizing yourself, and your relationships with other consultants, [how to write] good notes, and you... learnt about contracts and eventually, after a period, you can call yourself an architect under law.

Amarjit told me that he knew immediately that he was in the right place. He felt at ease in the airy, open-plan office overlooking the River Thames, which he described as run like a medieval guild where the less experienced learnt by working side by side with experienced masters - as in Leonardo da Vinci's studio in which pupils watched and copied their master artist's style of work, thus acquiring skills through a micro community of practice. The atmosphere was emphatically unstuffy. In the same way that Rogers' buildings were often characterized by splashes of primary color, in the office their designers often wore brightly colored shirts of lime green and red.

Amarjit described the whole experience as transformative:

> Your character develops. You are moving in a different world of new people – it just gives you confidence. I had hardly traveled and then you are traveling

to Europe. Richard would invite you to Sunday lunch. You had to make conversation. You could not just sit there. This was critical to your social skills.

Rogers, an Italian Jew, had himself arrived in the UK as a child and struggled at school with dyslexia; as Amarjit came to know him better, he realized that in many ways they shared similar experiences of prejudice, exclusion and marginality.

The office's space was open, and so was the practice's intellectual and organizational culture. RSHP describes on its website its collegiate, think-tank way of working:

> ...the choice of a completely open plan office reflects the democratic beliefs of the practice. There are no individual offices; partners sit with their architectural teams, and every Monday a weekly meeting open to all employees is held to discuss competitions, on-going projects and more.[8]

Amarjit respected the open and low-key style of his more experienced colleagues, who wore their seniority lightly rather than in an assertive, hierarchical manner (low-key was also very much his own style) and he valued the intellectual demands made on him:

> One of the precious things about working at Richard Rogers is that you are always challenged and are always challenging things. At the end of the day this makes things better not only for you but for everyone else. And the wonderful thing about being an architect is that you have the fantastic skill of realizing it.

While still a member of the Lloyd's building team, Amarjit was given his first project to lead on – a pumping station in the London Docklands in the east of London: "... then you are thrown in the deep end because people foresee your potential. This is ferocious – you learn to do everything yourself".

The Tidal Basin Pumping Station, Canning Town, was one of three pumping stations built to cope with rainwater run-off from the new streets being built to regenerate London's former docklands. Amarjit said he felt intimidated initially, as a young person of color, leading a team of engineers and builders:

> [I'm not] six foot tall and broad shouldered. They would see me turn up, an Indian, but obviously I was the architect in charge. At first, you used to feel threatened but after a while you realized that you are representing Richard Rogers... so that gave you a lot of confidence.

RSHP's website says that the intention with the building was to create "a visual delight, an oasis in the drab industrial environment of Silvertown" while providing a durable, secure space for the pumping machinery contained within.[9] The end result RSHP describes as "a bright and cheerful structure... imbued with a sense of joy". It's tempting to see the Malindi sky in the deep blue of the main cylinder and flame tree flowers in the scarlet of its doors, but this wasn't something I had the chance to talk to Amo about… "Joy" was one of his words, however: he talked about the "joy and use" that a well-designed building provides.[10] Meanwhile, his work was exhibited in the Young Architects exhibition, RIBA, 1983, and Six Young Architects, RIBA Heinz Gallery, 1984.

In 1988, Amarjit, still only thirty years old, was appointed a director of Richard Rogers's firm, and his career as an architect was fully fledged, progressing through a series of projects over the next twenty-seven years.[11] I want to explore in some detail how that career rested upon and fostered his supreme skill as a draughtsman and ability to capture the new; how it drew upon and expressed his background as a maker (a background shared with at least some of his colleagues, together with a respect for craft); his affinity for materials, steel in particular; his deep understanding of movement and flow; and his generous, collaborative, sharing style.

Maker skills: virtuoso draughtsmanship and capturing the new

Mangla, his daughter, told me that Amarjit was always drawing and sketching at home.[12] She described how he would draw on car catalogues and change the shape of the cars, reconfiguring their design to accord with his own aesthetics. Amarjit, too, talked to me about the pleasure he took in sketching ideas that were germinating in his head over the weekend while listening to jazz or the Beach Boys or the Beatles. In an earlier book, *Dangerous Designs* (2004), I made much of the fashion designer's sketches as the first encapsulation of an idea on paper, describing how fashion designer Bubby Mahil negotiated a design with her client through the in-the-moment sketch co-constructed, not imposed – so, for me, the salience of the sketch in Amarjit's story is particularly striking. It formed the focus of the obituary colleague Ivan Harbour wrote, published in both *The Guardian* and *Architects' Journal*: "His draughtsmanship was extraordinary, elevating technical drawing to an art form… The result was always a thing of beauty".[13]

In a simple drawing, Amarjit had the ability to express the spirit of a building, defining the form of landmark projects such as Terminal 5 at Heathrow Airport, London, and the undulating roof of Madrid–Barajas Airport. He was the midwife who shaped an idea in the immediacy of the moment for it to be rendered later in fully developed form based on subsequent drawings of organizational details. An article in architects' magazine *Building Design* praising the design for Capodichino subway station describes how: "[t]he form of the station and its 4,700 sq m roof canopy can be traced through a series of sketches".[14]

Ivan Harbour describes the process of the sketch as it took place in the office:

> During the animated meetings Kalsi would begin to draw in precise lines giving lyrical form to the emerging concept with his thin Rotring pen. He might draw a soaring roof profile such as Terminal 5 or Barajas, but he was equally adept at small details, such as the handrails that flow downwards on

FIGURE 4.1 Pump Room. Plan, elevation, section and detail, 1980–81 – a drawing completed by Amarjit Kalsi while a student at the Architectural Association, London

Source: Architectural Association Archives, London

> the beautiful stairway that forms the centerpiece of the now grade 1 listed Lloyd's building in the city.[15]

In these primal moments, Amarjit's exquisite command of the Rotring pen gave expression to the collaborative team discussion, a co-constructed moment of innovation and inventiveness, a still embryonic expression of the contours and the spirit of the building to be rendered. He had an ability to respond to the immediate context, an openness to the new, the what-is-not-yet-there, and gave it form – a powerful sensibility of those endowed with movement capital, which animates their creativity. This is a deep-rooted way of being in the world that emerges from liquid lives led amidst disequilibrium, a style of thinking and doing and making that Amo represented par excellence.

But these drawing and technical skills are also millennia old. Amo was reproducing an expertise that the community that produced him has carried for centuries. He honed it further, professionalized it and applied it to buildings with a high public profile. His forebears worked under European architects and were trained on the job – in the main, under British architects in colonial settings, where their signature was elided and their conceptual input unattributed, their technical skills unrecognized. A professional architectural education was closed to them. A number of men in my extended family had exactly this trajectory

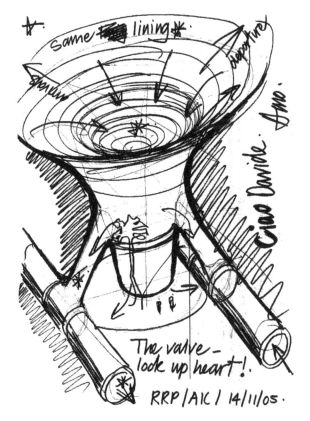

Same lining

partenza

Ciao Davide · Amo·

The valve –
look up heart!

RRP/AK / 14/11/05.

FIGURE 4.2 Amarjit's concept diagram for Capodichino Metro Station, Naples

Source: Courtesy of Rogers Stirk Harbour + Partners

of exquisite technical drawing without the professional credentials. They worked for British firms in East Africa and also in 1960s and 1970s Britain, their work submerged and unacknowledged. But for subsequent generations, the opportunity structure began to open up, and many have flourished, despite continuing racism. There are many architects and engineers in Amarjit's generation and the next; they may not have the profile of Amarjit, but they too are creating the cityscapes of the twenty-first century.

Makers and a respect for craft

Of course, as an architect at RSHP, Amarjit wasn't alone as a 'maker' who originated from a background of and having an aptitude for making as well as thinking – although he was probably the only one among his colleagues whose maker heritage dated back millennia. Both Graham Stirk and Amarjit's desk mate Ivan Harbour talk powerfully about themselves as practical, hands-on makers in the same way as Amarjit.

FIGURE 4.3 Capodichino Metro Station, Naples – an early sketch

Source: Courtesy of Rogers Stirk Harbour + Partners

Ivan Harbour describes himself as having always "…been very practical… as a kid in the countryside, we used to break up old cars, service them and get them running on the road. I just love making, investigating and actually building stuff".[16]

While Amarjit's grandfathers were carpenters, Graham Stirk explains that one of his was a magician who made "all kinds of dolls and props" for his magic tricks. Of himself, Stirk says that as a child himself he "used to make amazing cardboard structures… I used to do some amazing, very odd things".[17]

Similarly, both Stirk and Harbour have a strong belief in craftsmanship, expressed in discussion about the design and construction of the Lloyd's building. This was designed to provide a flexible space for the Lloyd's of London insurance market, where the dealing room could expand or contract, according to the needs of the market, by means of a series of galleries around a central space. To maximize space, services – lifts, stairs, air conditioning, heating, etc – are banished to the perimeter, forming the building's distinctive external shell, in the style first introduced by Richard Rogers at the Pompidou Centre in Paris.[18]

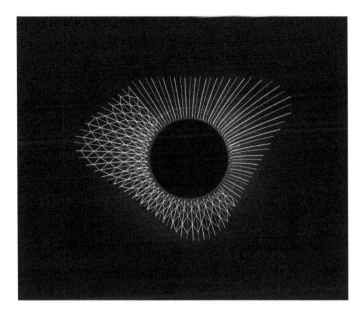

FIGURE 4.4 Model for the roof, Capodichino Metro Station, Naples

Source: Courtesy of Rogers Stirk Harbour + Partners

Talking about the Lloyd's design, Stirk notes:

> It's the power of the diagram and the relentless way in which it has been pursued throughout all its organizational detail. Lloyd's of London… is not an art piece… but all of its pieces are beautifully made.[19]

Harbour comments as follows:

> Lloyd's was built by a cottage industry, by genuine artisans, not by big conglomerates… We love working with the materiality. What we don't like is the idea that it's a pure art, that you construct an image. [The design] comes from technology, this idea that the most flexible space you can make, you want as little interruption or intrusion into the space that you can get.[20]

It is the craftsmanship and feeling for the materials used, as much as the designs themselves, that set RSHP buildings apart from run-of-the-mill twentieth and twenty-first century architecture – a craftsmanship and celebration of materials apparent in all of the projects in which Amarjit was involved, a key part of his heritage, and a design aesthetic shared by his closest colleagues. When opportunities for ambitious architecture were few in 1980s' Britain, the practice looked instead to continental Europe, winning competitions to design the European Court of Justice in Strasbourg and Law Courts in Bordeaux with plans drawn by Harbour and Amarjit. Amarjit described these as "formative buildings" for RSHP, when they started dealing with environmental and energy-saving issues, designing to allow the air to flow, ensuring natural ventilation rather than relying on electricity-hungry air conditioning.

Amarjit also demonstrated the perfectionism that is the core sensibility of the master craftsman, even to the point of exasperating his colleagues, according to his *Times* obituary:

> Kalsi had an obsessive nature and in meetings he would constantly question whether the practice had found the right approach to a particular project. Even his mentor Rogers could become exasperated by his perfectionism, but his passion was irrepressible.[21]

An affinity for materials: steel

Amarjit spoke about developing an affinity for materials in his grandfather's workshop. Then, it was wood, but it's his subsequent affinity for steel that I'm particularly interested in. His career coincided with the preeminence of steel as a building material, whether in beams girding the twentieth century's signature tower blocks, or in cables bracing the roof of the Millennium Dome and Terminal 4 at Madrid–Barajas Airport, or the lattice-work of the doubly curved hyperbolic paraboloid atop Santa Maria Del Piantro metro station,[22] or cladding the exterior of the Lloyd's building and the European Court of Human Rights - but what a beautiful coincidence that it's also a metal that occupies a central place in the Sikh symbols. It is the material of both *kara* – the bangle representing strength and continuity that all Sikhs wear from the time of their birth, and *kirpan* – the short sword, symbol of self defense and the fight against injustice. Steel, unlike gold, is an egalitarian, everyday metal, not exclusive to the rich and privileged. It reflects the key Sikh notion of *sarbhat dha pallah* (for the good of all) expressed in service to the community and the world.

Over the course of his career, Amarjit presented many lectures including to various national stainless steel associations, both in Europe and also in Asia. It's the German one I have a record of, delivered in Berlin in 2000, in which he spoke of "…the intrinsic physical and visual qualities of stainless steel".[23] The "most symbolic manifestation of these", he said, "is found on the Chrysler Building in New York".

He talked in loving detail and at some length about the process of finding the right finish for the Lloyd's building service towers:

> We investigated many coated aluminum systems, but none of these could sustain the quality of appearance as stainless steel when beautifully designed and fabricated… [W]e developed the design by having a tactile appreciation of stainless steel in the manner it can be cut, formed, machined, welded and finished. The Linen finish Grade 316 S16 stainless steel for the cladding panels is a result of having a finish which is not totally reflective, but gives a sense of flatness and precision.[24]

His feel and affinity for the material is also discernible from his description of the making of the European Court of Human Rights in Strasbourg in which he was centrally involved:

> For me the unique use of stainless steel on the Strasbourg Court of Human Rights project is how we manage to afford this material by design simplification… The finish we desired, i.e. non-reflective with a satin quality, we discovered by accident by processing the coil twice through the roller. The economy of this, together with the approach of only cutting and drilling the protected finished stainless steel sheet, resulted in the realization of the stainless steel cladding within the stringent constraints of the project.[25]

He talked eloquently, too, of his design for a stainless steel roof for Leuven Station that wasn't in the end made:

> For this station covering we created a roof of "dancing" arches… By using a standard coil material, which is a seam jointed by automatic machines on site, we had developed an economic roofing/structural system in beautiful leaf-like forms where the leaf veins are the seam joints. The roof sculpture of stainless steel, an expression of form and function, would have provided much joy and use to the people and visitors of Leuven. This is what the Chrysler building has done for seventy years and no doubt what Lloyds of London and the Court of Human Rights will do in the near future.[26]

Amarjit's feeling for the qualities of stainless steel are notable as a reflection and extension of his early childhood experiences with his carpenter grandfather, a comfort with materials intrinsic to his biography and inheritances and the culture of making and playing with materials rendered during the course of his career in some of Europe's most iconic buildings.

Flow – movement engineered, and as design aesthetic

Movement is central to Amarjit's biography, and also to the buildings he designed, structures which facilitate the flow of people, air and light through busy, highly trafficked sites – often, in fact, buildings which catalyze the movement of people: the airports, stations and transport hubs that constitute the essential infrastructure of a globalized world.[27]

His own personal story of movement underlies his desire to open up conduits of flow, travel and movement, welcoming the public and easing their lives as they transit from one site to the next. Capodichino, he told the journalist Will Hunter from *Building Design*, "[is] like Heathrow Terminal 5 – we're saying, 'here is the gateway to Naples'".[28]

In designing the subway station, his team used innovative engineering techniques to understand and decode travelers' pathways of movement at the micro level, as they moved between airport and subway, breakthrough techniques that reveal and can be rendered to ease and catalyze diverse traffic flows and traffics.

Amarjit explained to Will Hunter how they designed the building with a unity of structure and surface so that it would be easily readable by those passing through, so that they could orientate themselves without problem: "the problem with many stations is that they are designed as a structure, and then layers of linings and finishes are added later. Here, the structure and surface are one."

Working with the project's engineers, the design was facilitated by computer-generated algorithms and equations, as Amarjit explained to me:

> Usually when you design a roof you just do it to simple geometry but now… with these equations you can say, 'I want the roof to go from here to there and it needs shading from the sun and the sun is over here'. These equations can compute those two factors to produce geometry which is more like synthetic nature.

In his *Building Design* article, Hunter describes the resulting plans:

> …the roof is a vast vortex where both passengers and architecture follow irresistible flow lines from planes to trains… passengers spiral downwards on crisscrossing escalators while the roof's timber beams flow smoothly into the shaft's concrete ribs. In both engineering and concept, roof and station work as a single continuous swoop.[29]

Amarjit's biography of movement and his professional proclivity towards capturing flows are expressed in his architecture. His understanding of movement, both intuitive and mathematical, is evident in the practicalities – facilitating the flow of people through complicated spaces – but it is also present in the aesthetics of the buildings on which he worked, nowhere more so than in their roofs. In addition to the swoop at Capodichino, there are the light-filled curves at Terminal 5, Heathrow, London; undulating bamboo at Terminal 4, Madrid–Barajas Airport; and the "dancing arches" of the unbuilt railway station designed for Leuven, Belgium. His flowing structures embody a (positive) liquid modernity in both their function and form.

A generous, collaborative, sharing style

RSHP highlights on its website its generous, sharing style:

> [Our] collegiate approach extends to the wider world with a constitution that consciously brings a moral dimension to the work. This includes a staff profit-sharing scheme and significant contributions to charity, with staff members nominating the charities of their choice.[30]

"We have a constant belief that we can make people's lives better and I think that is what drives us", says Ivan Harbour in RSHP's film, *Thinking and Making*.[31]

It is an approach that Amarjit was in tune with. A long-time financial supporter of neighborhood outreach activities at the Indian Gymkhana Club close to where he lived, like his pioneering forebears, he also passed on his skills and expertise. He knew he had benefited from working alongside more experienced colleagues when he first joined Richard Rogers's practice, and subsequently shared his own knowledge in turn. "We guide students and take them to a different level", he told me. Ivan Harbour drew attention to Amarjit's openness and generosity in the obituary he wrote for *The Architects' Journal*: "His guidance and creative mind will be forever evident at the Heathrow Terminal 5 where his encouragement was not just restricted to his own practice but extended to every architect and engineer participating in the project".[32]

As well as working successfully in large teams of architects, engineers and builders on huge projects over many years, he also worked with outside companies to design lights (a special light for exhibition spaces, with Reggiani),[33] bus shelters (Adshel) and street furniture (Cemusa).

Like many of the creatives about whom I write in this book, Amarjit was particularly skilled at working collaboratively with others – the deep-rooted aesthetic of pioneering communities who have settled in new lands of unfamiliarity. To quote from his *AJ* obituary again:

> Amo the constant was never phased by the inevitable ups and downs of large-scale architectural projects and his singular spirit, marked by an infectious enthusiasm for his work, permeated the studio. Unflappable, he always has a wry expression or commentary on the process and was uniquely capable of offering both constructive critique and ingenious solution to problems met along the way.[34]

Conclusion

Amarjit Kalsi's work was influenced both by his biography of movement and the fine legacies and inheritances of craftsmanship that are the expertise of the group that produced him and are represented in his work. He translated his inheritances and legacies in the architectural designs he created, through his own brand of skills and sensibilities. Migrant communities have built and made objects of all kinds for many millennia in India and in the diasporas in which we have settled. We possess a social and technical capital that excels in building and making things. But Amarjit was rare in the way he opened paths into the mainstream architectural worlds of Europe and Asia, and in the ways he understood and used materials for new purposes and in innovative ways.

Notes

1 Ivan Harbour, 'Amarjit Kalsi obituary', *The Guardian*, September 21, 2014; 'Rogers Stirk Harbour and Partners pays tribute to Amo Kalsi', *The Architects' Journal*, September 16, 2014.

2 Amarjit Kalsi, lecture for a symposium on *Stainless Steel in Architecture* organized in Berlin by Euro Inox Brussels (Belgium) and Informationsstelle Edelstahl Rostfrei (Germany), 2000.

3 Originally known as 'Richard Rogers Partnership', it became Rogers Stirk Harbour + Partners in 2007.

4 *Civilisation: A Personal View by Kenneth Clark* (1969) [TV series], BBC Two.

5 *The Ascent of Man* (1973) [TV series], BBC Two.

6 *The Times – Obituaries*, 'Amarjit Kalsi, architect whose drawings first visualised the Millennium Dome, the Lloyd's building, and the roof of Heathrow terminal 5', October 17, 2014.

7 Architectural Association, *Spirit and Invention*, London Architectural Association, 1982, p. 68. The words of one of Amarjit's tutors in the same publication read as tantamount to an admission that they underestimated his ability: "In the last five years… [c]lever words and cute or historically bedded references have been the order of the day. By implication, the simply talented designer – the person who just works through non-verbalised intuition, or through craft-like talent – is at the moment undervalued. Foolishly, in the face of such as Ammo [sic] Kalsi" (p. 68).

8 Rogers Stirk Harbour + Partners, 'About us. Practice profile', www.rsh-p.com/practice/about-us/practice-profile/ (accessed August 6, 2019).

9 Rogers Stirk Harbour + Partners, 'Tidal Pumping Station', www.rsh-p.com/projects/tidal-basin-pumping-station/ (accessed August 6, 2019).

10 Kalsi, lecture.

11 Lloyd's building, 1978–86, www.rsh-p.com/projects/lloyds-of-london/; Tidal Basin Pumping Station, 1987–88, www.rsh-p.com/projects/tidal-basin-pumping-station/ Terminal 5, Heathrow, 1988–2008, www.rsh-p.com/projects/heathrow-terminal-5/; European Court of Human Rights, 1989–95, www.rsh-p.com/projects/european-court-of-human-rights/; Bordeaux Law Courts, 1992–98, www.rsh-p.com/projects/bordeaux-law-courts/; Millennium Dome, 1996–99, www.rsh-p.com/projects/the-millennium-dome/; Terminal 4, Madrid–Barajas Airport, 1997–2005, www.rsh-p.com/projects/t4-madrid-barajas-airport/; Capodichino metro station, 2006–under construction, www.rsh-p.com/projects/capodichino-metro-station/; Santa Maria Del Pianto metro station, 2006–under construction.

12 I interviewed Mangla, Amarjit's oldest daughter, in 2015. The family donated a set of Amarjit's student drawings – possibly those which first drew Richard Rogers' attention to him – to the Architectural Association in 2017: http://collectionsblog.aaschool.ac.uk/aa-archives-amo-kalsi-drawings-donated/ (accessed August 6, 2019).

13 Ivan Harbour, 'Amarjit Kalsi Obituary'; 'Rogers Stirk Harbour and Partners pays tribute to Amo Kalsi', *The Architects' Journal*, September 16, 2014.

14 Will Hunter, 'Naples goes with the flow', *Building Design*, September 8, 2006.

15 Harbour, 'Amarjit Kalsi Obituary'; 'Rogers Stirk Harbour and Partners pays tribute to Amo Kalsi'.

16 Rogers Stirk Harbour + Partners, *Thinking and Making*, www.youtube.com/watch?v=pXYeqogoV6c (accessed August 6, 2019).

17 Rogers Stirk Harbour + Partners, *Thinking and Making*.

18 The Centre Georges Pompidou was designed by Renzo Piano and Richard Rogers, 1971–77, www.rsh-p.com/projects/centre-pompidou/ (accessed August 6, 2019).

19 Rogers Stirk Harbour + Partners, *Thinking and Making*.

20 Rogers Stirk Harbour + Partners, *Thinking and Making*.

21 *The Times – Obituaries*, 'Amarjit Kalsi'.

22 Amanda Birch, 'Santa Maria Del Pianto Metro Station', *Building Design*, April 9, 2010: "The 2,300 sq m roof form… is a doubly curved hyperbolic paraboloid, ie the shape of a Pringle crisp."

23 Kalsi, lecture.

24 Kalsi, lecture.

25 Kalsi, lecture.

26 Kalsi, lecture.

27 A quaint notion, by the time of going to print, mid Covid-19 pandemic…

28 Hunter, 'Naples goes with the flow'.

29 Hunter, 'Naples goes with the flow'.

30 Rogers Stirk Harbour + Partners, 'Practice', www.rsh-p.com/practice/ (accessed December 1, 2020).

31 Rogers Stirk Harbour + Partners, *Thinking and Making*.

32 Harbour, 'Rogers Stirk Harbour and Partners pays tribute to Amo Kalsi'.

33 E-architect, 'Ambar light: Design for Reggiani', July 7, 2009; www.e-architect.co.uk/products/ambar-reggiani-richard-rogers (accessed August 6, 2019).

34 Harbour, 'Rogers Stirk Harbour and Partners pays tribute to Amo Kalsi'.

5

JASLEEN KAUR

Jugaadhan and artist-designer of border-crossing dialogue

Objects tell stories most historians would never write.[1]

At thirty-three years old, Jasleen Kaur is still developing as an artist, whose central role she says is "to help people see things differently", something she has done consistently, from 'Oil Drum Stools',[2] 'Chai Stall'[3] and the portrait of Lord Robert Napier[4] that she created while a student, to more recent works such as pseudo-documentary 'Yoorop',[5] installation 'He Walked Like He Owned Himself'[6] and video installation 'I Keep Telling Them These Stories'.[7]

Her current publicity describes her art in the following terms:

> ...an ongoing exploration into the malleability of culture and the layering of social histories within the material and immaterial things that surround us. [It] examines the hierarchy of histories and labour using a range of mediums and methods including sculpture, video, conversation and cooking.[8]

Her art performs the role of cultural interlocutor supremely well because of her combinational prowess and ability to transfer the aesthetics of her community heritage to new zones of engagement. She is a shaper of shapes who does not take contexts and objects for granted and resists established classificatory systems. She bends objects and social situations to create a new classificatory order and framing system, disrupting the conventions of the status quo. For me, her creativity is all about intersection, connection and combination, a dynamic hybridization, capturing both past and present as it discovers the new – and it bears all the imprints of Jasleen's migrant history. Her craft maker heritage is evident both in her skills, renewed and professionalized, and also her confidence, versatility and dexterity in working with a range of materials in a variety of mediums; her style and method of working is often quintessential *jugaad* – improvised, always combinational; and the content of her work reflects both explicitly and implicitly her family's particular story and the wider Indian-British history within which it is situated, while exploring and negotiating cultural boundaries and questions of identity.

Jasleen could also be characterized as a twenty-first-century situationist,[9] though this is not a term she uses herself. The way in which she recombines elements is not just *jugaad* – in certain cases it also exemplifies the practice of *détournement*, the situationist idea of recontextualizing an existing work of art or literature in order to radically shift its meaning to a new one which has revolutionary significance, as a means of breaking through the Spectacle. Jasleen's view of art as creating a landscape of interaction, a means of bringing individuals together to talk directly to each other, resonates strongly with the situationists' notion of "the construction of situations"[10] to reawaken and allow the pursuit of authentic desires.

Fourth-generation Scot: cutting keys in Hardy's Hardware, Glasgow

Jasleen was born in 1986, in Glasgow, one of the fourth generation of her family to live in the city. Jasleen's great-grandfather was a pioneering migrant in Scotland, arriving in 1950, and a founding member of Glasgow's first gurdwara. A carpenter from Ludhiana in the Punjab, in Scotland he picked up work on construction sites when he could, and also set up as a door-to-door salesman. He used his carpenter-maker skills to build a cart with which to transport his wares and successfully negotiate Glasgow's unfamiliar terrains and craft a new life for himself. Once he made some money, he replaced the cart with a car so he could travel further and sell more. He brought his son-in-law, Ram Singh, over from India to join him – Jasleen's grandfather – and then, in 1968, they were joined by Ram Singh's wife and their daughter (in time, Jasleen's mother). She, in turn, aged just seventeen, was married to Hardeep, a first-generation migrant from India, who became Jasleen's father. They worked on market stalls together before he joined his father-in-law in the family hardware store, building it up into a prosperous business.

Jasleen is very interested in her great-grandfather's life, describing him at the beginning of her career as "a flame in her" which flickers and inspires her. He died in 1986, just two months before she was born. He appears in family photographs, but very little else of his life was recorded, so she had to rely on the memories of other family members: "I asked stories about him and got all the relatives around so that I could build a picture of his early years but nobody has ever documented his stuff. I am so romantic about it. It is very significant to me".

She describes him as he appears in the photographs:

> He dressed like a real gentleman, like one of those proud-to-be-British types, with a well-kept moustache and a tweed hat (a modern replacement for his once traditional turban). He was an in-betweener, a hybrid of both Indian and British and, in his undecided state, functioned beautifully in his new surroundings.[11]

Elsewhere, she says of him:

> I really admire him, because he was so pioneering… He was involved in setting up the first temple, but he would also borrow the latest Bollywood film reels from friends in Leicester and screen them at the Odeon cinema after Sunday service. To me, it was [a] real survival and forward-thinking attitude that he had.[12]

As we shall see, he is the direct source of inspiration for much of her early work.

As a child, Jasleen worked with her father in the family hardware store – Hardy's Hardware, an anglicization of his name, Hardeep. (This part of Jasleen's biography, and its associated skills, are coincidentally shared with architectural artist Bhajan Hunjan, also a daughter of a hardware store owner whose story I have told in Chapter 3.) "I do remember being very excited to cut my first key when I was eight or nine", Jasleen told me. By watching her father, she developed an enormous familiarity and dexterity with different materials and tools and different ways of working with them – in particular, an ability to improvise a solution with whatever you have to hand.

This ingenuity was not just her father's. Her mother, too, improvised, re-upholstering their kitchen chairs in pretty, wipe-clean English floral fabrics, and of course her great-grandfather built his own cart from which to sell his wares door to door. It is about finding new uses for existing materials, the application of a flexible mindset – *jugaad* – a mindset that is inherited as part of movement and maker capital from forebears living in a needs-based economy, whether in India, or translated to East Africa or Europe.

Jasleen's father wanted her to study the sciences so that she could become a pharmacist but she rejected this choice because she already had a passionate interest in the arts. In high school, she spent every spare moment in the art studio. Her art teacher recognized her ability and told her parents they should allow her talent to flourish. So, instead of science, she studied silversmithing and jewelry design at Glasgow School of Arts, graduating with first-class honors. She then moved on to the prestigious Royal College of Art in London, from where she received a master's degree in applied art, goldsmithing and jewelry design. Since then, she has worked on a huge range of projects, rarely using the same tools or materials, thinking of herself initially as a designer and latterly as an artist. Yet these are categories that she has resisted: "I am not interested in hierarchies between art and craft or maker and artist. For me, it's about the maker's intentions. To do something artfully is to give it time and care".[13]

Nodding to the past and leaping into the future

Much of Jasleen's work is a conscious and explicit exploration of her British Punjabi heritage at the macro level of the historical relationship between India and Britain. When talking to me, she described her work as "nodding to the past and leaping into the future".

This exploration is often witty and playful. Early in her career, Jasleen several times "re-dressed" royalty and imperial aristocrats in *chunis* (the head scarf worn by Punjabi women and by women who wear *salwaar kameez*), turbans and in the jewelry she crafted. As a student she designed a locket case into which she placed photographs of Queen Victoria and King George V. In these photos, Victoria's head is covered with a saffron *chuni* and George has a turban on him of the same color. Similarly, a pendant consists of a framed portrait of Queen Victoria, in which Jasleen has covered Victoria's head in a *chuni* with gold embellishments and placed a gold Indian jewel on her forehead.[14]

In these designs, Jasleen subverts the sartorial styles of royalty – imperial power brokers of the past and symbolic of a certain view of Britain in the present – by re-clothing them according to her artistic whim, in the style and colors of the people over whom they once ruled; and in so doing also makes a wry political point about the end of the British Empire.

This is something she pursued further in a piece she prepared for her RCA graduation show, the portrait 'Lord Robert Napier'. To create the portrait, she wrote to the present Lord Robert Napier, progeny of the imperial Sir Robert Cornelius Napier, 1st Baron Napier of Magdala, who fought in the wars of the 1840s in which the British defeated the Sikh Empire and were thus able to annex the Punjab. A statue of the 1st Baron Napier on his horse stands outside the Royal College of Art in Kensington Gardens, part of the landscape Jasleen traversed every day as a student. While the statue was one source of inspiration for the portrait, another, equally important, was her great-grandfather.

In her letter to the current Lord Napier, she outlined the key themes of her work:

> My work is evolving as a means by which to comment upon the way in which immigrants like my great-grandfather... adapted to his new surroundings, and how subsequent generations of 'British Asians', including myself, retain their traditional roots whilst simultaneously experiencing a constant cultural evolution.
>
> The statue of your grandfather – Sir Robert Napier – stands next to the college. He was a central figure in the story of British India... someone who helped to open up the migratory relationship between India and Britain that enabled my Sikh great-grandfather to come to Britain. As part of my graduation work I would like for you to allow me to tie the revered turban of the Sikhs upon your head. This act, presented as a photograph, is intended as a celebratory statement of the dialogue between two communities of different cultures, religions and languages. With this intervention I will not be claiming to make a radical new statement, but simply to draw attention to a rich historical relationship and understanding between India and Britain.

When I interviewed Jasleen, she told me how the portrait came about:

> I wrote to [Robert Napier] and he replied and said yes. I asked my dad and wanted him to look stunning. We went to Wiltshire with a photographer. It

was surreal and so beautiful... We had roast chicken for lunch and he and his wife were wonderful. They showed us ancient photos of his great-great-great-granddad of his time in India. To me, this is just a lovely photo we did of him. We put a pink turban on him... Lord Napier from one walk of life and my dad from another, chatting at the dinner table having roast chicken and bread. I did not record the conversation – that was *the* project for me, not the outcome, but the engagement itself.

Her desire to promote an interaction, a social connection across borders through talk and conversation, is a recurrent theme in Jasleen's work, which resonates with the situationist practice of "constructing a situation".[15] As she states on her website, 'conversation' is a medium which she uses as an artist – this is a theme to which I will return.

The final portrait shows the twenty-first-century Robert Napier seated, wearing a pink turban with a *kalgi* (a turban pin, with a red fan) and, on the wall above his right shoulder, a small painted portrait of his nineteenth-century forebear, the 1st Baron Napier.

Jasleen's reading of the colonial history she took as her subject is ambivalent, not wholly negative. In a short film made to accompany her graduation show she says:

This history is so difficult to read, but it is amazing that I was born in this country because of all that stuff that happened during the Raj, which opened up the migratory routes to Britain. Britain could not have been the place to arrive to otherwise. For me, it's sweet and sour. It is just another piece of history and allows for new things to come out of it...[16]

In the same film, she also talks about how she wants to capture the story of her great-grandfather. His movement is central to her work. Jasleen is supremely conscious of her heritage and inheritance and the effort that went into the making of a life in a new site.

It is not *some* version of history. It is our *own* history. You can know the big picture of the Raj, which has its own place, but until you know what your own blood went through for you to be here in this position, you can't quite comprehend the value of your family heritage. I love it.

This narrative of extreme hard work that her great-grandfather, her grandfather, her father and her mother have undertaken to create a prosperous life in Scotland is something she reiterates many times as we talk, and which she honors consistently in her work. In Jasleen's case, the past is truly alive and it is not even the past. It is being rendered in her artworks. It is a defining fount and force, which she acknowledges explicitly, which inspires her and remains a fundamental part of her design sensibility.

FIGURE 5.1 *Lord Robert Napier,* 2010

Source: Rachel Louise Brown

Her portrait of Robert Napier, and the process of creating it, represent a considered intervention into the continuing relationship between those formerly colonized and their colonizers. "I wanted to tie a turban on his head as a visual marker of where we are now", she says.[17] The progeny of the member of a former colonized group reshaped the progeny of high-profile colonizers by encasing his head with the most powerful symbol of the Sikhs, the turban. What is significant is that the artist "ethnicized" him, as earlier she "ethnicized" and appropriated Victoria and George V for her artistic purposes. The placing of the turban on Robert Napier's head might have been only a temporary occupation of an aristocrat's person, but it was, nonetheless, an assertion of a new form of British-ness that led to a new conversation with people from opposite sides of the past – a conversation between people with opposite migratory histories and class backgrounds. This was an out-of-the-ordinary event, a reversal, a subversion that created a new moment – an ephemeral moment embodied permanently in the artwork of the portrait. It is from such micro-openings of spaces and people that the new emerges and the ground is laid for a shift in the status quo. Jasleen thus contests power relations to generate a conversation which is across borders and in so doing creates a new space of thought and action. Jasleen is a social revolutionary in this respect, in the tradition of the situationists, in creating a "situation", an experience of "real" life, enabling individuals to relate directly and authentically with each other. This, too, is a theme I will return to in due course.

Jasleen took her great-grandfather and Lord Napier as inspiration again some five years later in 'Marbled Busts', the work she created for the Jerwood Makers Open in 2015, an award offered to artists who combine "a high level of technical skill with imagination and intellectual adventure…"[18]

Her commission publicity read:

> Drawing parallels between Indian devotional sculpture and traditional Western portrait busts, [Jasleen Kaur] will create a trio of busts cast in hand marbled plastic which subvert both the material and subject from the revered to the everyday. Each depicted figure will represent a meeting point between opposing cultural ideas: Jasleen's great-grandfather, the first family member to migrate from India to Glasgow; Edward Said, a Palestinian American who lives between two worlds, and the current Lord Napier, whose grandfather played a central role in the story of British India.[19]

Jasleen says she conceived the idea while she was working at the Victoria & Albert Museum:

> It's a response to the sculpture corridor containing mainly traditional Western European portrait busts and on a tangent to the East Asian sculpture… This got me thinking: 'What is the Indian equivalent of these traditional portrait busts?' The answer is Hindu devotional gods, goddesses and Buddha. So it's not a poet or a writer or a lord – its religious gods. I love the contrast between the East and Western versions; on [the] one hand it's a way of revering, immortalising them through these untouched monumental objects, whereas Indian Gods are bathed in milk, offered fruit, put to bed at night and woken at sunrise – in acts which almost mortalise [sic] them.[20]

That the first of her subjects is her great-grandfather is unsurprising. She depicts him wearing a cap, with short hair, and the cap resembles that of Lenin rather than a Scottish working man (it is not a "flat cap"). The second is Edward Said, whose books she read while studying at Glasgow School of Art. She notes that he gave her "a sense of place as a practitioner" at that time, as the ideas he wrote about were what she, too, was "thinking and making about".[21] She told me, "He writes so eloquently about culture and what happens to cultures during colonization – what changes happen to their landscape and their mindset".

The third marbled bust she made is of the current Lord Robert Napier, on whom she had earlier tied a turban. She says, "including him in my trio of busts… represents how I work as an artist in moving the conversation [about the history of British-Indian relations] forward".[22]

She describes all three of her subjects as "everyday people" who "represent a meeting point in cultures, who straddle an in-between state". Elsewhere, she has said of the busts: "It feels like [they] represent a starting point, a mid-point – or a sense of place – and a sense of how I am working as an artist now to shape the dialogue".[23]

Again, Jasleen is engaging in reversal and subversion. She reversed the traditional forms of memorial statues created out of expensive and exclusive marble by rendering her own busts in marbled plastic sourced from the cheap, two-tone buckets sold in British ethnic markets or hardware shops (like her father's) – a perfect example of her powerful ability to improvise, bend and meld objects to create something new and her democratizing, egalitarian impulse to recast the everyday as art, as well as the way in which she quietly references and honors her family in her work.

'Making do with what you have at hand and making it work'

After graduating from Glasgow School of Art as a jewelry designer, Jasleen moved on to making functional objects because, she told me, jewelry did not "have enough power… the finished products were pretty to look at but did not engage anybody. I wanted people engaged in another function and in another story". At the RCA she was surrounded by product designers and was inspired by the "making of products and the process of making" functional objects.

As a product designer, she became *jugaadhan* par excellence. Her products fused existing found objects – conventional material culture present in the terrains we all occupy – to construct new forms. Notable examples include 'Oil Drum Stools' and 'Chai Stall', from her 2010 graduation show at the RCA, and her Duralex tea glasses with bone china handles and a saucer attached.

The inspiration for the upholstered stools came from Jasleen's mother and the seats of the kitchen chairs she covered in the wipe-clean English floral fabrics: Jasleen took the large, 15-liter cooking oil cans that are routinely thrown away by restaurants, cleaned them up and put a wooden seat on top, which she upholstered with the same kind of fabric as her mother used. Thus, Jasleen transformed the cans into durable pieces of furniture. "They are lovely to look at", she told me, "and I enjoyed making them… They are strong – it's to do with the structure of the metal…"

In the case of the Duralex glasses, Jasleen had gone with design students on a study trip to an English manor house where they were asked to design something for the shop. Reacting against the house's opulent style, she decided to make tea glasses with porcelain handles.

This hybridized product is made from Duralex Provence glasses, used for serving tea in Indian homes around the world, and the bone china handle of a British tea cup. Jasleen simply attached a handle to the glass with strong glue and added a bone china saucer at the base to catch the spills. The product remains an object to drink out of, but each of its components has moved into another cultural context. In so hacking the glass's design, Jasleen negotiates cultural boundaries: the tea-glass-with-handle incorporates both the context of her family and that of the country in

FIGURE 5.2 *Oil Drum Stools*, 2010

Source: Dominic Tschudin

which she was born and still lives, Britain, as well as the country where the tea is grown, India. She is a combiner par excellence.

Tea has been an important theme in Jasleen's work. For her graduation show at the Royal College of Art, she built a mobile chai stall which provided tea for visitors in fired terracotta cups. Each had her grandmother's recipe on its side for making chai. The tea cart itself was a mash-up of existing objects: a box, with wheels attached to the base and a tubular handle with which to push it; a gas canister and a burner; the handle of a spade made a flat surface next to the burner to hold the cups. She cut a basket in half and attached it to the side for the sugar and tea ingredients. Under the flat surface were two big bottles for tea bags and tea spices and sugar, with their lids screwed to the underside of the shelf.

Designs such as these demonstrate that Jasleen is a Punjabi *jugaadhan* through and through – a woman who improvises and uses *jugaad* as her regular practice, recreating and reusing objects to create new forms that don't necessarily look perfect, but function beautifully.

She emphasizes that her love of reusing and repurposing items is not about "just recycling": she is simply living her life according to the habits with which she grew up. It is a way of life, a way of creating and a way of being in the most natural way. In fact, she does not like her way of working to be categorized as "recycling" – for her, it goes beyond that; the reusing and purposing is a deep-rooted sensibility of everyday life. She says you:

make use of what you have in order to get the thing go on a bit further… We do that in the kitchen when we have got nothing left to eat… we take some chick pea flour and we get yogurt and we make curry. You can feed ten people if you want. This is ingenuity which is so ingrained in the way we live. You have run out of tooth paste or toothbrush – you get some salt and a bit of *dant-manjan* and clean your teeth. We don't rely on what is given to us… You have got something more than that – that is what is most valuable.

In reusing found objects and materials, Jasleen is subscribing to the currents of our times without setting out to engage in the environmental zeitgeist. She was socialized to this idea long before her training at a prestigious arts establishment allowed her to professionalize this aesthetic. Her improvisational work is about her lifestyle, her inheritance of *jugaad* and the styles in which generations past have lived, an essential element of her movement and maker capital – a durable cultural capital which has been renewed and reinvented.

It's an aesthetic Jasleen continues to use in her more recent artworks – e.g. 'Women Hold Up Half The Sky' (a doctored 1936 archival photograph),[24] 'He Walked Like He Owned Himself' (white plastic chair draped with a tracksuit with deconstructed Sikh Khanda on embroidered stripe),[25] and 'Yoorop' (a video composed of excerpts from Indian films).[26] She says that one of the reasons that she applied for the Jerwood Makers Open award was to move away from her practice of using found materials[27] – but even then she chose everyday buckets from a hardware store as the source of the polyurethane plastic out of which she cast her busts.

Her materials may be "found" but they are also "chosen" to say something about how she sees the world, and to encourage others to see it differently. "I design and refashion objects based on instinct and resourcefulness", she says – but, crucially, at the same time she is "reflecting a hybridity of national custom and reconsidering the realities of materiality, usage and everyday routine"[28] – as with the Indian/British ways of drinking tea.

Conversation as artistic medium and means of subversion

The tea stall has much in common with the Lord Napier portrait as a work of art, both in terms of Jasleen's situationist desire to facilitate/provoke conversation, and as another act of subversion.

Jasleen describes the tea cart as being "built to defuse the formal atmosphere of the RCA degree show". She says that often she feels uncomfortable in art galleries, and the cart was in part a means of counteracting those feelings of discomfort, both for herself and others. Inclusion is a central aspect of her creative sensibility and the tea cart again demonstrates the democratizing, egalitarian impulse that characterizes her work.

Describing the artwork as "a traveling chai tea stall that transfers the tea drinking culture from the streets of Delhi to a formal London gallery setting", she told me her immediate inspiration was the simple tea stand of a tea seller in Southall, whose

FIGURE 5.3 *He Walked Like He Owned Himself*, 2018
Tracksuit with deconstructed Sikh Khanda on embroidered stripe

Source: Love Unlimited

customers hung around the stand and talked. It struck her that his basic idea was so simple: a large pan, a cylinder-based gas burner and cups, plus the ingredients for tea, and his business was up and going. The cart can be packed up and taken to the next destination. It quenches thirst, makes money for its owner and also brings people together for interaction and conversation. It is a mobile business which encourages people to converse and engage. In a sort of meta-pun on the whole notion of migration, the object she designed encapsulates movement: it moves, and can be packed up and moved to another place entirely, as her family did, and it obliquely replicates the life of her great-grandfather, first-generation migrant to Scotland, who made a cart to help him earn his living.

But, placed in an art exhibition, Jasleen's pop-up tea stall does far more than this. Like the act of tying a turban on Robert Napier's head, it facilitates conversation between individuals who would otherwise never have met. The stall, and the act of buying and drinking tea together, prompt people to converse and engage and learn and come to know each other a little better than before. Jasleen's stall also enables information to be transmitted and passed on – in the recipes inscribed on the tea cups, as well as through exchanges between individuals. Thus, the stall, her work of art, is a mediator and an interlocutor, a bridge-builder, enabling border-crossing connections.

In this way, her "cobbled together", pop-up Indian tea stall achieves her aim of defusing the formality of the RCA degree show by subverting the established norms of an art exhibition. In a standard art exhibition, the visitors view the works of art in the gallery, and then, perhaps, go to the gallery café to drink tea; they rarely engage in conversation with any visitor they do not already know. The effect of Jasleen's tea stall was to break down these barriers, as the tea drinkers gathered round the stall within the exhibition itself and in many cases talked to each other. Again, as in the earlier encounter between her father and Lord Napier, she is contesting power relations by generating border-crossing conversations and in so doing creates new spaces of thought and action.

Jasleen talks consistently about her desire that her work should promote an inter-action. If it initiates a conversation – as in the case of the portrait and the tea stall – she considers her goal to have been achieved. Jasleen told me, "my products are vehicles that allow anyone to engage in something, my little way of doing art. It is not about Indian and white people; it is about any one and any other". She creates events, "situations", experiences of "real" life in which individuals are able to relate directly and authentically to each other. Jasleen engages in small revolutions by enabling border-crossing engagements, which have a transformative power. In this respect, she is a situationist social revolutionary. She is not an anarchist, but she has anarchic tendencies: she disrupts discreetly, implicitly and explicitly, without herself using any words.

Although Jasleen does not engage in an explicit political discourse, her politics are implicit in the way she works, the materials she uses, and in the pleasure she gets out of creating objects or happenings which encourage people to talk and produce conversation and dialogue. This is the exact notion of *sangat* in Sikh philosophy – engaging together in a community, crowd-sourcing knowledge, and sharing food while sitting or standing at the same level – a facet of egalitarianism and democratic sharing and a rejection of hierarchical social structures.

Food: measuring and sharing

Food is central to Jasleen's work. It is a big part of her practice: exploiting its universal and egalitarian nature to bring light to different cultural variations and to create 'situations' or events in which people can talk. "Food was one of the things I started using really early on", she notes, "a way of disrupting a formal space – it's becoming a tool, a really practical thing".[29]

After graduating, Jasleen was taken up by a commercial product maker – Tala – to make a cook's measuring cup for making Indian food: the Tala Curry Cooks Measure.[30] It reworks the traditional Tala Cooks Measure, which dates from the 1920s. While most Indian home cooks will measure their ingredients by eye and hand, the Tala Measure calibrates the quantities needed. In concordance with Jasleen's aesthetic of bending and repurposing existing objects, the curry measure recodes an existing object, and fits it into her cultural context, so that knowledge is more widely shared and those unfamiliar with the recipes will be able to prepare them successfully. The product was launched in February 2013. It neatly encodes a movement story: a product which is recoded and recalibrated for a different cuisine, itself now both Indian and British, and a legacy of empire – part of the same dynamic by which British Asian curries have displaced roast beef as the favorite British meal. The measuring cone is an exercise in both subversion and fusion – or perhaps it is the fusion which makes it subversive. It is another dialogue-enhancing product which creates bridges and crosses borders.

In 2014, she repeated the act of calibration for the *langar* (the communal kitchen where food is cooked by volunteers) in the Polloksheilds gurdwara in Glasgow, and also filmed the whole process.[31] With the help of friends, she then cooked similarly large quantities of food which she served at the 2014 London Design Festival, while showing *Balti*, the film she had made in the Polloksheilds temple, in a hired van transformed into pop-up cinema and taken from venue to venue around London.

Jasleen explains how a gurdwara provides food every day for anyone who walks in – the "free food ethos". She says, "Every meal time they cook for 100 to 1000 people and one thing that amazes me is that is that there's no recipe written down, there's no measurements, there is no such things as scales. They are all volunteers as well, there's not even a rota, so it's the most amazing thing to be part of".[32]

This is a Sikh practice, central to their egalitarian beliefs – the sharing of food while sitting or eating at the same level. There are *langar* vans which go out and serve food made at the temple to anyone who wants it, especially those in need. Sikhs volunteer services and resources all the time with no expectation of reciprocity. Such knowledge is learnt by being socialized into it from a young age – helping the community, both within and outside Sikh temples, which includes making and serving food.

While documenting on film the techniques used by the Sikhs at the Glasgow temple, Jasleen learnt the whole process, including the amounts of ingredients required to cook for that number of people. She said:

> Cooking alongside them, I made a version of the Tala Cooks Measure. I recorded the recipes by marking buckets with the volumes of each ingredient in order to create a series of measuring tools for cooking en masse… It relates to how people such as my grandmother have such an innate knowledge of quantities required for each dish… That project was about documenting something amazing that happens every day, then making the tools to be able to recreate [it] in a completely different context.[33]

FIGURE 5.4 *Tala Curry Measure*, 2013

Source: Dominic Tschudin

The knowledge of the quantities of ingredients needed to prepare the *langar* meal is implicit capital, undocumented, but passed on indirectly through observation and participation. It is the sedimented knowledge of centuries, carried by expert older men and women. Jasleen has become a transmitter of this expertise by concretizing the measures used for cooking large communal meals in the form of calibrated buckets (and the name of the film – *Balti*, a British Asian-created curry – is in fact the Punjabi word for 'bucket' – another of Jasleen's neat puns).

By screening the film and serving the *langar*-type food elsewhere, she transfers her Sikh traditions of sharing food and resources to generate conviviality and sociality, thus building bridges, making connections and alliances with a new set of people. Jasleen is a path-breaking innovator in formalizing and overtly documenting this knowledge both as a learner and reproducer of it. She represents the sharism and open, inviting aesthetic which dents monopolistic and hierarchical knowledge. Her egalitarian ways of working, and of sharing knowledge, are again part of her cultural capital. Jasleen carries these values and instantiates them in her creative practice and public creativity in potent and understated ways.

Subsequently, while also taking on prestigious commissions from the V&A and art galleries around the UK, Jasleen has worked with refugees and asylum seekers in Stoke-on-Trent,[34] with women in Middlesbrough,[35] and with children and mothers from the Portman Early Childhood Centre in London[36] – all in activities based around food. In Middlesbrough and London, as well as Stoke-on-Trent, the women who took part were often recent migrants with their own stories of movement and dislocation. In participating in such projects, Jasleen builds on her long-term creative trajectory of bringing people together through the sharing of skills, talk and food. This is a facet of both her distributive and contributive aesthetic and also her desire to engage in a participatory pedagogic mode, a sensibility she shares with other creatives I describe in this book. She is not only a designer of materiality but also of landscapes of interaction. Jasleen herself, in reflecting on her work with the children and mothers at the Portman children's center in a talk at the Serpentine Art Gallery,[37] says how she prefers to understand 'culture' in the sense of growing something, tending to people and relationships, rather than in terms of art or literature.

Conclusion

Jasleen's work encodes the journeys she herself has undertaken, as well as those of her family, now four generations' deep in Scotland. Her family's migration narrative is a defining feature of her creativity and her products. There is a unity in her life; how she lives and how she produces and the connections between her artworks. Her aesthetics and sensibilities are deep-rooted – inherited from her parents and grandparents and great-grandparents. It is a shared source code. Her family's legacy is fundamentally a part of the objects she designs, consciously encrypted, to encourage further journeys – in the minds of those who observe and discuss them. "Objects tell stories most historians would never write", she says[38] and each object she creates invites its viewers to see the world in a different way.

Growing up in and around a hardware shop, Jasleen acquired both an expertise and familiarity with materials, and also knowledge of selling to customers, understanding what they want and need. But her creative sensibilities, her technical skills and ease of use of materials are also part of her longer-standing maker inheritance, its technical skills enhanced through movement.

And, crucially, her art consists in creating events, as well as objects. Both facilitate conversations and interactions. She creates situations – low-key ones, which overturn the existing order of things. Her art makes strong political statements to break exclusivities and hierarchies through materiality without recourse to verbal gymnastics. Through these interventions, and the often playful attitude she has towards cultural identity, Jasleen questions and transcends cultural boundaries. Like her forebears, Jasleen's sense of tradition is open not closed, about renewal and reworking, adopting new ways of looking, making and doing in order to create anew. Her artworks are products of her forebears' migration history, inscribed in her design agendas and aesthetic sensibilities. She self-consciously and explicitly encodes these durable, translatable and transferable inheritances in her daily life, and specifically in her art practice. The past is a source of both inspiration and reassurance as she nods to it – and then leaps to the future.

Notes

1 Jasleen Kaur, 'Objects tell stories most historians would never write', February 23, 2016; www.britishcouncil.org/voices-magazine/objects-tell-stories-most-historians-never-write (accessed August 8, 2019).

2 Oil Drum Stools, 2010. Upholstered 15 litre oil drum cans with wipe clean tops;http://jasleenkaur.co.uk/oil-drum-stools/ (accessed August 8, 2019).

3 Chai Stall, 2010. Travelling chai tea stall. Royal College of Art graduation show 2010; http://jasleenkaur.co.uk/chai-tea-stall-2/ (accessed August 8, 2019).

4 Lord Robert Napier, 2010. "A turban tied by Jasleen's father on the head of the current Lord Robert Napier, whose great granddad (Robert Napier, 1st Baron Napier of Magdala) was an army officer in the 1st and 2nd Anglo-Sikh Wars in Punjab. Photographed by Rachel Louise Brown." http://jasleenkaur.co.uk/projectsaboutcontactc-jasleen-kaurlord-robert-napier-by-jasleen-kaur-artist-designer-royal-college-of-art-rca-degree-show-2010-lord-robert-napier-2011-dear-lord-robert-napier-i-am-a-postgradua/ (accessed August 8, 2019).

5 YOOROP, 2017. Video 5m 50s. "Commissioned by V&A Museum, Goethe Institute and British Council for 'Collecting Europe'. An account of Europe constructed from footage from popular Indian cinema, fabricating an image of European-ness from an alternative cultural perspective. Edited by Jasleen Kaur and Marianna Simnett, music by Leo Chadburn." http://jasleenkaur.co.uk/yoorop (accessed August 8, 2019).

6 He Walked Like He Owned Himself, 2018. "Commissioned by Love Unlimited for Glasgow International. Tracksuit with deconstructed Sikh Khanda on embroidered stripe." http://jasleenkaur.co.uk/he-walked-like-he-owned-himself/ (accessed June 22, 2020).

7 I Keep Telling Them These Stories, 2018. "As part of Where I Am Is Here, curated by Helen Nisbet for Hollybush Gardens. A two-channel video installation of sequenced diptych footage on family, identity, origins, memory and colonialism shot during travels and family gatherings in India and Scotland, combined with archival footage. Time and scale continually expand and contract, while topographies, flora and fauna merge with little regard for geography." http://jasleenkaur.co.uk/i-keep-telling-them-these-stories (accessed August 8, 2019).

8 Jasleen Kaur, 'About', http://jasleenkaur.co.uk (accessed August 8, 2019).

9 From the Situationist International – a revolutionary alliance of European avant-garde artists, writers and poets formed at a conference in Italy in 1957 (as Internationale Situationiste or IS) (see www.tate.org.uk/art/art-terms/s/situationist-international) and officially disbanded in 1972. Their ideas gained wider public prominence due to their influence on the students involved in the Paris riots of May 1968 (see www.spectator.co.uk/2018/07/how-situationism-changed-history/) and on the punk movement (see https://louderthanwar.com/situationism-explained-affect-punk-pop-culture/). In *The Society of the Spectacle*, the situationists' key thinker, Guy Débord, argues that we are all slaves to the Spectacle of images and objects, consumerism, entertainment, work, even politics. The idea, then, is to "construct a situation" to break through the Spectacle – moments of life deliberately constructed for the purpose of reawakening and pursuing authentic desires, experiencing the feeling of life and adventure, and the liberation of everyday life; https://en.wikipedia.org/wiki/Situationist_International (all accessed August 8, 2019).

10 Guy Debord, 'The Situationists and the New Forms of Action in Politics or Art', in Tom McDonough (ed.) *Guy Debord and the Situationist International: Texts and Documents* (Cambridge, MA: MIT Press, 2002), 164.

11 Interview with the author, January 15, 2015.

12 Interview with the author, December 20, 2013.

13 Elinor Morgan, 'Interview with Jasleen Kaur', Jerwood Arts 2015, https://jerwoodarts.org/exhibitionsandevents/writing-and-media/interview-with-jasleen-kaur-1/ (accessed August 8, 2019).

14 Queen of Great Britain – Empress of India, 2009. "Part of a series of pendants that comment on the rich, complex relationship between Britain and India. Selected by Monica Gaspar for Schmuck, International Contemporary Jewellery show, 2009." http://jasleenkaur.co.uk/jewellery (accessed August 8, 2019).

15 Débord, *The Society of the Spectacle.*

16 Royal College of Art Sustain Talks: Jasleen Kaur, https://vimeo.com/36423222 (accessed August 8, 2019).

17 Morgan, 'Interview with Jasleen Kaur'.

18 Jerwood Arts, 'Jerwood Makers Open 2015', https://jerwoodarts.org/exhibitions andevents/projects/jerwood-makers-open-2015/ (accessed August 8, 2019).

19 Jerwood Arts, 'Jerwood Makers Open 2015'.

20 MacPherson Shona, Artist to Artist Interview with Jasleen, Art Map, London, June 2015.

21 MacPherson Shona, Artist to Artist Interview with Jasleen, Art Map, London, June 2015.

22 MacPherson Shona, Artist to Artist Interview with Jasleen, Art Map, London, June 2015.

23 Morgan, 'Interview with Jasleen Kaur'.

24 Women Hold Up Half The Sky, 2019. Billboard commission curated by Freya Dooley for Spit and Sawdust. A doctored 1936 archival image of members of the 2nd Royal Battalion (Ludhiana Sikhs) in Waziristan, explores postcolonial gender roles. Tamed men precariously balance on each other's necks, propped up by Kaur's mother's hand: a gesture towards her research into the invisibility of women's voices and discovering non-masculine forms of resistance.

25 He walked like he owned himself, 2018, http://jasleenkaur.co.uk/he-walked-like-he-owned-himself/ (accessed June 22, 2020).

26 YOOROP, 2017, http://jasleenkaur.co.uk/yoorop (accessed August 8, 2019).

27 Morgan, 'Interview with Jasleen Kaur'. "I applied to shift my practice away from relying on found objects, so that while my work would still be informed by the qualities of found objects I would have more independence and agency."

28 Leonie Morris Q and A "Making Thoughts", The Saturday Market Project. September 10, 2014.

29 'Radical Kitchen 2018: Grain', www.youtube.com/watch?v=AJhOMQ3kffg (accessed August 8, 2019).

30 Curry Measure, designed for Tala, 2013. "The new Curry Measure is a redesign of the iconic 1920s Cook's Measure. But where the original measures dry ingredients without the use of scales, the Curry Measure acts as the scales and the recipe book. Designed to get you back to cooking intuitively, without the millilitres and grams but by eye – just as my mum and gran taught me. The innovation has been such a success for Tala, they have used the concept for other cuisines. Stockists include John Lewis, SCP, Selfridges and my dad's hardware shop." Graphics by Hurricane Design; http://jasleenkaur.co.uk/tala-curry-measure/ (accessed August 8, 2019).

31 BALTI, 2014. Video shot on iPad, 7m 50s. "Filmed by Rachel Louise Brown, titles by Christina Foreman. Balti (ball-tee) noun. 1. A bucket 2. A type of curry. This film documents the daily process of cooking *Langar* in the kitchen of Polloksheilds Sikh Temple in Glasgow. The cooks' intuitive methods of preparing food in mass quantities is an unwritten skill known only by a handful of members in the community. Cooking alongside them, we recorded their recipes by marking buckets with the volumes of each ingredient to create a series of measuring tools for cooking en masse. *Balti* was screened at various venues during the London Design Festival 2014 from a portable cinema screen designed to fit perfectly into the back of a ZipVan." http://jasleenkaur.co.uk/balti-unmeasured-measurements/ (accessed August 8, 2019).

32 BALTI, 2014.

33 BALTI, 2014.

34 "Artist Jasleen Kaur has been working alongside members of the Jubilee Club, a group of refugee and asylum seekers who meet at a luncheon club in Burslem." – British Ceramics Biennial, Stoke-on-Trent 2015.

35 Residency at Middlesbrough Institute of Modern Art (MIMA), 2018, as part of New Mappings of Europe, www.newmappingsofeurope.si/en/news/jesleen-workshop_16 (accessed August 8, 2019).

36 'Learn – Changing Play', www.serpentinegalleries.org/learn/changing-play/jasleen-kaur. "Throughout 2018 children and mothers from the Portman Early Childhood Centre have been working with artist Jasleen Kaur, using the micro-politics of cooking and eating together to collectively consider and respond to issues facing the local community." (accessed August 8, 2019).

37 'Radical Kitchen 2018: Grain', www.youtube.com/watch?v=AJhOMQ3kffg (accessed August 8, 2019).

38 Kaur, 'Objects tell stories'.

6

RISHI RICH, FEARLESS SOUND SHAPER, AND JAY SEAN, PATH-BREAKING SINGER-SONGWRITER

We have got to make our own noise. We have got to do what we want to do.[1]

Rishi Rich and Jay Sean are both musicians who grew up in London during the 1980s and 1990s. Their backgrounds include an eclectic mix of all sorts of music, both contemporary and inherited from their multiply migrant kin. For British Asian fans, it was with Juggy D that Rishi and Jay achieved their finest musical moment, performing *Dance with You/Nachna teray Naal* together as the Rishi Rich Project in 2003 – but it was only by moving to the United States and then, in Rishi's case, on to India, that they have been able to develop their individual musical identities and exploit their global reach in order to sustain their careers over the longer term.

Jay Sean, R&B singer-songwriter, moved from the UK to the United States in 2008, and benefited from this migration by making alliances and recording with powerful and creatively daring African American music producers who sound-engineered his songs to take him to the top of the Billboard 100 in 2009 with their first release *Down* – making Jay Sean the first-ever Asian to occupy this number one slot. (Or, rather, the first self-declared Asian: Freddie Mercury, aka Farrukh Bulsara, who was also an Indian but had hidden his Indian-from-Zanzibar-East-Africa-UK ethnicity had two number ones as the lead singer of the band Queen.[2]) Jay's migration to Los Angeles, United States, unleashed his creativity in new ways and in a new opportunity structure in which he was not read as an Indian, nor reduced to an ethnic slot. There, European musical hierarchies were impotent to exert their power over his courageous creativity and he escaped the powers of classification which had been hindering his growth in the UK. Jay is not into Punjabi music or the use of this language in his music; he is into R&B par excellence. When the grip of the US record company again constrained his creativity, Jay moved on once more, now based in New York and distributing his music via his own company Kamouflage Records and multinational Sony to a global audience.

Rishi Rich is a musical producer and combiner par excellence though an organic, in-the-moment inventiveness which has deep roots in his migration inheritance from India to Africa to Britain and his own movement as an adult to the United States and then on to Mumbai, India, with a base in London – a deeply rich legacy of four continents that undergirds the soundscape he generates. His musical language reflects the diasporic, richly cosmopolitan musical milieu in which he grew up, with multiple influences from East Africa, India, the United States and the UK. Like other case studies in this book, Rishi is a radical hybridizer, an innovative remixer, a maker of recombinant forms in soundscapes that produce and capture the new. It is his courageous inventiveness, technical expertise and fluency in arranging a multitude of sounds that have made possible the careers of many others, including Jay Sean and Juggy D. His mastery of sound engineering, its samplers and computers, brings out the best in his artists in a symbiotic, synergistic way. About his music he says, "I don't really care if it sells or not… I just want to put it out there and let the world share it".

A cosmopolitan London childhood

Jay

Jay Sean was born Kamaljit Singh Jhooti in Southall, west London, and his family then moved the short distance to Hounslow. His grandparents and parents came to the UK from India but other relatives moved to London from East Africa in the late 1960s and 1970s. His grandfather helped establish the first gurdwara in Southall.

Jay describes his background as "a normal traditional Punjabi Sikh family". His father does not wear a turban but is a devoted Sikh and is well versed about Sikh religious texts, scriptures and rituals. Jay admires him for his openness and support of his son's career while also being comfortable with his religion and ethnicity. Growing up, Jay and his brother went to the gurdwara with their mother to listen to *kirtan* (devotional songs; he and his brother learnt the Sikh prayers and would pray in the morning before school).

Alone among my case studies, Jay attended a private school rather than the local state comprehensive, which was "99 per cent Indian", he told me.[3] Jay cites his parents' decision to send him there as "the crucial turning point in my life" as it brought him into contact with a wider range of people and influences than he would otherwise have encountered:

> …I had white friends, black friends, Chinese friends, Japanese friends, English friends, and Polish friends – a mixture of friends… It made me very open, to be able to talk to people of all walks of life.

Jay talks about how open he has been with his parents and has not had to hide anything from them. He brought his girlfriends home without censure and both his parents supported his move from a safe and prestigious medical career to the unpredictable and not-yet-trodden path of music. In fact, they have delighted in his career and every triumph he had. He learnt from them the value of hard work, and the value of money. "One thing they knew about my personality", he told me, "is that I don't give it less than 110 per cent in anything I do".

Rishi

Rishi Rich – Rishpal Singh Rekhi – was born in Croydon in south London, an area which is home to many of his kinsmen from East Africa. His maternal and paternal families are from Tanzania, though originally from North India. His mother was born in Dar es Salaam and migrated to London as a young woman and married his father who had arrived there as a teenager from Kenya.

Rishi's father died when Rishi was still a child and his mother moved with him to Harrow to live near her brothers. A formative dynamic in Rishi's life has been being raised by a single mother and living on a council estate where, even if you were not conspicuous with a turban, bullying of Asian men was rife. This is a common theme in the lives of so many British Asians. Rishi told me: "It was just that we were Indians. I was bullied a lot. I decided, 'We have to make our own noise. We have got to do what we want to do'."

Radical remix: heterogenous musical inheritance

Jay

Jay was exposed to popular mainstream music even before the multi-ethnic cosmo-politanism of his secondary school. He listened on his Sony Walkman, the gadget of the time. Lionel Richie was an early favorite:

> I fell in love with soul music so much. I was eight to ten years old and I fell in love with Lionel Richie. It is weird that you are so young and listening to Lionel Richie – that kind of music at such a young age… That is how I learnt to sing.

He was already, through his Punjabi background, exposed to bhangra[4] music of all kinds and Hindi music from Bollywood, but he got into R&B because his friends in school listened to it, and so did his uncles and aunts:

> My heart took to it, I gravitated to it… When cable TV came through, I started watching MTV religiously, obsessed with all the music videos… I used to watch these rappers. I used to listen to how they rap, fascinated by how they were able to do it.

Jay was inspired by many African American role models, not just Lionel Ritchie – people like Will Smith (Jay and his brother knew whole episodes of *The Fresh Prince of Bel Air* off by heart), James Brown, Michael Jackson, Stevie Wonder and Jay Z.

This was Jay's induction and seduction into African American music and artists. Through the global entertainment industry, African American creative people dominated his life.

When he was twelve he began to record himself singing:

> Myself and my brother discovered how we could record our voices onto a cassette player on our [sound] system… Eventually we would play it to mum and dad. They would say, 'I didn't know you could sing'.

He would be brought out to sing after every meal when guests and relatives came from India and Canada. He became the "entertainer of the house"; he had got the bug and was already a performer, honing skills he would use in the future.

Jay told me he takes after his Baba, his paternal grandfather, who loved to sing in Punjabi and Hindi. Once Jay started composing songs, his Baba would listen and comment on them in a nuanced way. His parents would celebrate their son's music, but his grandfather would give him a detailed critique. According to Jay, he was like the "Simon Cowell of the family".

> When I would bring home a song… Mum and dad would love it because it is their own son. Baba would listen to it carefully, listen to the melody choice, listen to the words… and would change a bit of this and ask, 'Why are you putting this here and not there?' He would really listen.

Rishi

Rishi's family was particularly into music – listening, singing, and playing instruments. Rishi's uncles had a music-making evening almost every Sunday in one or other of their homes. Before they came to the UK, Rishi's great-aunt played the guitar at home and also on *Voice of Kenya*, the local radio station. Other relatives hosted singers from India who went on to become internationally renowned, for example, Jagjit and Chitra Singh who were the pre-eminent ghazal singers of the times.[5] His parents and their cousins grew up listening to all the famous Europe-based musicians whose recordings traveled all over the world, Bollywood, and African American singers such as James Brown, Ray Charles and Stevie Wonder.

His paternal grandmother had taught classical Indian music in Dar es Salaam, and taught Rishi when he was a child. She sang in the temple on public occasions and at weddings and pre-wedding celebrations, *sangeet*. She also performed popular Bollywood film and Punjabi folk songs and Urdu ghazals, as did many people in that generation, in which code-switching and moving in and out of different languages with unselfconscious ease was the norm. All in the older generations of Rishi's extended kinship network are speakers of Swahili, the language they were raised with and spoke in East Africa in public and at home, combined with English and Punjabi and sometimes Urdu and Gujarati and also often Hindi. Rishi's generation of young people born and raised in Britain have not had direct exposure to Swahili and do not speak it themselves, but hear it all the time in the Swahili-influenced Punjabi this group speaks. For Rishi, although he told me he has never seen Kenya as his home, "it is in [his] blood":

> My mum coming from Africa was already quite fused… I grew up in a house where she was playing Indian music one minute and James Brown the next, so my mind became soaked in musical fusion.

The rich and organically multicultural milieu that both Jay and Rishi were socialized to was sophisticated and complex, musically as well as linguistically mixed to a high degree. Their exposure to a vast range of music underlies their radical combinational powers and ability to fuse different genres. This music emerged from the complex legacy of movement of their own families.

Youthful improvisation and experimentation

Jay

When Jay was sixteen, he acquired proficiency and confidence and managed to get himself heard in a small way, which sowed the seeds of his later success:

> There was a radio competition going on [on Choice FM, the biggest black music radio station in London]. You would call up and you got twenty seconds to… do some singing. You either got a flushed… toilet sound or… applause. The first time I did it, I… was flushed. I called back and back and had another go. It was a fast rap and a melody this time. I cured it and got the [applause].

It was after this that he had the confidence to rap publicly. He had formed a rap group with his cousin Pritipal Rooprai, called *Compulsive Disorder*. Their first-ever performance was to an aggressively critical audience at Jay's school's band night. But the crowd loved Jay and Pritipal's performance, which gave them the confidence to perform again. They put their music on tape and handed it out, so that it started to "get a little noise around that area".

> Me and my cousin, we are two Indian boys doing rap music. We were fearless. We were young. What did we have to lose?

They were placed in the top twenty of a talent show contest organized by Choice FM. All twenty bands had to perform at a club in Peckham, south London. As Jay explains:

> In terms of standing out, we were two Indian boys surrounded by 100 percent black talent. Every other competitor was black. We were doing hip hop. I was sixteen…

They came third, and continued performing at local events. But the turning point, Jay says, "was when I bumped into Rishi Rich".

Rishi

Rishi learnt Indian classical music from the age of six and when he was eleven years old his mother bought him a portable Casio keyboard. He loved this keyboard, played it all the time and performed with uncles, cousins and friends at the frequent family musical events. When he was thirteen, he got a job in a recording studio and bought himself another keyboard on which you could sequence music as well as play, because he wanted to make his own music, drawn from his sensibilities. He was constantly recording on tape at home. He went as lead keyboardist with a school band to Germany, where he accompanied a pioneering bhangra fusion group led by Sanj.[6] This was the beginning of his journey beyond the soundscapes he was inducted into as a child. A key influence was Apache Indian (aka Steve Kapoor who made his mark with his bestselling bhangramuffin style [reggae and bhangra] which combined Jamaican patois and Punjabi).[7] As Rishi explains, Apache was "amazing" for a generation of musicians who were a decade younger and indeed he was a path breaker, influential for Asians all over the diaspora and in India, too.

When he was fifteen, Rishi bought a fusion record by a producer called Pankaj Jethwa, who was originally from East Africa. The record cover showed the name of the studio which produced this album: it was only a few streets away from Rishi's mother's home. Rishi went to see Pankaj and gave him some of his music. Pankaj loved it and invited him to use his studio when he himself was not using it, which was most evenings. Pankaj showed Rishi how to use the studio equipment and then Rishi figured things out for himself.

Rishi describes having a feeling for machines, how they work and how else they could be made to work – the notion of engineering as craftsmanship, and the innovation that comes from experimenting with technology. (This is something he shares with fellow musician Kuljit Bhamra – see Chapter 2.) He has a natural ease with technology and a proclivity to "putting things together and tinkering with machines and sounds". He also has a respect for what he calls "learning the craft".[8] In Pankaj's studio, Rishi said he learnt how the music he liked should sound and technically how to balance it:

> Even though I used to make the music, Pankaj used to engineer it and make it sound amazing. That was our team. We became a group and we did a lot of Hindi mixes together.

They worked with singers from India on Indian songs which they reinterpreted and remixed with new instrumentation from other genres – that was Pankaj's hybrid working style. While these singers failed to break into the UK market, locally born people like Bally Sagoo, Talvin Singh and Nitin Sawhney, among others, were emerging and making a big impact. Rishi told me:

> I used to hear all these different sounds and think it was amazing... I loved composition. That is what I really wanted to do... I tried to construct music which I heard but fuse it together. But it took me a little while.

He gave up a place at university to study computer science and engineering in order to pursue his musical career. From the beginning, he wanted to create his own soundscapes through tinkering and experimentation and manipulating machines, the technology of musical engineering. He had a highly developed musical ear and a deep confidence in his abilities. Despite opposition from other relatives, he had his mother's unfailing and public support to pursue his passion for music. Rishi views this unquestioned backing from his mother as critical to his success. She loved and enjoyed her son's soundscapes and friendships without disapprobation. She would welcome his friends in the world of music and cook for them, which catalyzed his ability to develop connections with musicians beyond the immediate Asian ethnic enclaves. Even now, she is the first person to whom he sends a new composition.[9]

He became Rishi Rich – RR – when his then manager told him to come up with a name. He did not invest a great deal of energy into this:

> I didn't think my name would be a brand. I just wanted people to listen to my music... I like being in the background... People... don't need to know too much about me. They need to know my music.

Rishi is part of the power behind the performer but is not into being out front. This is a recurring theme among the people I am writing about: they are not self-promoting but work creatively in the background; they don't seek the limelight but create unobtrusively and innovatively.

Rishi's talented black manager, Brian Wilson, played a crucial role in introducing Rishi to a wider black British network and thus extended his exposures and sonic range. Rishi explains that "learning from him was good because he opened my eyes, and doors – in the sense that I met a lot of other people who were not just from the Indian industry... [for example,] radio DJs from Choice FM".

This station gave Rishi the chance to make alliances with R&B sounds which were outside the landscapes of the Asian community; like Jay, he looked to US R&B and African American musicians rather than British white and mainstream musicians.

Aged twenty-four, Rishi set up his own studio in Perivale, west London. He funded it, persuading a record company that he'd done work for with Pankaj to pay him to do "Asian garage music with Hindi songs and Punjabi songs" – as garage music was popular at the time.

Word spread about his work. Another local record company started to send artists to him, primarily the bhangra groups, but also other singers, and the studio started paying for itself:

> I used to work day and night… I was living with my mum but I was always in the studio. If I had one or two clients, that paid the rent and I would use the rest of the time to work on the music and send it to… different companies.

It was around this time he met Juggy D and Jay Sean: "We all got on and knew we all got on and I wanted to work with them. That was it".

Combinational daring: the Rishi Rich Project

Rishi and Jay met at a *mela* (a large public fair) where Jay performed and Rishi told him his performance was "sick". This was when Jay was fully entrenched in the beat box, hip hop culture and still in medical school at the University of London. Rishi was already well known and had just done a mix for the singer Craig David who at that time, as Jay comments, "had taken the country by storm – the biggest pop star in the UK. Rishi, an Indian guy, had done the remix. I thought it was so awesome".

FIGURE 6.1 (*Left to right*) Juggy D, Rishi Rich and Jay Sean, c. 2015, in Rishi's west London studio

Source: © Raj Ghai, www.mediamoguls.com/"www.mediamoguls.com

Jay asked Rishi if he could visit his studio and work with him, and Rishi took Jay under his wing. Jay explains the exact moment of radical innovation when they created *Dance with You / Nachna teray Naal*:

> In the beginning it was just an English song... It was just me and Rishi. And at the time, Juggy D was becoming quite a sensation – a bhangra sensation. He was also one of Rishi's artists. So... Juggy came into the studio. There was great energy, amazing energy – incredible energy... We just hit it off instantly. We became friends so soon, so quick, so easy. Juggy said, 'Let me listen to some these songs you are doing, man. Seeing as you are Rishi's new boy...' I said, 'Yeah, we're writing this song *Dance with You*'. He heard it and he started to sing along but translating everything I was saying in English into Punjabi. So we – me and Rishi – looked at each other and said, 'That's pretty cool, actually – it's different. Me singing in English and him coming back in Punjabi. Wonder if it's even been done'. So we got him behind the mike and recorded his bit. Before we knew it, we had done something groundbreaking. We had... made a song that had really connected organically – it was just organic. It was not mixing – it just happened. It was two different voices, two different languages, two different cultures coming together in this one song.

For Rishi, it was the perfection of a sound he had been experimenting with for some time.

> At that time, I just knew that 'this is exactly what I have been working for' – this sound in *Dance with You* was unique... The beat really didn't change but the flute mixed and married with the base and the drums... Jay singing in R&B and Juggy singing in Punjabi. Putting that together – that kind of started the whole thing... For me this was what I work for...

The moment that Jay describes is what Basil Bernstein calls "a recovery of something not yet spoken, of a new fusion";[10] it is the capturing of a new fusion as the moment unfolds without knowing in advance what the new terrains will throw up. This is the power of Jay and Rishi – to capture the moment in the moment and so produce the new form. They created a new form of influential music, through a process of tinkering and playing around with sounds and language. Bernstein's book describes this terrain which leaves the old sacred behind and has the power to discover and capture the moment in its new becoming. Their organic innovation came from this power of tinkering and experimentation – the "triumph of tinkering"[11] and the notion of "bricolage" that Levi-Strauss[12] talks about.

This story of Rishi and Jay is resonant with the temples of corrugated iron that the pioneers built with no template to follow and with whatever materials they had, using all the principles of *jugaad*, the sensibility they had inherited and developed further in the diaspora where they had to work with what they had at hand. This is a facet of movement capital, a fearless experimenting to discover and make the new. Across the generations, they are all – the great-grandparents, grandparents and parents – courageous, patient tinkerers and experimenters, trying out novel ways to build, and create and improvise in new post-migration sites. This is what you have to do when there are no well-trodden and tested paths. It is indeed the triumph of tinkering, as Sherry Turkle puts it,[13] because there is no other established way of creating and crafting. It was in this organic way that Rishi, Jay and Juggy D came up with their winning sound – the bricolage aesthetic combined with Rishi's techno-logical musical prowess; the ethnographic moment of organic hybridity.

Rishi, Jay and Juggy performed the song at the Southall Mela and knew as soon as they had performed that they were a hit. Jay, who was the least well known at the time, was followed around by the young women who were enamored by his singing, his style and his looks:

> We came on stage and sang this song. Came off the stage and to my surprise, we had a ton of screaming girls chasing me. I thought, 'Why they are doing this? I am not even famous'.

Jay's fan base is, he told me, 99 percent women and this remains so to the present day.

Dance with You / Nachna teray Naal went to number twelve in the British chart; 500 Asian youngsters queued outside the HMV shop in Birmingham to buy the record on the day of its release. Then Relentless Records, a division of Virgin Records, got in touch to sign the song – and decided to sign Jay as well. He explains:

> They wanted to officially release the song mainstream, but they met me and decided perhaps we can sign this guy as an artist rather than just the song… This was mindblowing for me… Most people try and try and [in] god knows how many different ways but this one record company wanted to sign me on the back of this one song.

He was twenty-one at the time and was given a £1 million record deal. His parents gave him their blessing and support even though it meant giving up his medical career. Jay Sean had "the whole package", as Rishi says: the sound, the looks, the voice and the sex appeal – that made Virgin focus on him.

Two diasporas – an African American and a British East African Asian one – met in *Dance with You* and it took both Jay and Rishi to new heights. Rishi continued to produce Jay's music during his time at Relentless Records, while also working with a whole range of other singers – Britney Spears, Mary J. Blige and Ricky Martin were among those who now sought out his production skills.[14] Rishi's pioneering sound traversed many borders, putting his sonic brand onto *Top of the Pops* and into the British music charts.

Rishi explains:

> [*Dance with You*] was the first of its kind. The song had grown without any video and without any publicity or anything like that… It was the song that

changed British Asian music, I was told by young people who heard it at the time, as MTV was playing it frequently.

The appeal of Jay, Juggy and Rishi was that they were young British Asians, and their sound was different. Rishi told me:

> When we originally got together, we were just three friends from west London trying to make music. We didn't realize the impact it would have. The Rishi Rich project really shaped all three of us…

In 2015, twelve years after the release of *Dance with You/Nachna teray Naal*, the three friends released a new track, *Freak*. Rishi has described it as follows:

> We are like brothers, always have been and always will be. Working on *Freak* was amazing. It's hard to find artists who are really tuned into each other's skills and bring the best out of each other.[15]

Diasporic alliances: in the United States and beyond

Jay

The euphoria of signing a contract with Virgin Records did not last. In 2004, after two UK top ten singles hits in the same year, they released his first album, *Me Against Myself*. Favorably reviewed in the UK, it sold best in Asia. Jay recorded sixteen tracks for his second album, which Relentless then refused to release. The UK record company limited him both geographically and creatively. According to the terms of the contract, Relentless, via Virgin, sold his music only in Europe. But Jay knew his appeal was global:

> …the internet started to go crazy and YouTube had just started, every sound I had put out, the rest of the world could see. There are Indians everywhere. I was shocked. I was getting phone calls from Hong Kong, from Greenland – gas stations and 7/11s in Greenland.

In places with substantial Indian diasporic populations, there were South Asian promoters who could attract audiences of over 2,000 people, after informing them of Jay Sean's visit. Many had seen him on television, and information about him traveled along transnational diasporic networks. His shows were selling out and Jay was frustrated that Relentless was not putting out his CDs to thousands of potential buyers. He alerted his record company to these diasporic markets, including a large one in India, but it proved to be a frustrating attempt on his part to educate his handlers. Relentless's myopic understanding could not decode this new, international fan base. They and their parent company Virgin did not understand the power of diaspora audiences beyond Britain.

FIGURE 6.2 Jay Sean, 2020

Source: Courtesy of Amit and Naroop, www.mediamoguls.com

Creatively, Jay's relationship with Relentless Records soured because they wanted to impose musical categories on him. They wanted classificatory control of his creativity according to their frames rather than according to how Jay saw himself. He saw himself as an R&B artist while the record company were pushing him to go in the direction of rock. Instead, he set up his own company, Jayded Records, through which he produced and marketed his next two albums, *My Own Way* and *All or Nothing,* using the power of YouTube and social media; he resisted narrow classifications with the help of the digital domain.

The classificatory myopia of recording companies is a central dynamic of how Jay Sean was marketed and read in Britain. Virgin were into the markets they already knew and they could not navigate unfamiliar terrains. Nassim Nicholas Taleb[16] in his book *The Black Swan* writes about how people understand situations and issues through knowledge they already have, which might not be applicable to anything that is happening now – yet it is on this that they base their future decisions. In the same way, Virgin had no idea of the diaspora markets that had opened up for Jay and were unable to capitalize on them. Jay was creating a new diasporic landscape of music but the British record company did not know how to sell to these new audiences around the globe. In some ways, this was an aspect of racism, a sort of classificatory raj, the ability to only see people through a narrow lens, rendering invisible the aspects of Jay's creativity which lay outside it.

By creating a path for himself, through his own company and use of the internet, Jay has much in common with the other creative agents in this book, as well with their path-breaking ancestors. Like his grandfather who set up the first gurdwara in Southall, Jay too was a pioneer. At 30 million views for his YouTube videos, US hip hop recording company Cash Money Records got in touch with Jay, offered him a contract and got him over to the United States – a move that proved crucial for him, further unleashing his creativity and changing his opportunity structure. At that time, despite his success with the Rishi Rich Project and his solo singles and albums, Jay Sean was not yet a household name in the UK. But he became one after moving to the United States and the release of *Down*, a huge hit on both sides of the Atlantic, topping the US Billboard Hot 100 and reaching number three in the UK charts.

In achieving success at home only once he moved abroad, Jay is similar to Henrik Ibsen and other artists who are not recognized in the site of origin that produced them until they make it elsewhere. Migrating to the United States released Jay from the narrow categories that Britain imposes – black, white and brown. In Britain, he could not override these restrictions – it was too hard to change the entrenched frames. In the United States, however, his Britishness worked in his favor; in addition, the South American markets opened up for him a big way:

> The minute I opened my mouth, they heard the British accent... The girls would go crazy: 'You are cute. You are from England'. Radio people loved it because it was so cool, a different voice on radio. It worked for me.

As a performer, Jay has never used his Sikh name – Kamaljit Singh Jhooti. He points out that in this he resembles many other performers, like Jay Z and Snoop Doggy Dog, who do not use their birth names. But his choice of name is made to counter others' lack of open-mindedness, and racism: "We judge immediately on looks, on a name, on skin color", says Jay. He cites the example of his grandfather and his uncles, first-generation immigrants, who worked in factories in which racism was rife. They gave up or anglicized their Sikh names, often using names attributed to them by bosses or co-workers:

> My uncles are Gurdial and Harbhajan, 'but you can call me Bobby'. All my uncles and my granddad have Western nicknames.

He thinks his compromise is no different:

> ...if my Baba had to make a sacrifice of cutting his hair just to work in a factory, that doesn't mean that he was not proud of being an Indian, that just means he had to do what he had to do to survive. In my career, I would love to say... 'I am Kamaljit Singh and I am an R&B singer'... As it is, the odds are stacked against us to make it in this field where I stand out like a sore thumb. I believed... let me just be great at what I am doing. [If] I have that power, earn that name and that platform – I can do so much more for my community, for my background and for my religion and for my race... For me, it was – let me concentrate on being a great artist. I sing in English, I sing

pop and R&B music. If I succeed in this field, I will be doing something that has not been done before.

Jay credits his success in the United States to working with African Americans whose music inspired him in the first place – again, that coming together of two diasporas. The US influence for Jay meant working with eminent African American urban producers J. Remy and Bobby Bass. Jay explains the differences between working in the United States and Britain:

> …America… understands how to make great R&B records, in the sense that America has more *tools*. It has access to a greater bank of songwriters; the best R&B mix engineers… Which is why, for that big, heavy R&B sound, America is the epicenter of where it goes down.[17]

But, while Cash Money Records gave him a major break, producing the song that took him to number one in the US Billboard Hot 100 and two subsequent albums, they too subsequently put restrictive categories on him and in 2014 Jay left the company because they were no longer enabling him to make the type of music he wanted to. Having defied classification in the UK, he defies it in the United States as well:

> Unless I can do the music I want to do – and it's going to get the push it deserves, more importantly, the push and the support from a record company to allow me to do that – I am not going to do it anymore…

All his musical career, Jay has fought to resist the categories record companies have wanted to cast him into to make him conform to their classifications. Instead, he has created his own paths according to what he felt comfortable with. He said that for him there was no book to follow or a person whose guidance he could seek. He had to do his own thing in his own way and capture the moment as it unfolded for him. He had no one to guide him or to show him the ropes and tell him how to operate in the unfamiliar terrains of record companies and commercial music making, especially as an Asian man who was into hip hop, rap and R&B music, which is centrally the domain of black artists.

Rishi

After his success in the UK, Rishi also made alliances with US musicians. In 2014, just as Jay Sean was parting company with Cash Money Records, Rishi moved to Atlanta to work with musical innovator and Grammy award-winning producer Teddy Riley, himself the originator of the New Jack Swing Sound[18] – "I just wanted to come and learn about music again", Rishi has said. As in Jay's case, migrating to the United States allowed Rishi to expand and sophisticate his technological expertise further and in new directions, in alliance with African Americans who are product of an older diaspora. It was an opportunity for complex, multiplex diasporic capitals to come together in the contemporary generation of hybridizing music makers.

Two diasporas – one which had slave roots and another rooted in labor recruited to build the railways of British imperial power in East Africa – are meeting, colliding, collaborating and improvising: a potent alliance of two once-marginal groups. Rishi's complex musical genre encodes and renders the sounds of twenty-first-century urban America produced by a West African diaspora, together with the soundscapes of a British Asian with an inheritance of Indian and East African musical influences infused with all the contemporary sounds of his childhood and youth in the UK.

For both Rishi and Jay, movement to a new site dramatically aided their musical development in so far as they were then read much more expansively, unrestricted by narrower British frames of classification. Their music was marketed to new audiences they acquired through conduits that were beyond the comprehension of established British record companies who were unable to see the significance of the emergent sonic landscapes that these new kids in the block were strumming. Their move across from the Atlantic opened up new vistas and visions and widened further their social connections.

I underscore the point I have made throughout this book: that movement facilitates opportunities in ways which are not possible in the sites of birth. There, the existing classificatory frames cannot read the emergence of the new; rather, there is an attempt by those in power to curb and destroy such creativity. However, a well-established African American music industry could see both Jay's and Rishi's creative potential and as a result their music has traveled in ways they could not have expected.

White music producers were not into the development of R&B and rap. These fields were outside their interests and so it is in these areas that black musicians have emerged as record producers, as managers, as singers, as musicians of all types. It is this area beyond the purview and control of the mainstream gatekeepers – the marginal outside – which has created a space for the emergence of Asians who combine R&B, rap and bhangra. These British Asians are inspired by the American black musicians and have absorbed their African American influences into their own music. African Americans in locations and situations of power are able to diminish the impact of restricted categories and help others to flourish, co-constructing paths to new sonic landscapes. People who are products of movement – in one case forced and in the other voluntary – meet, meld and resonate to create the new on the basis of the new. They bring together different diasporic aesthetics to create a new sonic landscape. People of color who have been racialized are meeting to produce music across continents and in domains where one has already influenced the other.

The dynamics of this creative alliance between African Americans and British Asians (one of them also with an East African inheritance) are interesting. They echo an earlier Indian migrant–African alliance, when Indian artisans shared their skills with their fellow African *fundis* (craftsmen) and, with them, established the first trade union in British colonial East Africa (see Chapter 1). The Indian migrant experience of colonization in East Africa, a land not their own, was different from that of those they left behind in India. To be colonized in one's own land has the feel of a take-over, which it is. But in the East African context, Indians helped and also exploited Africans and were exploited by the British in their turn – but they were also co-builders of enterprises, cultural institutions and the infrastructure of East Africa. They were therefore not taken over but were co-constructors side by side with the colonizers and also with Africans.

When I think of Rishi's contract with Teddy Riley and Jay Sean's with Cash Money Records, I see the origins of these cross-Atlantic alliances in Africa and the settlements of Indians there – including Rishi's grandparents on both his maternal and paternal sides who, having already crossed the Indian Ocean, then moved from Africa to England. I am also reminded of the experiences of an earlier generation of British Asians. Writer Hanif Kureishi, son of an Indian father and white British mother, who like me grew up in the south London suburbs of the 1970s, has described eloquently his youthful identification with African Americans rather than anyone in the UK: "As I planned my escape I read Baldwin all the time, I read Richard Wright and I admired Muhammad Ali". On seeing images in a magazine of Eldridge Cleaver, Huey Newton and Bobby Seale with their guns, he replaces the pictures of the Rolling Stones and Cream on his wall with the Black Panthers': "These people were proud and they were fighting. To my knowledge, no one in England was fighting".[19]

Rishi in Bollywood

In 2015, Rishi moved to Mumbai, India. Working with Universal Music India and EMI Records as their in-house producer, he is widening the reach of his musical brand in new directions.[20] He produced music for *Gully Boy,* a film about a twenty-two-year-old street rapper from the slums of Mumbai, directed by Zoya Akhtar, which was released in 2019.[21] Hip hop has been around in India for some time, but not in its films, so Rishi Rich's US hip hop expertise – honed by his time in the United States – is highly prized in Bollywood.[22] Rishi has also come together with his London pal of old, Juggy D, and produced a single, *Get Down,* in 2018 ("Juggy D's fiery vocals coupled with the raw rap of Rishi Rich and IKKAA make 'Get Down' a super hit hip-hop release" – www.bizzasialive.com).[23]

In making a quadruple move to India, Rishi carries with him the cumulative experiences of a multiply moved diasporic life of music making. He takes these deeply ingrained experiences and his sophisticated musical expertise back to India, the land from which his great-grandparents came. This completes a circle of complex and multiplex creativity which is a product of four continents, now encoded in new music for a powerful film industry which is seeking fresh directions. Rishi's border-crossing life, both the one he has inherited and also one he has engaged in personally, and his resultant expertise amassed and advanced in the UK and United

FIGURE 6.3 Rishi Rich, Mumbai, 2020

Source: Kiran Dhanoa, www.mediamoguls.com

States, is helping to define Bollywood's emerging sonic scapes. Sound shaper Rishi Rich's movement and maker capital are playing a determinative role in reinventing an influential, transnational movie-making machine. His particular hip hop expertise is unique in Bollywood and could only have come from an outsider. He is now located inside the domains of Bollywood, collaborating with Bollywood insiders, a scenario that is different from the past, when innovative British Asian music created in Britain was hijacked by Bollywood without acknowledgement. Bollywood film makers are now inviting diasporic creatives like Juggy D and Rishi to work on the inside, with a base in Mumbai, the heart of Bollywood films. Both maintain their home base in London and in the case of Rishi his US connections as well.

Despite being an outsider to an established film industry with defined musical conventions, Rishi has maintained his style of music on his own terms while adapting it to the task at hand:

> Don't get me wrong, when I am working on certain projects that require a more 'filmy' Bollywood approach, sometimes my heavy hip hop-influenced

drum patterns don't suit the brief I have been given, but I always try and retain some sort of sound in everything I work on so that my vibe is there.[24]

Rishi's journeys, which traverse four continents, are a product of diverse musical landscapes and paths, including an inheritance of movement which originated in India in the first place. This is a similar pattern to that of *Riverdance* and *Lord of the Dance*, in which American Irish step dancers were the central agents in making hybridized Irish step dancing an internationally celebrated phenomenon and so catalyzed Irish step dancing in Ireland itself. New York and Chicago-based Irish diasporics hybridized an ancient dance form and gave it new impetus in its place of origin. They are intervening in and defining the performative cultures of the homeland in the same way that Rishi's diasporic musical ingenuity is disrupting and forming Bollywood's music anew.

His life is now lived across three continents as he travels back and forth from Mumbai to London, and to the United States. He has said he had always wanted this "triangle" of the United States, the UK and India and he does not "chase it" but it now comes to him with great ease because people can see what he has already accomplished. He is now described as a "legendary music producer"[25] and the triangular transnational life of creative work is happening as he desired.

Notes

1 Rishi Rich, interview with the author, August 18, 2014 and January 30, 2015.
2 Queen's number ones with Freddie Mercury as lead singer were: *Another One Bites the Dust*, April 1980, and *Crazy Little Thing Called Love*, February 1980.
3 Interview with the author, April 12, 2012.
4 Bhangra developed in the UK during the 1980s and 1990s, as a fusion of Punjabi folk rhythms and Western pop styles. The musical genre became a thriving and vibrant transnational musical industry, adopted by the Bollywood film industry and many musicians within the diaspora. See Chapter 2, which tells the story of Kuljit Bhamra, who was one of the genre's pioneers.
5 A husband and wife duo who performed together during the 1970s and 1980s, known as the "king and queen of ghazal". As composer, Jagjit Singh (1941–2011) is credited for the revival and popularity of ghazal, an Indian classical art form. Chitra Singh (1945–) stopped performing after the death of the couple's son, aged twenty, in a car crash.
6 Kuljit Bhamra, 'Decades of music': "With the success of remix album Bhangra Fever, Sanj and Amit were signed to Multitone Records in 1990 to remix their Bhangra music stock. Over the next four years, ten volumes of the Extra Hot remix albums were released, with five produced by Sanj and Amit. Sanj's career was in full swing, touring Europe as a Bhangra-fusion specialist DJ. A booking from Germany in 1994 enabled him to take a young school band with him, led by 13 year-old keyboardist Rishi Rich." www.thesouthallstory.com/decades-of-music/ (accessed August 8, 2019).
7 Apache Indian's music reached the top of both the reggae and mainstream charts. Apache Indian was brought up in Handsworth, Birmingham, where he lived in a racially mixed neighborhood of Black and Asian communities and the music of reggae bands and close black pals. He carved a new and influential trend that was copied by many musicians from

Asian diaspora as well as by the Bollywood music industry, which not only borrowed his style but also hired him for some film songs.

8 The Drum, 'What is creativity?': "I was learning Indian classical music from the age of six and got a job in a record studio at 13, where I worked for 10 years learning the craft, before even putting a record out." www.thedrum.com/news/2015/05/22/what-creativity-music-producer-rishi-rich-inspiration-going-stateside-and-working (accessed August 8, 2019).

9 Amrita Tanna, 'Rishi Rich: fortunate to have been able to collaborate with so many artists', April 12, 2019; www.bizasialive.com/rishi-rich-fortunate-to-have-been-able-to-collaborate-with-many-artists/ (accessed August 8, 2019).

10 Basil Bernstein, *Pedagogy, Symbolic Control and Identity: Theory, Research and Critique* (Lanham, MD and Oxford, UK: Rowman and Littlefield Publishers Inc, 1996, 2000), Chapter 4, 76.

11 Sherry Turkle, *Life on the Screen: Identity in the Age of the Internet* (Simon & Schuster, 1995), 51.

12 Claude Lévi Strauss, *The Savage Mind* (Chicago, IL: University of Chicago Press, 1962), 11.

13 Turkle, *Life on the Screen*.

14 See, for example, 'Britney Spears – Me Against The Music (Rishi Rich's Desi Kulcha Remix (Audio)) ft. Madonna', www.youtube.com/watch?v=g9K98_hP1wo; 'Love @ 1st sight, international version, https://open.spotify.com/album/1EyahtWnvqs5j2Hmiqhbtw; 'Ricky Martin remixed by Rishi Rich', www.dnaindia.com/entertainment/report-ricky-martin-remixed-by-rishi-rich-3592 (all accessed August 8, 2019).

15 Raj Baddhan, 'Rishi Rich soon to come back with Freak!', www.bizasialive.com/the-rishi-rich-project-soon-to-come-back-with-freak/ (accessed August 8, 2019).

16 Nassim Nicholas Taleb, *The Black Swan* (New York and London: Random House, 2007).

17 Pete Lewis, 'Jay Sean on top of the world', www.bluesandsoul.com/feature/509/jay_sean__on_top_of_the_world/ (accessed August 8, 2019).

18 The Drum, 'What is creativity?' www.thedrum.com/news/2015/05/22/what-creativity-music-producer-rishi-rich-inspiration-going-stateside-and-working. "Teddy… produced the [Michael Jackson] Dangerous album. In his house he had a plaque saying 'presented for 13 million albums'. Whenever I walked out of my studio into his, that was so inspirational. He created New Jack Swing, a sound named after him!" (accessed August 8, 2019).

19 Hanif Kureishi, *The Word and the Bomb* (London: Faber & Faber, 2005), 3.

20 Tanna, 'Rishi Rich: Fortunate'.

21 Jasleen Kaur, 'Exclusive: Rishi Rich journey to Gully Boy', www.dissdash.com/2019/02/22/exclusive-rishi-rich-journey-gully-boy/ (accessed August 8, 2019).

22 See, for example: 'Badshah and Rishi Rich to work in another Bollywood film soon', https://timesofindia.indiatimes.com/entertainment/hindi/music/news/badshah-and-rishi-rich-to-work-in-another-bollywood-film-soon/articleshow/65114517.cms (accessed August 8, 2019).

23 Raj Baddhan, 'In Video: Get Down by Juggy D Featuring Rishi Rich', October 19, 2018; www.bizasialive.com/video-get-juggy-d-ft-rishi-rich/ (accessed August 8, 2019).

24 Tanna, 'Rishi Rich: Fortunate'.

25 See, for example: Baddhan, 'Rishi Rich soon to come back'; Daniel Pillai, 'Music producer Rishi Rich talks fusion music & cultivating talent', www.bizasialive.com/the-rishi-rich-project-soon-to-come-back-with-freak/; www.danielpillai.com/interview-music-producer-rishi-rich-talks-fusion-music-cultivating-talent/ (both accessed August 8, 2019).

7

THE SINGH TWINS

Multifaceted makers and defiant disruptors of the artistic status quo

Don't let them get you down. Stand up and fight your corner. Don't give in to them – it's the Punjabi spirit.[1]

The Singh Twins, Amrit and Rabindra Singh, are artists and disruptors of convention. Their self-styled "past-modern"[2] work acknowledges and centrally uses an ancient, highly developed tradition of painting to explore and comment on contemporary cultural, political and global events, and so creates something exquisitely new.

Using a narrative, decorative, symbolic and witty style, the Singh Twins have revived the Indian Mughal miniature tradition within modern art practice. In their own words:

> Our work bridges many worlds, the ancient and the modern, fusing big Western and Eastern aesthetic elements... using an ancient art form to deal with contemporary issues. Our aim is to introduce wider audiences to the beauty, richness and continuing value of our heritage within contemporary art and society.[3]

In the courts of the Mughal empire, miniature paintings were produced collaboratively by a team of artists[4] and the Twins' artworks are likewise joint creations. Although by definition small, each painting is the painstaking product of many, many hours of work and latterly the Twins have combined the traditional techniques of hand-painting with digital technology.[5] Multifaceted makers since childhood, the Twins are now taking their art into multiple domains – from film and animation to textiles, fashion and ceramics – translating it so it has wider exposure and also as a commercial venture, putting me in mind of nineteenth and twentieth-century artist-craftsmen-entrepreneurs William Morris and Mariano Fortuny. Novelist and critic A. S. Byatt writes of them: "They were both men of genius and extraordinary energy. They created their own surroundings, changed the visual world around them, studied the forms of the past and made then parts of new form" – a description which rings just as true of Amrit and Rabindra Singh.[6]

The Singh Twins are British artists locally born and produced. Based since childhood in Liverpool, in the north-west of England, they work within the British milieu dealing with contemporary social, political and cultural issues that impact local, national and global domains. Their brand and rendering of the miniature style is no longer the purely Indian tradition of painting that they were initially inspired by. Additional influences include the pre-Raphaelites, Art Nouveau, William Blake, William Morris and Aubrey Beardsley:[7]

> We very much see our work as being part of the British art scene in the lineage of British Art. We have developed the British style in such a way that it is no longer purely that tradition. But also we are dealing with very contemporary social, political and cultural issues in our work. The commentary in our work is what makes us the artists we are.[8]

In common with my other case studies, they are also makers with a legacy of making, and have taken this background of creating and making into their artwork. Rejecting individualism in art and the European Renaissance legacy, the Singh Twins have played a powerful disruptive role in the face of virulent opposition from establishment power brokers, the institutional pedagogues and consecrators of art. Their "twinning" way of being in the world was denigrated and public institutions rejected their artistic style as backward and outdated. It is amazing to me that they have resisted and survived this since the outset, from their time as undergraduates during the 1980s.

Where does their resilience come from? They attribute it to their grandfather's courage of moving from a Punjabi village to unfamiliar and cosmopolitan Britain at a time when there were few Asians around, to the ways in which their grandfather and father worked as door-to-door salesmen in hostile environments carrying suitcases of household goods to sell, suitcases so heavy that it felt "like their arms were going to come out of their sockets", and to their grandmother who used the park railings as a loom on which to weave the cord for her *salwar* (suit trousers). The Singh Twins were not crushed by their own struggle and rejection because, they say, they have the spirit of Punjabi migrants. They translate this inheritance and socialization – buttressed by the support from their father and their extended family among whom they have lived all their lives – into their art. They have translated their movement capital into artistic capital and a defiant way of being in the world, debunking and defying conventions of art and life. In conducting and making their lives on their own terms with daring and defiance, they have made their mark and have become one of the most recognized and honored contemporary British artists.

The Singh Twins: their art and style

In July 2018, the Singh Twins' exhibition 'Slaves of Fashion'[9] took as its subject the history of textiles shared between India and Britain from the time of Empire to the contemporary period. Its focus was described in the publicity material as "Indian textiles, empire, enslavement and consumerism". The exhibition featured nine paper works, and eleven fabric artworks displayed on lightboxes, the latter further developing the Twins' use of digital technology which previously they had only used for composition.

It is the first time that the Twins have produced work on this scale:

> With this particular project we wanted… something that was pretty large-scale compared to the detailed small-scale work that we're known for. Digital seemed like the only way we could do that.
>
> To create the eleven mixed-media works in the show it has taken us three years. If we'd wanted to paint them all by hand on the same scale, it would have literally taken a year per piece.[10]

Each artwork in the exhibition is the result of long hours of meticulous research and then minutely detailed, equally meticulous draftsmanship that both delights the eye and draws together the threads of many individual and global histories. A departure in terms of size and scale, Slaves of Fashion draws and expands upon a theme central to many of their works – an exploration of notions of "East" and "West" and the long relationship between India and Britain that effectively deconstructs the West.

With this exhibition and those over the past twenty years, the Singh Twins have now mainstreamed. They have been invited to galleries like the prestigious National Portrait Gallery in London where in 2010 they had an exclusive exhibition of twenty-seven of their paintings for visitors to view in relation to work in 'The Indian Portrait 1560–1860' exhibition and other portraits within the gallery's permanent collection selected by the Twins;[11] their work was part of the 'Artist and Empire' exhibition at the Tate Britain in 2015/16[12] and much more. "This was great for us", they say, "because it makes us feel we are finding a place for this work we have been doing within the whole scheme of the history of art – which was our main aim when we started off many years back as artists".[13]

In 2015, the Twins were acclaimed as "the artistic face of modern Britain" by high-profile professor of history and art history Sir Simon Schama in his book and five-part TV series *The Face of Britain*, which accompanied an exhibition of the same name at the National Portrait Gallery in London.[14] He compared the Twins' work to that of eighteenth-century English painter and printmaker William Hogarth who, Schama said, "would have had no trouble seeing the Singh twins, Amrit and Rabindra, living and working in the Wirral and marrying the formal patterning and jewel-like figure painting of Mughal miniatures to the carnival of contemporary Liverpool, as heirs to his swarming London tableaux".[15]

FIGURE 7.1 The Singh Twins with their Slaves of Fashion series triptych artwork *Jallianwala: Repression and Retribution*

Source: © The Singh Twins, www.singhtwins.co.uk

He was keenly aware of the struggles behind their achievement.

> [The Singh Twins'] story is… very important because they came through art school in the eighties in Liverpool [where they were told it would be a mistake for them to pursue their art through the tradition of Mughal and Indian painting]. I cannot tell you how many ways in which they fought this – and their work is an unforced union between their traditional culture and the life they lead fully of Liverpool and fully of Britain.[16]

Even before this accolade, the Twins were chosen as the artists to interpret Liverpool's history and mark its status as European Capital of Culture in 2008,[17] and were Artists in Residence for the 2002 Manchester Commonwealth games.[18] They have exhibited at galleries up and down the UK, as well as in Canada, the United States and India (other than Henry Moore, they are the only British artists ever to have had an exhibition at the National Gallery of Modern Art, Delhi).

Awarded honorary citizenship of their home city Liverpool in 2009, an MBE from the Queen in 2011 "for Services to the Indian Miniature Tradition of Painting in Contemporary Art", and honorary doctorates by the University of Chester for their "outstanding contribution to British Art" in 2015, the Twins have mainstream recognition and establishment success – but not yet, they say, the benchmark prizes of the art establishment, such as the Turner Prize and the Italian Venetian Arte Laguna Prize.

Growing up in a maker family

The Singh Twins live on the Wirral, just across the River Mersey from the city of Liverpool, within an extended family which supports their artistic goals in the face of opposition and which has also supported them materially and economically. They live with their father, their life force and staunch supporter, and also encouraging aunts and uncles (their father's brothers – their *chachas* in Punjabi), and their cousins.

The Singh Twins highlight the critical role played in their artistic career by their extended family and in particular their father:

> Our success has not been alone. We would not be who we are without the support of our family and particularly our father who has always been behind what we do. Whenever we have had struggles, he has been in the background saying 'Don't let them get you down. Stand up and fight your corner. Don't give in to them – it's the Punjabi spirit.'

They recall one of their *chachas* telling them: "Don't take no for an answer. If people reject you, it's their problem. It's about believing in yourself and what you are doing. Push the boundaries".

Born in 1966 in London, the Twins were seven years old when they moved with their family to Liverpool. When we talked about strong women in their background,[19] they spoke of their paternal grandmother, who was among the first South Asian women to come to the UK, in 1947, seeking refuge from the murder and chaos of Partition. She lived in Ancoats, a poor part of Manchester, where her husband, the Twins' pioneering grandfather, had settled after a migration journey which took him from a Punjabi village to Singapore to Sri Lanka (then Ceylon), arriving in the UK in 1939. Their grandmother traveled alone from India with their three children to join him, and landed at the port of Gravesend on the River Thames south-east of London in 1947 (in fact, the port in the nineteenth-century paintings of British soldiers who sailed to India to put down the Indian Mutiny, to which the Twins' painting 'EnTWINEd' is a response). She was one of that generation of Asian women in Britain who carved out an existence and demonstrated their resilience despite, as the Twins put it, "not knowing the language, the customs, the food. They had to be strong resourceful women".

They recount how, when she needed a new cord – *naalas*, like a pajama cord – to thread through the waistband of her *salwar* (suit trousers), she went outside and used the park railings as her loom to weave it. What is interesting to me is the way in which she used a public space – the railing of a park – not designed for weaving, but which she had the imagination and expertise to adopt, applying her highly developed skills of *jugaad* acquired in the Punjab.

Their grandmother also made them and the other children little cloth parrots from discarded fabric pieces, left-over suit material which she would recycle into toys – in much the same way that American pioneering women made quilts out of left-over cloth or old clothes.[20] Women knew the value of cloth as often they had woven it themselves; it was precious, to be used with care and supreme economy.

The Singh Twins imbibed the maker culture of their grandparents and rendered it from a young age, for example by making their own boxing mitts using imitation leather, and a punch bag also. One of the twins told me, "I even made my own punch mitt. I said I am not going to buy that. I figured out how to make it and I made it in imitation leather. If someone else can make it – I can make it". Later, they made their own clothes, laying an existing garment out on the cloth and cutting round it, not needing to use a commercial pattern.

They describe a childhood that fostered an expertise in craft – a "hands-on" upbringing, as they call it:

> Our toys were always very mechanical, whether it was Meccano or dolls or making birds' houses. That is how we occupied ourselves. That is how people passed their time at that time. It was very hands on and we didn't sit in front of televisions. Maybe it was part of our generation.

This expertise in craft came from their father, too. They describe how he "could look at a machine and figure out how it worked always... He has got a very mechanical mind. He could work out anything and figure out how to repair anything that needed to be mended or fixed".

Their father is central to their lives and is the focal point of many of their early paintings. He was the one who, when they "scribbled on the wall" as small children, bought them their art materials. He has been the backbone of their lives and a force behind their creativity, believing in them when the world was against them. He is the one who spurred them on when they were challenged about the art form they wanted to work with.

He is also significant because of the struggles of his own life, which have been legion. He himself was adventurous, and accepted neither the conventions of his own community nor the stipulations and restrictions of the wider English community that was his social context. He had observed, since his arrival in Britain as a child of nine years old, that doctors received more respect than any other profession. He wanted that kind of respect more than anything else. This was his goal, a determination reinforced by his experiences growing up and then working with his father as a traveling salesman in the 1950s, during which period turbanned Sikhs and South Asians in general were seen either as "coolies" or as "Maharajas". The Twins recount his story:

> He basically was not going to be told that he is [sic] not good enough. That is where his motivation came from. He wanted to do better and do medicine...
> He was not going to be told he was a "coolie" when he was a citizen, when

he was doing door-to-door salesman work and found himself in an alien environment and having doors shut in his face because of prejudice.

This desire to be – as the Twins put it, "somebody of substance", who commanded respect – was his motivation to qualify as a doctor, not so much for the economic benefits but because he wanted a job that commanded respect regardless of race. He studied medicine while helping his father in his door-to-door salesmanship – an arduous and difficult route into medicine – and became the first to become a doctor in his community, the Bhatra Sikhs, who were the earliest Sikh settlers in Britain and in many parts of the world.

Their father's ability to fight for what you want and to live on your own terms and assert these terms is a key characteristic that the Singh Twins have inherited and used in their own fight against cultural prejudice and virulent institutional opposition to the ancient Indian miniature art form they contemporized and made their own.

The Twins' education: a Catholic convent and a road trip to India

The Singh Twins attended a Roman Catholic convent school where, as the only Asian pupils, their religious and ethnic difference was accentuated and emphasized: they were considered to be "pagans" unable to go to heaven because they were not baptized as Christians. Initially excluded from religious service, they fought to be allowed to choose for themselves and to be treated like their school mates. When eventually allowed to join the services in the chapel, they became leading members of the choir and found the services to be beautiful and inspiring enough to choose subsequently to study comparative religion and ecclesiastical history. In their book *Making of Liverpool*, they talk about the deep "lasting impact" of their convent education on their lives which inculcated a deep interest in the Catholic religion's art and iconography, which can often be seen in their own artwork.[21]

As far as being twins was concerned, they say, "initially, we were allowed to sit in the same class and quite quickly we were put in separate desks well away from each other. We would always want to sit together… People feel there is something a little weird about twins…"

It was while they were still in secondary school, in 1980, that they went to India with their father, his first visit to the country after more than three decades and their first exposure to their Indian heritage. "Our father was always very forward looking", they note. "His idea of education was a real education – just seeing the world at such a young age first hand". Their father felt they needed to know about their background and indeed this trip to India turned out to be a life-changing experience for the Twins.

Using very significant maker capabilities and with the help of his brothers, the Twins' father converted a Bedford van into a motorhome robust enough to survive the road journey from Liverpool to India across Europe, the Middle East (during the Iran–Iraq war…), Afghanistan, through Pakistan to North India; and then a further nine months touring India. The van had belonged to the local fire brigade, had all kinds of equipment and tools needed to perform the supporting tasks for fire engines, and was battered. One of the Twins' uncles had a car repair garage and helped extend the chassis and then made the carapace out of aluminum sheets. They added a kitchenette with chairs and a table that folded down to make a double bed, and a toilet. Since their father and uncles had made the vehicle, they could also repair it on the road when it broke down. This inheritance of improvisation is central to the Twins' lives and their skills as artists and makers of whatever things they needed, a *modus vivendi* and *modus operandi*.

On this audacious long trip were five people – the Twins, their father and two uncles. The journey was, the Twins say, "a huge adventure". It was a transformative experience for them and a turning point for their later creative style. During their nine months in India, they experienced the diversity of its artistic and cultural styles, and were also imbued with a sense of connection and belonging:

> It was a life-changing experience for us… We were exposed to the feel, the whole of India in its diversity – not just our Punjabi specific cultural heritage. We travelled around India, visited galleries and palaces, caves… Something instantly connected… with us – [a] connection with the land of our forefathers. Before we went to India, we had always grown up in a Western community where there were a handful of Asian families… We had always had the peer pressure on us to conform to Western ways of living and dressing and socializing because our school class mates came from that background… When we were in India we were full of pride. We came back thinking "nobody's going to tell us our traditional Indian heritage is inferior to Western culture".

The trip also gave them their first encounter with Mughal miniature painting, a style popular in India between the sixteenth and eighteenth centuries, which had its origins in China and was introduced to India from Persia during the Mughal empire and then hybridized:

> It was at this time that our journey as artists started… We were completely bowled over by the exquisiteness of the paintings. The sheer craftsmanship, the detail, drawing and the decorative aspects that came with that tradition…

They were also drawn to the storytelling, humor and political satire often present within traditional miniature paintings. The Twins kept a diary while they were away in which they recorded their observations in words and drawings as they absorbed the enormous regional diversity of the religious, linguistic and cultural life of India. They say that their drawings before they left for India were "very Christian orientated", but that their imagery changed as they traveled. They also visited contemporary art galleries where they were disappointed at the high level of "aping Western trends in art" and lack of interest in India's own artistic traditions, commenting later as adults: "It seemed to us that the miniature genre in particular had been totally rejected by India's contemporary art establishment – which we felt was a great shame".[22]

From secondary school, the Twins moved to Chester College, then part of the University of Liverpool, to study Comparative Religion and Ecclesiastical History, with a subsidiary in Twentieth Century Western Art History. They had told their teachers that they wanted to become doctors but were discouraged from doing so, on the stereotyping assumption that their choice was the result of parental pressure. Subsequently, they studied Religion and Art at the University of Manchester, where they specialized in Sikh Art and Iconography as graduate students. During this time, they also won an INTACH (Indian National Trust for Art and Cultural Heritage) scholarship to conduct a year's field research in India.

Defiance of European artistic conventions and notions of individuality

As far as the Singh Twins' use of the Mughal miniature tradition is concerned, they are self-taught. Demonstrating the sensibility of *jugaad* par excellence, in common with others in this book, they taught themselves how to emulate the distinctive style without help from expert art teacher or institutions. They decoded the method and learnt the brush strokes by examining how they were done in the past using blown-up photographs they took of existing miniatures – very much the idea of the craft of Art. They taught themselves this way of painting just as they had previously taught themselves how to make what they needed, whether toys or clothes:

> We went to Delhi and found a book profiling Indian miniatures. That was our bible for a long time. Then we had a chance to study the original miniature paintings at museums in Britain and later on we did scholarship research in India. We looked at original miniatures there, too, and started to photograph those... and see how the brush strokes had been placed and how layering the colours, outlining all the details had been done. Trial and error, persevering and teaching ourselves.

But they faced enormous opposition to painting in their chosen style, even though their contemporized version was highly relevant to and captured their own British context and the global cultural and political trends of the times.

They say the fact that:

> ...we were inspired by a non-European ancient tradition was a real problem for our tutors in the art course... It seemed quite clear to us from the feedback we had from our tutors at the university that the kind of art we are doing was not real art.

But this in turn helped them clarify what they wanted to do as artists as it "really got us thinking about the whole notion of what is art and who defines what art is and how it is valued in society today". They describe how their art teachers criticized the Indian miniature style as "outdated, backward and as having no place in contemporary art". For the Twins:

> This was an extension of the prejudice we had grown up with all our lives – the constant pressure to conform and be accepted – "the West is best" syndrome – the colonial British superiority attitude [that it is] the Western world that leads the way.

Nonetheless, they did try to comply with their art department's expectations, returning to British influences such as the pre-Raphaelites, William Blake and Aubrey Beardsley but they were still criticized for their interest in the decorative and romantic.[23]

They faced very major educational opposition, both to their way of painting and also to their way of being as twins. Although their tutors recognized that they had exceptional ability, there was high-level pressure for them to express themselves individually and produce what their tutors classed as individualized creative work. An external examiner snapped at them, saying that they should be different from each other and that they were too compliant with each other's aesthetics. This was when they realized that twinning really was a transgressive and a problematic category for some. As the Twins point out, among their contemporaries, they were the ones treading a different path:

> All our peers were compliant with Matisse and Gaugin etc.... but it wasn't okay for [the two of] us to be interested in the same thing... We were doing something quite different from everybody else.

The irony was that the very artists that were touted as role models, the big names of the Western canon, in particular, Manet, Matisse, Gaugin and Picasso, had themselves been influenced by the artistic and creative aesthetics of both Asia and Africa:

> The artists they were putting forward to us... had themselves been innovators because they had been inspired by non-European forms from Africa, from Japan, from India. We thought Western art had progressed the way it has... was because of non-European influences. We were simply doing the same – what was so wrong about it now?

The Twins' mission from that moment was to prove their tutors wrong about their chosen artistic style, but also to challenge and subvert the concept of "individualism" and identity:

> That's when we started wearing the same clothes and challenging the whole notion of individuality. We were told individuality is something to be valued... [We] challenged the notion of what it was to be an individual.

They contested the notion of being separate and resisted the conventional valorization of individuality – a view underpinned by Sikh philosophy where community comes before self. The Twins fought for their space and their right to be themselves by adopting an explicit and deliberate stance of celebrating their sameness, both in the way they dressed and also by calling themselves "twindividuals" and presenting themselves as "the Singh Twins" rather than by their individual names. They argue that their sameness is their individuality: "Our twinness sets us apart from other people and that's what makes us unique".[24]

Many of their early paintings celebrated extended families, domestic scenes and family weddings, and their father as the patriarch of the large extended family[25] – in opposition to the individualism that was being foisted upon them. The Twins have also wittily defended their painting style, which they came to call "past-modern", using the ancient Indian traditions of their heritage but in a vibrant, contemporary way to tell stories and make political statements about the world now.

In so doing, they went against the establishment's and the power brokers' deep structures of thought and artistic and creative styles. They had similar battles with the curators of museums and art galleries who wanted to classify and reduce them to ethnic slots or allow them space in the "Indian Season" because they could not see the relevance of their work as part of the lineage of British art per se as it was "too culturally different".[26] The milieu the Twins were in was virulently hostile and potentially traumatizing for them. All these are experiences that politicized them and racialized them and have been further expressed in their paintings.

The Twins have been creative and defiant on multiple fronts and courageously adhered to the values of their upbringing. In their fight against institutionalized cultural prejudice, they have deployed their creativity to defy the classificatory categories that were being imposed on them by the educators, consecrators and gatekeepers of the worlds of art pedagogy and artistic display. Despite their tutors initially dismissing the Indian miniature tradition as passé, the Twins' success has ultimately proved their own instinct right.

> It's about valuing tradition in the modern world… We stick with that style because we are trying to provoke the art world into accepting other art forms. Modernity travels with tradition. It's also a modern lesson in the value of sticking to your guns… Our work speaks for itself in terms of individuality, but it has been accepted with [our traditional] roots. We have not changed ourselves to be accepted.

They say that their courage in rendering their art in opposition to their tutors and the art establishment came in part from their grandfather – a traveling salesman in 1940s Britain – who shares a similar trajectory to Jasleen Kaur's grandfather, "a flame in her life", in Chapter 2. "If you have the courage to leave the village environment…," the Twins say. They have a huge admiration of their grandfather's courage to migrate from a Punjabi village to Singapore to Ceylon (Sri Lanka) to the UK and to settle in Manchester as an early pioneering settler, and of their father's struggles to qualify and work as a doctor.

They understand the importance of migration as an inheritance and the ways in which it makes people courageous, resilient and adaptable:

> It forces you into an alien environment. You have to learn to defend yourself. If you fail, you have to claw your way up and make the best of a bad situation… We get a lot from [our father's] determination – to… be the best you can be or better because you try to take it one step further to break the mould of what people expect you to be – to get acceptance on your own terms and not be pressured to conform to fit into a particular mold.

The Singh Twins in India

Before the Singh Twins, the miniature genre was little admired in contemporary domains of art in India art.[27] However, India's high consecrators and connoisseurs have come to admire the Twins' rendering of the Indian miniature style: a distinctive reinterpretation of the genre by Europe-based diasporic artists who engaged in a radical and daring combinational hybrid form that is highly politicized and racialized, capturing both the British landscapes in which they are located and contemporary global cultural and political events.[28] It is a new form which comes out of Britain and represents the diasporic experiences and creativity of two British artists. The Twins are radical recontextualizers and have created this new form, which has its origins in Indian miniature paintings.

The Twins' creativity has its fount in a deep-rooted inheritance that comes from movement and the experience of living as minorities in contexts of hostility and prejudice. To the Singh twins, it is striking that it was Europe-based migrants who have revived a neglected tradition of ancient India:

> The irony is, why can't India set its own standard? Why does it always have to follow the West, seek the Western stamp of approval? The irony is that is has taken two artists perceived to be from the West to come over and show value to an Indian tradition and then they suddenly did take notice of it.

'EnTWINed' (2010): from Rule Britannia to Cool Britannia

'EnTWINed' is a painting that particularly engages my imagination.

The Twins were commissioned by the Museum of London in 2008 to respond to two paintings in its collection by British artist Henry Nelson O'Neil: 'Eastward Ho! August 1857', showing British soldiers embarking a ship bound for India to fight the Indian Mutineers in what came to be known as the First Indian War of Independence (1857–1859); and 'Home Again, 1858', which depicts the war-torn, disheveled soldiers disembarking on their return.[29]

The Twins' response, 'EnTWINed', subsequently displayed as part of Tate Britain's 2016 exhibition 'Art and Empire: Facing Britain's Imperial Past', looks at the historical event "from an Indian perspective".[30] Where O'Neil depicts British soldiers, in

FIGURE 7.2 EnTWINed

Source: ©The Singh Twins, www.singhtwins.co.uk; Collection Museum of London

the Twins' painting, the heroes disembarking from the ship are all Indian figures, who "largely represent… the freedom fighters of India".[31] These include Mahatma Gandhi, Indian soldiers from the First and Second World Wars and British Sikh centenarian marathon runner Fauja Singh. Taking inspiration from their own personal history, the Twins have painted among the disembarking figures their grandmother and father.

The Twins explicitly state that their painting is absolutely part of the British art lineage and that, with this work, they "have developed the British style".[32] Indeed, they have. The painting reworks the Indian miniature tradition in a style that is not backward or outdated but a modern expression of elements that are at once old and new. The Twins are no longer simply recontextualizing the miniature form but have advanced it and created a new British artistic style that can address contemporary social, political and cultural issues, including the deep history of empire. It is a diasporic intervention by the progeny of migrants, whose courageous creativity against the odds has reinvented an art form that was not valorized in contemporary India, but which has been vibrantly reimagined in the diaspora.

In terms of content, the painting is about movement, displacement and arrival; shared identities and heritages and deep connections which are old and new; a celebration of Indian immigrants as heroes, in a reversal of O'Neil's British soldiers deployed to ensure Indians' subjugation. It is also about the persistence of colonial traces and the resistance by Indian immigrants – who are British citizens and insider subjects – to unchanged attitudes of empire. It puts colonial struggles in a historical context by exploring Britain's connections with India pre-Empire and the colonial legacy of trade and migration that sustains Indian influence on British culture today and has helped transform "Rule Britannia" into "Cool Britannia" (the Twins' terms).[33]

A central theme of the painting is what the Twins call the "hidden connections between British identity and Indian identity".[34] It is about what India and Indian immigrants have contributed to Britain and its culture through the conduits of empire, from languages, to commerce, to food, to fashion. These connections are invisible to most people and yet so potent in styles of consumption. Borrowed words like *pyjamas*, *shampoo*, *bungalow* (inscribed, with others, in delicate curlicues around the main image) are about a shared identity further undergirded by the contemporary contributions of immigrants from India. The painting deconstructs "the West" because it shows, as the Twins say, that "the West has never been distinct from the East"; as the painting's title implies, for the Twins, the histories and identities of the two are "entwined" together.

They place their own figures within the main image, holding their paintbrushes and coolly observing from its bottom right-hand corner. They are clad in the Singh Scottish tartan – another twist of the legacy of empire – and their presence is a knowing nod to tradition, for painters of the Mughal court often depicted themselves within their paintings, too.

My favorite piece is the adapted Bedford Van used for their journey to India, also at the bottom right of the painting in the border area, an allusion to the life-changing journey they took to India with their father as teenagers which introduced them to Indian miniature paintings and wowed them powerfully enough to make it their creative form, a form for which they have battled the art establishment and that now defines them as "the new artistic face of Britain".

Multifaceted making: a nascent Singh Twins brand

In 2014, the Singh Twins joined forces with the famous Indian fashion designer Tarun Tahiliani in a collection of high-end clothing which appeared on the catwalk for Spring/Summer 2015. The Twins already knew and liked his work and they "couldn't have got a better collaboration in terms of profile and the respect he has in the fashion world internationally", they say. Best known for his bridal couture designs, Tahiliani was hugely inspired by the Twins' paintings:

> I went into a hypnotic trance when I first saw [The Singh Twins'] work. In a way, I suppose I responded fully to their Past-Modern work, as our own philosophy is "All that we were and more". It was a wonderful, novel, intellectual take on patterns and layering, with such wit and finesse. I could not wait to put a collection of ready-to-wear easy pieces together.[35]

Strikingly, it was a diasporic interpretation of miniature paintings that inspired him, however, rather than the traditional miniature paintings already present in the Indian subcontinent.

For the Twins, this was a direction they had wanted to go in – to take their designs into the world of commerce – and this was their chance to work with a highly respected, high-profile Indian designer. Tahiliani translated selected motifs, patterns and elements from the miniature painting of the Singh Twins into digitally printed fabrics and clothes and interpreted them according to his own design signature. For the Twins, this first collaboration with a fashion designer was:

> ...a wonderful experience. We saw his work. We have a lot in common between our own aesthetic taste but also the way he is taking something that is very classically Indian tradition but making it relevant for the modern audience. One of the things we wanted to do was... to try and prove how ancient traditions – whether Indian or otherwise – still have a continuing relevance in contemporary society...

The Twins want – and need – to diversify. It is hard physically to work on their labor-intensive and painstakingly detailed miniature paintings. When using solely the traditional techniques of hand-painting, they can only produce two or three of these a year. While before they would share long days in shifts, sometimes as long as eighteen hours, as they get older this is not something they can easily do. They already had a commercial bent – they have previously sold their work as prints, posters and postcards – now they wish to take their designs into the realm of everyday artifacts, beautifully made and encoding their design aesthetics.

In the same vein, the Twins have visited the Potteries in Stoke-on-Trent in search of a ceramics manufacturer with the color range and technical expertise to reproduce the vibrant colors and the complex, richly detailed imagery of their designs. They gained experience and honed their expertise in these directions when the National Museum of Liverpool asked them to design jewelry and ceramics for the museum shop. At that time, the Twins say, "the project fell flat on [its] face" as they were unable to find a manufacturer who could create these products at a high enough quality and a price the museum could accept. The Twins were interested in fine bone china: "We wanted it produced on items that would value the work".

Despite the failure of this earlier venture, the Twins remain keen to produce commercially viable, well-designed, high-quality artifacts which have their imprimatur and which would be available to a wider public which liked their design signature and aesthetics but could not afford their original artwork. They have polymath maker ambitions much like Mariano Fortuny and William Morris – who were artist-makers and also commoditizers and entrepreneurs. William Morris embroidered, painted and designed wallpaper and textiles, Fortuny is known for his lamps and exquisitely pleated gowns; they both had a brand. Morris, in particular, aspired to make things of beauty available to the masses though in practice both men's goods were only affordable by the better-off.

The Twins' desire to develop their art as a brand springs in part from their desire for more people to own some bit of their art through their products – a democratizing creative imperative. These commodities in the past were paper products – the prints, postcards and books. They say, "We have always felt the work needs to be out there. Not everybody can afford a painting, an artwork… something for everyone".

In the summer of 2020, they launched their new online shop as part of their website, offering special edition prints, limited edition tapestries and art posters.[36] In December 2020, they extended this enterprise, describing it "The Singh Twins Art Mechandize" all made in Britain using organic cotton. These textile gifts include aprons, face masks, tote bags and cushion covers depicting their signature artwork.

Conclusion: their work speaks for itself

The Singh Twins are disruptors par excellence. They have disrupted artistic classifications and conventions buttressed by art consecrators, educators and art galleries to become the new "artistic face of Britain". They have also resisted definitions of what twin-ness should be.

These battles to classify themselves in accordance with their own worldview and preferences remain an important dynamic in their artistic creativity and in their personal politics and sartorial style.

Their battles were on both fronts in Britain and India. They found that there was little respect for miniature painting in either location as a style that could be reinterpreted and recontextualized for contemporary art.

The Singh Twins' consciousness of their Indian heritage and their contestation and rejection of "West is best" have helped them to resist being pigeon holed and the dynamic that applies to all ethnic minorities that they should give up their cultures and integrate. The Twins have fought not to be ghettoized as ethnic artists and not be forced by art institutions into showing only in regional and peripheral museums.

They demanded acceptance on their own terms – they did not change to be accepted – they say their work speaks for itself.

Notes

1 The Twins' father, as quoted by the Singh Twins during an interview with the author, January 22, 2015.
2 "Past Modern" was the title of a major retrospective of the Singh Twins' work at the Walker Art Gallery, Liverpool, in 2005, which also toured to India. www.liverpoolmuseums.org.uk/walker/exhibitions/singhtwins/ (accessed August 8, 2019). They define their use of the term as follows: "we term our work as 'past modern' which is something that brings together the traditions of the past and elements of modern expression but also trying to make a statement about how those traditions have a relevance to today and are not backward or outdated" – Tate Britain, 'The Singh Twins on Empire and their work',

En TWINed, 2016; http://media.tate.org.uk/context-comment/video/singh-twins-on-empire-and-their-work-entwined (accessed August 8, 2019).

3 'Why we describe our artwork as "PAST MODERN"', www.singhtwins.co.uk/about/inspiration.html (accessed August 8, 2019). Professor Deborah Swallow, Director of the Courtauld Institute, identifies their sources of inspiration as follows: "Western fairy tales richly illustrated by Arthur Rackham, Edward Burne-Jones, and Edmund Dulac, and the myths and legends of the "ancient world" –the civilizations of the Sumerians, Babylonians, Egyptians and Greeks", quoted in the Twins' own book: Amrit Kaur Singh and Rabindra K. D. Kaur Singh, *Twin Perspectives: Paintings by Amrit and Rabindra K.D. Kaur Singh* (United Kingdom: Twin Studio, 1999).

4 Saloni Mathur, 'Diasporic Body Double: The Art of the Singh Twins', *The Art Journal*, Vol. 65, No. 2 (2006): 38: "Miniature painting in India, a narrative tradition that encompasses both religious and secular storytelling practices while often blurring the lines between them, was itself a unique confluence of Persian, Indian, and European art when it was established in the sixteenth century during the Mughal rules in the subcontinent. Miniature paintings were produced collaboratively in the context of the imperial courts by a team of artists inhabiting a *karkhana* (workshop), some specializing in portraiture, others in birds and animals, and others skilled in ornamentation or the 'border work' at the margins of the painting."

5 For an overview of their work, see www.singhtwins.co.uk (accessed August 8, 2019).

6 A. S. Byatt, *Peacock & Vine* (New York: Knopf Publishing Group, 2016), 6. The backgrounds of Fortuny and Morris are, of course, very different from that of the Singh Twins: Fortuny, a wealthy descendant of Spanish aristocrats and a mainstream man who came from a lineage of artists and craftsman and lived in a palazzo in Venice with more than one hundred craftsman producing his textile designs; Morris, also a mainstream man (his father had made a fortune in tin mining), bourgeois, bohemian and a socialist.

7 The Singh Twins, *The Making of Liverpool: Portraits of a City by the Singh Twins* (Liverpool: Twin Studio, 2010), 19.

8 Tate Britain, 'The Singh Twins on Empire and their work', *En TWINed*.

9 Walker Art Gallery, Liverpool, January 19 – May 20, 2018; Wolverhampton Art Gallery, July 21 – September 16, 2018.

10 'Interview: Reowned Wirral-raised artists The Singh Twins', February 23, 2018, http://ymliverpool.com/interview-singh-twins/31555 (accessed August 8, 2019).

11 *Contemporary Connections: The Singh Twins*; National Portrait Gallery, London, March 11 – June 20, 2010.

12 Tate Britain Exhibition, 'Artist and Empire', www.tate.org.uk/whats-on/tate-britain/exhibition/artist-and-empire (accessed August 8, 2019). Their work EnTWINed was loaned from the Museum of London.

13 Tate Britain, *The Singh Twins on the Impact of Empire: Artist and Empire,* http://media.tate.org.uk/context-comment/video/ (accessed August 8, 2019).

14 As well as the book and TV series there was an exhibition at the National Portrait Gallery, London.

15 Simon Schama, 'From masterpieces to selfies: Simon Schama on portraits of a nation', *Financial Times*, September 11, 2015.

16 'Indian twins are face of British art', www.telegraphindia.com/india/indian-twins-are-face-of-british/cid/1513059-2015 (accessed August 8, 2019).

17 The Twins' paintings to commemorate Liverpool's history were 'Liverpool 800: The Changing Face of Liverpool' and 'Art Matters: The Pool of Life'. They also produced a book, *The Making of Liverpool*, and collaborated in the making of an animated film, *Liverpool 800*.

18 They produced their SPOrTLIGHT series, which examined the relationship between the worlds of sport, media and celebrity. It features sporting icons such as Venus Williams, Muhammed Ali and David Ginola.

19 The Twins never talk about their white British mother, who doesn't appear in any of their paintings.

20 See, for example, www.quilting-in-america.com/ (accessed August 8, 2019).

21 The Singh Twins, *The Making of Liverpool*, 13. Their Catholicism is particulary evident in their documentary film: *1984 and the Via Dolorosa Project*; see www.cultureunplugged. com/documentary/watch-online/play/52458/Nineteen-Eighty-Four-and-the-Via-Dolorosa-Project (accessed August 8, 2019).

22 Interview with the author, January 22, 2015.

23 The Singh Twins, *The Making of Liverpool*, 19.

24 For Saloni Mathur, the Twins' exploration of their "twinness" is the most interesting aspect of their art: "My suggestion is that the significance of their work rests ultimately in the strategic assertion of their status as identical twins, within both their painting and exhibition practices… I argue that it is the performative power of their twinness that exists in tension with the more optimistic celebrations of multiculturalism in their work and gives their practice in the broadest sense its political distinctiveness and critical charge." Mathur, 'Diasporic Body Double', 36.

25 See, for example, 'Daddy in the Sitting Room' (1987), 'Wedding Jange II' (1991), 'All That I Am' (1993–94), 'The Last Supper' and 'Indian Summer at Dhigpal Nivas' (1994–95), 'Tel' (1997) – as discussed by Saloni Mathur, 'Diasporic Body Double'.

26 "Too culturally different" was the phrase used, the Twins told me, when their painting was ruled inadmissible to a national televised art competition that they entered as young adults, although their entry complied with all the judging criteria.

27 Pakistani-born, New York-based artist Shahzia Sikander has experimented with the genre using video, sound and digital technologies. Mathur, 'Diasporic Body Double', 35.

28 2002/03 *Past Modern*: Paintings by the Singh Twins; A major India touring exhibition which showed at galleries in Delhi, Mumbai and Kolkata.

29 'Eastward Ho! August 1857', https://collections.museumoflondon.org.uk/online/object/737945.html and 'Home Again, 1858', https://collections.museumoflondon.org.uk/online/object/737946.html (both accessed August 8, 2019).

30 Tate Britain, 'The Singh Twins on Empire and their work', *EnTWINed*.

31 Tate Britain, 'The Singh Twins on Empire and their work', *EnTWINed*.

32 Tate Britain, 'The Singh Twins on Empire and their work', *EnTWINed*.

33 Tate Britain, 'The Singh Twins on Empire and their work', *EnTWINed*.

34 Tate Britain, 'The Singh Twins on Empire and their work', *EnTWINed*.

35 Shruti Thacker, 'All you need to know about Tarun Tahiliani S/S15', *Elle India*, March 2015.

36 'Shop', www.singhtwins.co.uk/shop_2020/index.html (accessed 26 November 2020).

8

SUNEET SINGH TULI

Technologist seeking the maximum good – computing power for the billions

Every experience is meant as a learning experience and it's important not to take it too hard, not to take it personally.[1]

Suneet Singh Tuli is a visionary philanthropist and tech entrepreneur, co-founder of Datawind, a company dedicated to eradicating the digital divide.[2] Suneet's wider ambition is to "impact poverty" by bringing internet access to the billions across the world who are currently excluded.[3]

Datawind was the company behind the Aakash, launched in 2012 as "the world's cheapest tablet computer"[4] in a deal with the Indian government, with an ambition to facilitate nationwide internet use in schools. Suneet's brother, Raja, was the technical brains of the operation, while Suneet was CEO and Datawind's public face. In 2014, *MIT Tech Review* listed Datawind in its "50 Smartest Companies List",[5] and by 2016 the Aakash's commercial successor, Ubislate, had a larger share of the Indian market than any other tablet.[6] But then came demonetization and changes to the tax regime. These disproportionately affected Datawind's target market and by 2018 sales had slumped and the company had to cut production and lay off workers from its Indian factories.[7] In April 2019, it changed its name to Jeotex and announced it was withdrawing from the manufacture of devices to concentrate instead on providing low-cost mobile internet connectivity: its technology "enables a broadband experience even on legacy 2G networks still prevalent in some developing countries".[8] A month later, Suneet and Raja had stepped down from the board. But the new company retains Suneet's original philanthropic aim: to bring "social and economic benefits for the billions of people for whom an internet connection was previously out of reach".[9]

The Aakash was a path-breaking device which has made Suneet the educational revolutionary of his time. All projects have a finite life span. Part of his movement capital is having the resilience to move on from the demise of one project to the

FIGURE 8.1 Suneet (*right*) with his brother, Raja

Source: Suneet Singh Tuli

FIGURE 8.2 Suneet with the Aakash tablet computer

Source: Suneet Singh Tuli

rise of the next. When asked in an interview in 2018 about dealing with setbacks, Suneet referred to his experience as an engineer:

> In engineering everything is an experiment until you get to the result you are happy with – it may not be the result you are hoping for – every experience is meant as a learning experience and it's important not to take it too hard, not to take it personally – how would you do it differently next time? Every step of the way it's a learning experience. Sometimes the guru has a different plan for you.[10]

Suneet and his brother seem to revel in negotiating obstacles, even when they seem insurmountable. They make mistakes but also make enormous strides. None of this is easy. It is painful and needs courage and resilience, and a high level of risk-taking – a motivation not to follow the paths already created, but to create new paths which have widespread implications for society and the world at large.

Out of Canada

Suneet Tuli is a product of multiple migrations: born in India, raised in Iran and then, from the age of eleven years, in Canada, and now operating out of London, Montreal and Toronto.

The family moved from the Punjab to Iran in the 1970s, migrating again at the end of the decade, during the Iranian Revolution. Initially, Suneet's parents went to the UK while the children returned to India, before they settled together in Canada, the only Sikh family living in a small town in Alberta.

Suneet is supremely conscious of how his family's multiple migration and eventual residence in Canada has opened up opportunities for them, catalyzing their technical creativity, and allowing it to flourish in multifold directions. His early experiences as a child in India – playing with the son of the *mali* (hired gardener) and socializing with a range of people from different classes and castes – widened his horizons, but he believes that he and his older brother Raja would never have been as innovative and daring if they had remained there.

Their paternal family background was in engineering and building. Biba, their mother, told all her children they had to succeed, and their father urged them not to study any "arty-farty" (Suneet's term) subjects like history, which Suneet was in fact very interested in. He went on to study engineering at university and Raja chose computer science. The expectation of success was drummed into them. His mother took care of the children until they grew up, and then their father took over. He was the person who believed in Raja and Suneet's first innovative ventures and gave them the seed money needed to develop the devices they were inventing and perfecting.

Suneet subscribes to orthodox Sikhism. As a grandson of a judge in India (his maternal grandfather), he is fearless about asserting his rights – he sued his Canadian secondary school when they did not allow him to wear a *kirpan* (a small sword, one of the five Sikh symbols). He won his case.

He is supremely cognizant of the egalitarian and anti-hierarchical ethos of the Sikhs – the sharing of resources and food, tithing 10 percent of your income and participating fully in society wherever you live by collaborating and passing on all kinds of knowledge and skills. Collaboration, sharing and teaching others what you know is central to Sikhism. This style of being in the world is meant to benefit not only the Sikhs, but also the world at large. This is a highly developed practice of Sikhs in the diaspora, especially among the pioneering communities, where sharing their skills and helping each other was essential to becoming established. In these situations, in new lands, every social institution and enterprise – technical, cultural and philosophical – had to be started from scratch.

The sharing ethos of pioneers, new settlers and migrants was essential for starting life all over again in places where there were few other Sikhs or Asians, and people had to rely on their own resources and whatever skills they had. Collaboration and thinking of the good of all is exactly what is reflected in Suneet's *modus vivendi* and *modus operandi*.

Multiple movements are a recurring theme in Suneet's life. Even now, his business is globally dispersed across several continents. Suneet's sensibilities are not those of the mainstream. Culturally and religiously, he and his family were, and are, outsiders – both now in Canada, and in Iran where he went as a child. This outsider status has spurred him to think innovatively on many fronts. His instinctive understanding of the new is reflected in the way he has marketed his products and the ways in which he and his brother Raja have developed their products. They are hardware, marketing and business model innovators.

Becoming a tech entrepreneur

Both Suneet and his brother Raja are serial innovators and entrepreneurs. By their forties, each had more than two decades of experience of making low-cost devices in the field of communication technologies.

Raja's breakthrough invention at the start of their careers was a fax machine capable of transferring large architectural and engineering drawings. They had identified a need for it in the offices of their father's building firm. They called the machine Widecom and Suneet used a ruse of getting it in *The Guinness Book of Records* as the world's largest fax machine, which won them high-profile publicity and many orders as a result. The Xerox company wanted to buy the patent but the brothers refused to sell. They would have become multi-millionaires in their twenties, but Suneet believes that it would have arrested their instinct to innovate further.

Subsequently, their business moved into digital technologies, initially specializing in the transfer of large data sets, and then developing battery-powered mobile printers and a handheld scanner. The scanner was super-thin, inspired by a trip to the dentist where Suneet was caught in the waiting room tearing an interesting article out of one of the magazines. Again, when sales were slow to take off, Suneet contacted *The Guinness Book of Records* – and the scanner is still in its pages as the thinnest in the world.[11]

Next up, the PocketSurfer smart phone and the Ubislate (Aakash) tablet. The brothers and their father now hold a hundred or so patents in the field of communications technologies – in particular, for data compression, which vastly reduces the amount of data required for web browsing (by as much as 97 percent).[12]

The brothers are innovators on many fronts – not only in creating and providing hardware and software, but also in their business model of providing low-cost access to the internet together with the device (also at other times they have experimented with providing free access to the internet) with the aim of making money from advertising and their own app store.[13] They are disruptors par excellence. Before the launch of Aakash, brothers Suneet and Raja were completely unknown in India – they succeeded as outsiders from the diaspora.

The Ubislate/Aakash story

The arrival of the Aakash ("Sky") tablet in India was high profile and beset by controversy – an excellent launchpad for its commercial cousin, the Ubislate.

Suneet told me how he was on a flight from Amritsar when he read in an Indian newspaper that the government of India had opened a tender for a low-cost educational computer. He found out that they had advertised before but had been unsuccessful in finding a company to make the devices at the price stipulated.

None of the big Indian technology companies had bid for the tender – they were not interested, despite the fact that they could have entered, or rather created, new markets.

Suneet's explanation of why Datawind was successful in its bid when Indian companies did not even take part lies in part with Datawind's own strengths as an agile start-up and his particular interest in impacting poverty: "Breakthroughs sometimes happen with start-up companies", he told me. "This made a big difference. We were looking at poverty alleviation, because we had patented tech around delivery platforms – we had a unique position".

Of the larger firms, he notes that they lacked the expertise, and that it would be against their own interests to undercut their existing products and prices: "Some of the largest international competitors did not bid on it because it was so far out of their league – also it would have impacted their current pricing in the market".

But he also blames the culture of the Indian business environment, in particular the amount of effort it takes just to negotiate the system before you can start being creative. While Indians do really well in California's Silicon Valley, he says, "the Indian corruption, the bureaucracy, that whole culture that continues to exist in that environment... consumes most of the entrepreneurial energy that exists there. The energy and resources that it takes to figure out how to get past these issues, that is the reason you don't see so much innovation come out of India".

Raja was initially against bidding for the tender, but Datawind's other board members voted in favor. The mainstream banks were not interested in funding the venture but eventually Suneet secured backing from a group of venture capitalists based in London, high net worth investors who believed in Suneet and Raja's enterprise.

Datawind's contract with the Indian government was to supply 100,000 Aakash tablets to the IIT (Indian Institute of Technology) in Bombay. Costing the Indian government $50 per tablet, each would be available to students at a government-subsidized price of $35. The Indian government had pledged in 2009 that it would introduce a super-cheap laptop in order to improve the quality of education in India through technology – a pledge that had proved difficult to keep.

Datawind fulfilled its contract, but the process was not straightforward. The delivery date was delayed by seven months when the Chinese manufacturer of the device's touchscreen let them down: the brothers designed their own and at a lower cost than the original design from China. There was also controversy about the extent to which the Aakash was an "Indian" product. The Indian government had announced that the tablet was to be manufactured in India, giving a boost to the country's nascent digital hardware industry, so the Indian press was put out to learn that the new tablet's motherboard, among other parts, was in fact made in China. Suneet deftly recast the Aakash as a story not just of Indian innovation but, with its hardware-manufacture partly subcontracted to its near-neighbor, China, "a story of global innovation led by India".[14] What Suneet did not tell his audience was that the innovator of the device was an Indian from the diaspora.

But orders were also open to the public to buy the Aakash commercially – as the Ubislate – for $60. With all the publicity that the Aakash itself had already earned, orders sky-rocketed: millions were ordered. Initial enthusiasm for Suneet's tablet was contagious. His agenda was to create an affordable device, but the demand for the tablets far exceeded expectations. The markets he entered did not develop as scaled markets which were gradually built over time, but those which emerged overwhelmingly and immediately, fully fledged. But Suneet – and his company – coped: "[I am on] a journey which I have decided not to drown in but am surfing the waves of that breaking dam", he told a Tedx audience in 2014.[15]

By 2014, Datawind was marketing upgraded versions of the tablet sold through the retail network – because many of the target market relied on paying in cash. Each purchase included unlimited free access to the internet via the state-run BSNL network. By 2015, the company was opening manufacturing plants in Amritsar and Hyderabad financed by its flotation on the Canadian stock market which raised $30 million. By 2016, Datawind had secured a greater proportion of the Indian tablet market than any other company – 34 percent with Samsung the next largest at 21 percent[16] – a position it maintained until the second half of 2017.[17] Suneet was optimistic with plans to take the tablet to the equally promising markets of Latin America and Indonesia.

But at this point the project was already being disrupted by external factors beyond Suneet's and Datawind's control. First up was the Indian government's policy of "demonetization" in a bid to curtail the shadow economy and bring the cash thought to be held at home in large quantities into the formal banking system: on 8 November 2016, prime minister Narendra Modi announced on live television that all 500 and 1,000 rupee notes would be banned in four hours' time. There was a period of several weeks during which people were able to swap their cancelled notes for new notes at banks, but they were insufficient, and could not be printed fast enough[18] – and the policy hit the millions who lived entirely within a cash economy hardest – among whom were the Ubislate's target market. "[Demonetization] impacted primarily our customer base", Suneet told me. "They were people who lived off cash and [they] lost the ability to use cash". Ubislate remains the most-bought entry-level tablet – but the absolute number of entry-level purchases has declined. As Suneet notes, "We are still 65 percent of that segment, but that segment has shrunk significantly".

Datawind was also hit by the Indian government reforms of the tax system. Whereas previously the Ubislate was in a zero tax bracket, under the new regime of the Goods and Service Tax (GST), it now has a tax on it of 18 percent, so increasing the price to the consumer.

Suneet and the board of Datawind – the company still carrying large amounts of debt – were thus forced to change their strategy: reduce their manufacturing capacity in India, and reorientate their business towards its core strength – its technology in data compression and enabling web browsing with less bandwidth.

But the Tuli brothers' venture did succeed in disrupting the market – and it was their migrant, outsider status both in Canada and in India that pushed them to be innovative in this way. The existing mega-successful technology companies in India had not innovated in this domain, nor did they want to. But Suneet and Raja wanted to design a technology product to fulfill the needs of the millions of ordinary people and not just for India's burgeoning middle class.

Suneet Tuli wants to close the digital divide and provide internet access to the vast majority of the world's population that still does not have it. The user interface on touchscreen devices has become so evolved, Suneet says, that it is possible to create solutions on touchscreen devices without having literacy as a pre-requisite for internet access. So affordability is the critical dynamic that excludes the poor from accessing the web. The cost of an iPad is $300–500, which is around two to three days' salary for an average person in the United States and Europe. But for a billion people in rural India, that cost is three to four months' salary.

Suneet gives the example of the cell phone. It was adopted widely in India as soon as they became affordable. It took India sixty years to adopt 30 million landlines, but it took only six to seven years for 900,000 million people to adopt the cell phone – more than 80 percent of the population – once its cost dropped to between $23 and $35, a week's salary for Suneet's target customer.

Suneet wants to bring low-cost internet and computing to those who cannot afford an iPad or smart phone. He is not interested in competing with Samsung or Apple. His desire is to bring "good-enough" products that are not over-designed or overpriced to those who cannot afford to pay huge prices. He told *Forbes*, "I don't care about creating the iPad killer. I care about the 3 billion people who can afford [Datawind's] device".[19]

In the end, the top-end devices are not that different from the good-enough ones in their later iterations. The good-enough ones catch on and provide an adequate interface and experience, just as good, for example, as the early iPad. On its launch in 2012, Ubislate resembled the first generation of iPads – same number of gigabytes, same amount of memory. It had a 7-inch touchscreen, an ARM 11 processor and it ran under the Android 2.2 operating system. But it cost just $60. Datawind sold solar chargers, too, to remove a further barrier to tablet and internet access.

Datawind's fundamental disruption in the market was that it provided a good-enough device, which the billions could afford, in order to access the internet. The concept of the "good-enough" product, which is the disruption the Ubislate creates, is fundamentally connected with *jugaad* – the improvised solution and flexible mindset: "a unique way of thinking and acting in response to challenges; it is a gutsy art of spotting opportunities in the most adverse circumstances and resourcefully improvising solutions using simple means… about *doing more with less…*"[20]

It is a concept that Suneet is very familiar with. In his 2014 Tedx talk, he referred to *jugaad* as a "word that reflects how entrepreneurial kinds of businesses get done, especially from those at the bottom of the pyramid". He described how villages manage with the tools and equipment they have and how machinery is improvised to perform functions other than those they were designed for; villagers "get by" by "improvising solutions". For Suneet, it also summed up the process by which Datawind's technology could transform the world, with a "good-enough" tablet affordable by the billions – that, he said, is the Ubislate's disruptive power within the market.[21]

He has talked about how his experiences and passions have come together in ways he could not have predicted, referencing Steve Jobs' comments on the same theme, how "the dots in his life" came together without him thinking of the "broad agenda".[22] Jobs' visions and aesthetics are encoded in the products he has designed and the sensibilities he has engaged. Suneet's experiences are similar. He and Raja's cumulative life experiences – their disruption through migration twice from India to Iran and then to a small, almost exclusively white town in Alberta, Canada and then to Toronto – are all experiences rendered in the products they create and market. His life experiences of disruption through movement and his own technologically disruptive tendencies – which started in his teenage years – are exactly what is reflected in the disruptive markets he has created, in terms of the affordable product, the novel business model and the marketing of the Aakash as an educational revolutionary.

The impact of Suneet's work on the world and education

Suneet's guiding philosophy is undergirded by his subscription to Sikh religious and cultural ideology: good for all of mankind regardless of hierarchies, class, caste, color, religion. A belief in the egalitarian principles. These are defining themes of his work and of the technology he is pushing. This idea is similar to the philosophy of the founding fathers of the United States of America – maximum good for the world at large and equality of opportunity. These ideals have enormous implications on the domains of the twenty-first century – they are defining them.

The invention of a low-cost tablet *is* a business enterprise, but one that is designed for the benefit of the billions of people in the world who cannot access the internet because they cannot afford the device or the subscription to access it. The Aakash/Ubislate tablet is a truly revolutionary product; a facet of diasporic invention, even though the request for a cheap computing device came from the Indian government originally.

Even while marketing the Ubislate more widely, for Suneet, the issue that he is centrally concerned with is education and the availability of his devices for India's 220 million students. Within India, dramatic growth of the youth population is predicted. In 2011, the population of the group aged between fifteen and thirty-four years stood at 430 million. By 2021, it is predicted that this figure will be 464 million. Among this youth demographic, inequalities are rampant. Low-cost internet access, designed through the impulse of *sarbhat dha phallah* [wishing the best for all], will do a great deal to reduce the persistent inequities, especially for students in small towns and rural areas.

He told me that he objects to the boast that some Indian politicians and elites make when they say, "The next century is ours", and their suggestion that this demographic potential "offers India and its economy an unprecedented edge" and will "reap dividends in future by providing a dynamic labor force and a 2 percent per capita growth in GDP each year for the next twenty years".[23]

India's demographic dividend is frequently mentioned at Harvard Business School conferences and is much touted in the press. Yet, the *Economist* magazine, in an article published on May 11, 2013, refers to "Angry young Indians – What a waste". India is "throwing away the world's biggest economic opportunity because young people do not have access to an appropriate quality education to equip them for a 21st century economy… Many of India's young leave school ill prepared even for rudimentary jobs". The article talks about how India has "too few of the right sort of firms or workers and too many of the wrong rules".[24] Suneet has said, "Every rickshaw wallah in India wants to educate their children so that they don't become rickshaw wallahs themselves".[25] Parents certainly do not want their children to become rickshaw wallahs – a back-breaking, low-paying, bottom-of-the-ladder job – and want their children to be educated so that they can earn a better living. But while quality education is available in the big cities which attract the best teachers, these opportunities decline markedly for rural areas in which the educational system is poor and there is no access to the internet. Deteriorating educational opportunities, teacher absenteeism and large classes in Indian government schools are the norm.

By the fifth year of schooling, only half of rural pupils can solve a calculation like 43 minus 24 and barely a quarter can read an English sentence like "what is the time?" "India's Century" is not inevitable, says the *Economist* because, "it's a giant opportunity that India is in danger of squandering".[26]

It is for this reason that access to educational opportunities through a computing device that connects these vast millions to a quality education is a critical agenda for Suneet. "The quality of the education that you get is directly dependent on your economic class", he has said. "Access to the internet is an equalizer of sorts."[27] The digital divide yawns as wide as ever for millions of youth. The need to provide educational resources to make the world a little more equitable is urgent, and therein lies the revolutionary potential of the low-cost tablet.

Suneet's belief is that such devices will empower both the students and the teachers significantly through their ability to access the internet, to help with teaching and comprehension of complex topics. He is not alone in thinking this. Hardeep Singh Puri, India's then permanent representative to the United Nations, in his speech at the New York launch in 2012 said, "Using Aakash 2 teachers and students in the remotest parts of India can join a classroom, benefit from lectures delivered by the best teachers".[28] The flipping of the classroom is already in progress in schools in North America where the students watch a video of the lecture prior to coming to class and actually do their homework in class time. The big benefit for them is the ability to rewind and listen as many times as it takes for the material to sink in and be understood.

Consider the case of Malala Yusufazi, who was shot in the head by the Taliban for daring to go to school. It is important to acknowledge that the internet allows home-based learning, which is necessary, in some cases, until security issues are resolved. Suneet knows that providing students with internet access will continue to be revolutionary in the future, and that enabling this to happen could transform the educational systems of many countries. He has worked closely with the state government of the Punjab in particular. The Aakash 2 was trialed in schools there. The devices were funded by the Punjab government, which has said that it is fully committed to strengthening education in the rural areas. Datawind has subsequently been involved in "smart classrooms" (smartpunjab. com), which aim to provide free digital learning in state primary schools. The provision includes specially prepared apps for teachers who can use these in the classroom to explain concepts to students in class by means of a classroom screen and laptops.[29]

Suneet explained to me that working in India has been harder than he expected – not just in terms of manufacturing, but also negotiating the bureaucracy of customs clearance and the corruption still inherent within the system. The reason Datawind was able to get the price of the Aakash down, helping them to win the tender, is that they did not include the cost of bribes in their estimates, which the other competitors did. Bribes are needed, because even though the device is supposed to be a duty-free product, Datawind pay 40 percent customs, otherwise they delay the parts and product – part of the reason that Datawind was unable to meet initial demand for their products.

Conclusion

Suneet is a revolutionary inventor and democratizer of digital and computing technologies using Sikh traditions of *sarbhat dha pallah*. These traditions are revolutionizing twenty-first-century landscapes technologically but also with a deep and positive societal impact around the world.

He and his brother are serial entrepreneurs – they have been inventing devices and figuring out how to market them innovatively since they were teenagers, when they were recent migrants in Alberta, Canada, where there were very few Indians and Sikhs. They were assertive and daring from the time of settlement. Raja invented the world's largest fax machine as an undergraduate. He changed the landscape in which he operated and that has been his *modus vivendi* ever since. Both Raja and Suneet have the ability to negotiate the new on the basis of the old in new landscapes, despite the opposition and obstacles.

Just as they are ethnically courageous, they are technically and technologically bold and take high-level risks. They transfer their ethnic and cultural boldness into the field of developing technical objects that are useful for the many. The technical prowess which these technically orientated diasporics have inherited is being further honed in the diaspora in new ways. This is the point that Ricardo Hausmann, who is himself Venezuelan, makes – that the existing expertise base evolves in new directions with the entry of an outsider group; the skill base diversifies and evolves in more "complex and more advanced"[30] directions. The incomers, too, develop their own skills, even as they help to diversify the skill base into which they move. Advancement of already existing skills becomes possible in new settings. Suneet and Raja reskilled themselves for new purposes. Their entry into new contexts required them to apply their skills in new ways, in pioneering contexts in which they had to build and make every sphere of their social and economic lives.

Suneet and Raja take note of criticism they receive – they have had a great deal of it – but they incorporate these critiques of their method and products, taking into account what needs to be improved in their work, but defend themselves in areas in which they are correct. They have demonstrated their capacity for resilience time and time again: when the Chinese company due to supply their touchscreens went bankrupt just before the Aakash's launch; riding out the criticism they received when they were unable to meet demand for their Ubislate and some of the device was made in China; then dealing with demonetization and tax changes and reorientating their business again. This kind of over-riding of obstacles with further invention is a facet of their movement capital and innovative creativity. It is the negation of existing norms and conventions and negotiating a way around these establishment expectations that makes them migrant creators par excellence. Suneet told me that none of this would have happened if they had not moved to Canada and had stayed in India.

While he says that the cheapest, most affordable tablet computer is indeed an Indian idea and that the final assembly is done in India, their ability to render this idea in the form of a $60 tablet computer would not have been possible had they stayed in India. A testament to the truth of this statement is that no Indian company, big or small, bid for the Indian government's tender. Suneet and Raja as Canadians bid for it, ignoring the conventions: they had no idea that they were supposed to include bribes in the cost of the computer, and they were outsiders. It is their disrupted, migrant lives which allow them to innovate and disrupt existing modes of technology and also ways of being in the world and reading the social and technical landscapes around them. People who have led disruptive lives can deal with dissonance and disequilibrium, and can create disruptive markets and products in turn. The brothers are discoverers of landscapes yet to be formed. In fact, *they* form and build these new landscapes, navigate technological landscapes in new ways, and in discovering the new, they make a deep impact on society and culture.

Notes

1 Sikh Channel, 'Business Show interview with Suneet Singh Tuli of Datawind', January 14, 2018; www.youtube.com/watch?v=rYPGUQZVHGU (accessed August 6, 2019).

2 Datawind, 'Datawind, Bridging the Digital Divide', www.datawind.com (accessed August 6, 2019).

3 Sikh Channel, 'Business Show interview'.

4 Rajini Vaidyanathan, 'India upgrades "world's cheapest tablet" Aakash', *BBC News*, June 25, 2012; www.bbc.co.uk/news/world-asia-india-18580131 (accessed August 6, 2019).

5 *MIT Technology Review*, 'Press release: MIT Technology Review releases 50 Smartest Companies List for 2014', February 18. 2014.

6 Pranbihanga Borpuzari, 'Riding the wind: How Suneet Singh Tuli powered DataWind to become top tablet player in India', *Economic Times*, August 11, 2016; https://economictimes.indiatimes.com/small-biz/startups/riding-the-wind-how-suneet-singh-tuli-powered-datawind-to-become-top-tablet-player-in-india/articleshow/53646908.cms (accessed August 6, 2019).

7 Muntazir Abbas, 'Demonetisation and GST-hit DataWind shuts Hyderabad facility', *The Economic Times*, May 10, 2019; https://economictimes.indiatimes.com/tech/hardware/demonetisation-and-gst-hit-datawind-shuts-hyderabad-facility/articleshow/69260432.cms?from=mdr (accessed August 6, 2019).

8 Jeotex press release, 'Jeotex Inc. announces board resignation', May 29, 2019; www.accesswire.com/546608/Jeotex-Inc-announces-board-resignation, (accessed August 6, 2019).

9 Jeotex press release, 'Jeotex Inc. announces board resignation'.

10 *Sikh Channel*, 'Business Show interview'.

11 Borpuzari, 'Riding the wind'.

12 Jeotex press release.

13 John Pavlus, 'An anti-iPad for India', *MIT Technology Review*, March 11, 2013; www.technologyreview.com/s/511801/an-anti-ipad-for-india/ (accessed August 6, 2019).

14 *The Economic Times*, 'Aakash manufacturer dismisses controversy over Chinese parts', November 29, 2012; https://economictimes.indiatimes.com/tech/hardware/aakash-manufacturer-dismisses-controversy-over-chinese-parts/articleshow/17415189.cms?from=mdr (accessed August 6, 2019).

15 TEDx Talks, 'Frugal innovation for impact: Suneet Sing Tuli at TedxSITM', April 5, 2014; www.youtube.com/watch?v=LzyVt15Hux0 (accessed August 6, 2019).

16 Borpuzari, 'Riding the wind'.

17 Sanjay Singh, 'Datawind sold 5 million tablets in 2017: Suneet Singh Tuli', *Tech Observer*, February 2, 2018.

18 Michael Safi, 'Demonetisation drive that cost India 1.5m jobs fails to uncover "black money"', *The Guardian*, August 30, 2018.

19 *Forbes*, 'Impact 15: Suneet Singh Tuli', 2012; www.forbes.com/lists/2012/impact/suneet-singh-tuli.html (accessed August 6, 2019).

20 Navi Radjou, Jaideep Prabhu and Simone Ajuja, *Jugaad Innovation: Think Frugal, Be Flexible, Generate Breakthrough Through Growth* (San Francisco, CA: Jossey-Bass, 2012), 4.

21 TEDx Talks, 'Frugal innovation for impact'.

22 ICFvideo, 'The 2014 Visonary of the Year, Suneet Singh Tuli, accepts the award at the 2014 ICF Awards Dinner', June 12, 2014; www.youtube.com/watch?v=r5nmcOBoCJs (accessed August 6, 2019).

23 Danielle Rajendram, 'The promise and peril of India's youth bulge', *The Diplomat*, March 10, 2013; https://thediplomat.com/2013/03/the-promise-and-peril-of-indias-youth-bulge/ (accessed August 6, 2019).

24 *The Economist*, 'What a waste – how India is throwing away the world's biggest opportunity', May 11, 2013; www.economist.com/leaders/2013/05/11/what-a-waste (accessed August 6, 2019).

25 TEDx Talks, 'Frugal innovation for impact'.

26 *The Economist*, 'What a waste'.

27 Eccles Health Sciences Library Digital Publishing, 'MC: Social entrepreneurship: Suneet Singh Tuli – Equalizing education in developing countries', October 5, 2015; www.youtube.com/watch?v=SO237YeWwaM (accessed August 6, 2019).

28 Ministry of External Affairs, Government of India, 'Remarks by Permanent Representative of India at the launch of the Aakash 2 at the United Nations', November 19, 2012; www.mea.gov.in/Speeches-Statements.htm?dtl/20854/Remarks+by+Permanent+Representative+at+the+launch+of+the+Aakash2+Tablet+at+United+Nations (accessed August 6, 2019).

29 G. S. Paul, 'Phoolka takes smart class concept to border areas', *The Tribune*, August 23, 2018; www.tribuneindia.com/news/punjab/phoolka-takes-smart-class-concept-to-border-areas/641305.html (accessed August 6, 2019).

30 Ricardo Hausmann, in discussion with Paul Solman and Eric Weiner, January 2016, www.pbs.org/newshour/show/hotbeds-of-genius-and-innovation-depend-on-these-key-ingredients#transcript (accessed August 6, 2019).

9

JATINDER VERMA

Cartographer of spectacular, inclusive theater

> *There is nothing more epic than to leave one country and go to another… It changed all of us irreducibly.*[1]

Jatinder Verma is a theater director and co-founder of theater company Tara Arts. The first person of color to direct a play at the Royal National Theatre (*Tartuffe*, 1990), in 2016 he achieved his long-held ambition of a permanent home for the company: the Tara Theatre, south-west London. In the 1890s in Kenya, his grandfather collected together and bound the maps of the railway then being built by his fellow Indian workers; since the 1970s in Britain, Jatinder has been a cartographer of performative spaces and "a binder of performative landscapes" (his words). Jatinder has mapped a route through a twentieth and twenty-first century experience of migration, loss and gain by means of dramatic storytelling – and Tara Theatre is now his means of binding those maps together.

Jatinder has a cosmopolitan sensibility and is also politicized and racialized by his migration from East Africa to Britain and the racism he experienced once there; he translates these into performative domains. Migration and racism are the defining elements of his innovative creativity, though his theatrical productions are about far more than this. His leitmotif is a notion of "sustained theatre"[2] that can help people to understand those whose culture, ethnicity or experience is different from their own:

> What theatre has the power to do is to make connections between the performers and the audience, connections which also open people to the fact that another person's experience, or the way they look, or the way in which they articulate, is actually not that far removed from one's own.[3]

Tara Arts, set up initially as a community theater group, in 1982 became the first professional Asian theater company to be funded by the Arts Council. Under Jatinder's

FIGURE 9.1 Jatinder Verma, inside the Tara Arts Theatre

Source: © Talula Sheppard

direction, it has explored Indian and other non-European theater techniques, for example collaborating with Anuradha Kapoor from the National School of Drama in New Delhi in a production of *The Government Inspector* (1988); it has undertaken eclectic reinterpretations of European theater classics, for example the production of *Tartuffe* at the National Theatre, and also *Oedipus the King* (1991), *Troilus and Cressida* (1993) and *The Bourgeois Gentilhomme* (1994); it has created new works such as *Journey to the West* (2002), a trilogy of plays reflecting the experiences of the British Asian diaspora.

Throughout all of his work, Jatinder's sensibility and aesthetic is fundamentally about a bridging capital – "to make imaginative connections across cultures through theatre".[4] As well as being a connector, in common with many of my case studies, he is a distributor and sharer of his skills, knowledge and resources – Tara Theatre is designed to welcome a diversity of people of all kinds. But, having established a permanent base for Tara Arts, a lifetime's work and struggle against the odds, Jatinder now wants to be elided from this enterprise. His legacy is in place and, like the music producer Kuljit Bhamra, he wants to become irrelevant. The performative space that he has created will enable the making of vibrant new connections which will in future flourish, and nourish new generations of British people of which Asians are a part, British to the core. They will promote this space of performance and much more and take it into new directions and create new landscapes of drama and performance.

Again, like the other case studies I have explored, Jatinder also has movement capital – a skill set of resilience, a cultural dexterity and sophisticated management of minority status, as well as the ability to deal with extreme dissonance and disequilibrium. Jatinder has translated this capital into storytelling through drama, establishing inviting spaces of performance which generate generosity and connections across borders, so developing further bridge-building capital.

The rupture of migration

With his mother and sisters, Jatinder left Nairobi aged fourteen in 1968 even as the Labour Government under Harold Wilson was drawing up an Act of Parliament to restrict the entry of Commonwealth British citizens into Britain.[5] The legislation did not apply to the white Kenyan settlers who could return to Britain at any time. It was a racist law specifically aimed at keeping the "coloured immigrants", as Kenyan Asians and other people of color were then referred to, out of Britain.

In 1963, when Kenya became independent, a minority of the Asians living there formally became Kenyan citizens. So in 1967 when the Kenyan government decreed that anyone not holding Kenyan citizenship would have to apply for an "entry certificate" to remain in the country and a permit to work, moving to Britain was the logical next step. The total number of British passport-holding Asians in Kenya numbered fewer than 200,000, but, alarmed by an increase in the number of Asians entering Britain each month and the angry, fearful reaction of many Labour voters, Wilson's government introduced the Commonwealth Immigrants Act, which came into force on 1 March.

Many families left within a few days to get into Britain before the legislation came into effect.[6] Jatinder said he carried a blanket onto the plane; otherwise they brought very few things. He has come to view it as a life-changing event of ultimate dissonance and disequilibrium – and it has been the source of much creativity for him and his whole generation.

At the time, Jatinder was excited by the possibilities; he did not feel exilic – it was a positive thing even though they came with nothing. He quickly grasped the geography of London by extensive travel on the Tube – in a way, he was a cartographer then, too. He progressed well academically, moving on from his state comprehensive school to study history at the University of York a few years later.

But he felt differently about it once he was older – the turning point being the murder of Gurdip Chaggar by white British thugs in 1976, of which I write below. In adulthood, Jatinder has likened the experience of sudden migration to the Hindu rite of passage he had undertaken not long before leaving Nairobi, that of having his hair shaved off to mark his transition to manhood. For Jatinder, both events constituted an entry into the world of "otherness" and "an act of incredible brutality".[7] He has also written poignantly of the "loss" of his mother, forced by the process of settling in Britain to see her as a sexualized woman for the first time:

> I had grown up in Nairobi with an idea of her as a housewife, dressed in a certain way, in a sari. On her first day in a factory she was told she could only work there if she wore slacks and a blouse. No saris allowed. So the next morning I saw my mother in slacks and a blouse. For the first time I saw her

shape, and she was no longer my mother – she was a woman. Again my world had crashed…[8]

At other times he has likened the process of his migration to "a rebirth":[9] he began one life in Africa and a second in Britain. Talking with me, he described it as an event of epic proportions (we were discussing Tara's productions of Indian and Greek epics): "There is nothing more epic than to leave one country and go to another. There is no bigger journey to make. It is major and has huge consequences. It changed all of us irreducibly".[10]

He talked, too, of a lingering sense of betrayal – "betraying my culture… by being here" – and the irrevocable loss of home:

> As a first-generation migrant – there is no home for me. I will die with that… What I mean by that is – not that I don't have a home. Of course, I have a home, a partner and all the rest of it. But life cannot be recovered. It's like childhood can't be recovered. You can live in the same country and visit your childhood. In the first generation's case, there is not re-visiting – that is a kind of chopping of the head.

But, he said, the way that loss has manifested itself is in his life's work in the theater: "the only home I have is plays I do. That is the only real home".

He referred to the condition of the migrant in our twenty-first-century globalized world in terms reminiscent of Zygmunt Bauman:

> The modern condition is that we have all been forced into feeling like strangers in our own homes. The more globalized we are, then the more we leak into each other, the more the question becomes, "Can I rest comfortable in an unquestioned sense of my home life?" I don't think any of us can. But certainly I know in myself that, as a migrant, that's something which is constantly beating ahead – that I haven't yet found home.

A rupture animated the rendering of a new kind of creativity. Jatinder translated his inheritance and experience of movement and migration into a new theatrical capital of politicized storytelling which is relevant to the many. Migration and the discourse around it and the experience of it represent the zeitgeist of the times globally. Stories about journeys, migration and movement have defined many of the theatrical performances he has created – and his work remains still urgent, still relevant today.

Double migrant: African influences

Jatinder described himself to me as a "double migrant". His mother's side of the family left India for East Africa during the late nineteenth century. Her father became the binder of the railway's maps. Jatinder's father came from Rajasthan to work on the railway as a guard in the twentieth century (and then worked for British Rail when he came to the UK). Jatinder was born in Dar es Salaam, Tanzania, before moving with his family to Nairobi.

His experiences as an African-born Asian, not a direct migrant from India, are important to his work. That is, his performative aesthetics as well as his sensibilities are informed by his childhood in East Africa. For him, Africa is an older significance. His inheritance, his place of birth and childhood, which he has re-signified with renewed vigor in performative creativity as well as being rendered in the physical innovative physical environs – the earth floor of Tara Theatre, for example.

But initially, as a boy and young man, he dismissed the African part of his heritage, largely because it was too complicated for his white British peers:

> My parents came from India to East Africa. I am born there. I grew up knowing nothing else except some idea of India. Then I arrive here. Part of the process of arrival here… meant that for quite a number of years that part of me had to be killed off… And the only thing that was relevant was an Indian identity or a sub-continental one because it was tiresome to explain to someone – "How come you are brown and you came from Africa?"

He is now increasingly conscious of the importance of Africa in his creative work, especially as he gets older. He has talked about his memories of his mother braiding his sisters' hair in Nairobi, Kenya, before they left and used it as a metaphor to explain his own identity:

> [I] realize that the braids of myself are three spaces, Africa, England, and India – and that of the three, one is entirely imagined space, and ironically that's India. India exists in my head; sure, I've been there, but it's virtual, in my head – and that the home I create [in the plays I produce] is a kind of braiding of these three worlds.[11]

As an East African Asian, the notion of return is non-existent from the point of departure.[12] To me, describing his migration trajectory, Jatinder said:

> There was an absolute consciousness *at the moment of leaving*, that there is no return. So in other words, the place is dead. Then you have entered the other process, which is here, of reinventing yourself… Now it took me thirty years to own up to myself that [Kenya] is that land which has up to then, and continues now, to inflect my soul in intimate ways, inflect the way in which I look at theater. So, to give you an example, I think there's a particular kind of color palette which I now recognize comes from Kenya: it is to do with the soil, it is to do with a combination of the earth and the flora and fauna that I still remember from there.

He thinks that the experience of being an Asian from East Africa has not only affected how his work looks, but also its content, in terms of being open to a variety of cultures, languages and texts:

> There was a pioneering sense in Kenya… you were completely open to modernity, to a variety of cultures because you had no choice, that's what you did, that's how you lived your life. Equally, that you are as a matter of course negotiating across several languages without [it] being an issue, and those two things have materially affected how I am, and how I approach theater. If I look at the sheer diversity of the texts that I look at, that comes from that African homeland.

He also has a consciousness of and exposure to African traditions – the *ngomas* – dances with powerful drum sounds.[13] Jatinder explained to me his childhood memories of these and their presence now in his work:

> *Ngomas*… were large circular affairs where there was dance and music, but actually also a kind of text was being recited. I know that that sense of movement, and rhythm really keeps coming back to these experiences… and the sense of a shared dynamic, which as a child was my only experience of it, a communal activity. This sense of communal movement, and therefore a communal sharing of a story – it could be a story in the conventional sense of a narrative, or in the sense of a proverb that was being reinforced. I haven't got it from anywhere else except from Africa itself.

These are emergences – sparks of a life lived in Africa – which surface and are ever more potent than before when he first started a new life in Britain and had to get on in a world in which you did not look African and are Asian born and brought up in East Africa, an identity most people in Britain found hard to decode and understand – Asians who were products of Africa for a few generations.

Resilience: racism and the murder of Gurdip Chaggar

For Jatinder, race has been central to his life. Since coming to the UK, it has been the air that he has breathed.[14] And it was a shock.

> In Kenya, I had been taught English and Englishness. In my dusty Nairobi classroom I heard about green meadows and red buses, fair play, parliament and Shakespeare. Arriving in England in 1968, I felt I was on home ground. But I was not prepared for the reaction to my colour.[15]

1968, when Jatinder arrived in the UK, was an iconic year. Hanif Kureishi, who like both Jatinder and myself was also fourteen years old at that time, remembers it vividly: "that year of newness, experimentation and hope, when people were thinking in new ways about oppression, relationships and equality, but also when the racial temperature was in megawatts".[16] Being called "Paki" and "Nig-Nog" on a daily basis was common, especially for the men.

Jatinder has described how he and his family "stepped off the plane straight into headline news, part of what the press was describing as the 'Asian exodus', one of the most significant waves of mass migration in modern times".[17]

Again, his experience was refracted through the prism of his love for his mother:

> What I saw was my mother struggling with four children in a strange land, wading through torrents of abuse, repeatedly refused rented accommodation because of the smell of her cooking, disparaged and devalued by shopkeepers and landlords, stripped of her sari and her dignity on the factory floor.[18]

And only two weeks after Jatinder arrived, Enoch Powell, then the MP of Wolverhampton South West, in a declining industrial town in the British Midlands with an existing Indian migrant population, made a speech which was recorded and reported on the television news. In it, he expressed fears that immigration would result in racial and ethnic violence.

Kureishi describes Powell in his article recapturing the experiences of that year:

> A middle-class, only child from Birmingham, socially inept and repressed, Powell had taken refuge in books and 'scholarship' for most of his life. He was perhaps happiest during the war, spending three years in military intelligence in India. Like a lot of Brits, he loved the empire and colonial India, where he could escape his parents and the constraints of Britain... Like most colonialists, Powell was a bigger, more powerful man in India than he'd have been in England... On his return in 1945, Powell went into politics.[19]

The speech – "as I look ahead, I am filled with foreboding; like the Roman, I seem to see the River Tiber foaming with much blood" – and the way in which it was reported in the media, following on from the Labour government's immigration act, emboldened white racists to be overtly and aggressively racist. This was the background against which Jatinder and the rest of our generation lived our teenage years.

But it was the racist murder of Gurdip Chaggar in 1976 that Jatinder cites as the key event in his post-migration "rebirth". It happened in June, just as Jatinder was finishing his history degree at the University of York: only eighteen years old, Gurdip Chaggar was stabbed to death in Southall, west London, by racist white thugs. At the trial a year later, two white teenagers pleaded guilty to manslaughter and so were acquitted of the murder; the judge said it wasn't a racial killing and sent them to prison for just four years.[20]

The murder was an event that politicized a generation of Asians and was a turning point in our lives. It led to the formation of the Southall Youth Movement, which was the first of its kind and very effective: young Asians along with Afro-Caribbeans took to the streets and organized themselves against racist violence and police harassment. The murder and reaction to it catalyzed a politicized creativity in many fields and in the political styles and *modus operandi* of my generation.

Indeed, Gurdip Chaggar's death was the initial impetus for Jatinder and four friends — Praveen Bahl, Ovais Kadri, Sunil Saggar and Vijay Shaunak — to set up an Asian theater, Tara Arts, which gave a voice to that generation of Asians and those following.

Jatinder says his initial reaction on hearing of the murder was to break down in tears, and that he has been "making sense of those tears ever since. It is my way of saying [Gurdip Chaggar] lives on. This is how Tara began: to keep the memory of that event and the impact of that murder in which the all the thugs from the gang who killed him were acquitted".[21]

Tara Arts: from 1977 and into the twenty-first century

Tara's first production was staged the year after Chaggar's murder. The choice of play was *Sacrifice* — an anti-war play by Nobel Prize-winning Bengali poet Rabindranath Tagore. In common with other early productions, it explored questions of iden-tity and cultural hybridization. Reflecting in 2008 on Tara Arts' trajectory, Jatinder said: "When we formed Tara, we became accidental exponents of 'Asian theatre': at that time, we were the first and only example of it."[22] The political imperative was "to find a voice".[23]

During the 2000s, there was an explicit focus on the notion of epic journeys: *The Ramayan Odyssey* (2001) and a trilogy about the migration of Indians from India to Kenya to Britain, *Journey to the West* (1997–2002). Jatinder's interest in the epics wasn't just the result of his experience of migration, however. There is a further biographical aspect, as his father narrated the Indian epics and myths to Jatinder when he was a small boy. "When you hear, as I did as a child, the stories from *The Mahabharata* orally, told to me by my father, it marks you", he told me. This led him to an interest in the Greek myths and epics. "What I found with the Greek plays is a kind of equivalence to the grand epics of Indian literature, the *Mahabharata* and the *Ramayana*." In addition, like Amarjit Kalsi, in 1969 Jatinder watched the BBC Two television series *Civilisation: A Personal View by Kenneth Clark*.[24] But Jatinder watched it with an uncle, who made him realize that there was much elided in this series and gave him an alternative view to the one presented which ignored the earlier and more sophisticated civilizations of India and China. His uncle urged him to read the *Gita* and the epics again and with new eyes and with care. Jatinder had to scour the London libraries to find these, which he did and devoured them; and this biographical interest and a relative's timely and important intervention was subsequently reflected in Tara Arts' choice of productions.

Jatinder speaks about the differences between Indian and Greek epics with depth of knowledge and deep thinking. He sees epics as land and "earth" based, in the case of Indian epics like the *Ramayana* and *Mahabharata*, and "water-based" in the case of the Greek myths in which seas are crossed. Both deal with central "elements of nature – earth and fire – so these are extraordinarily potent metaphors". In the Indian epics there is movement within the continent from north to south to the island of Sri Lanka "mapping India" and in the case of Greek myth, the movement within the Greek sea-faring empire and world.

In 2008, when staging Shakespeare's *The Tempest*, Jatinder identified the thread running throughout Tara's work up until that point as "a dialogue between the past and present, between ethnicity and nationhood, between a sense of belonging and of alienation". In its productions of Indian, French, Greek, Russian, English and contemporary Asian plays, the company had promoted this dialogue, Jatinder wrote, "by claiming ownership of the world's stories".[25]

Jatinder's presence in mainstream circuits and his style of performative creativity was a transgression for some of the establishment consecrators of British theater. He describes how Tara Arts' right to interpret Shakespeare was questioned:

> At a conference last year, an outraged academic asked why my company was producing Shakespeare at all – and if we were, why could we not "do it straight"? Another wondered whether we were going to "Bollywood-ize" it, complete with cod–Indian accents.[26]

Jatinder has also had to struggle against his work being always reductively read, seen only in terms of his ethnicity. Comparing the comments of the critics about his own serialization of the Sanskrit epic *Mahabharata* for BBC Radio 4 to those made about the stage and film version by older British director, Peter Brook, Jatinder told me, "Peter Brook can… be hailed as a world director. I do it and I re-confirm my status as creator of 'ethnic theater'".[27]

We also talked about his production of *The Merchant of Venice* (2005), with which he sought to challenge critics' reductive readings. The production was in English, the language of the power group, but set in sixteenth-century Kerala. Jatinder was pushing the boundaries and, in a way, challenging the hegemony of the RSC. He was attempting to force the powerful belief consecrators[28] that legitimize these domains to take him seriously on his terms, through his frames. He reframed the play and this immobilized the existing frame and so created it anew; he was not trying to stabilize the past to create the future. His agenda is not retrospective but, rather, future orientated. He creates new frames, new ways of seeing, and therefore discovers the new as it emerges, the contours of which are not known in advance; rendering new fusions in the moment as the moment is recovered through its emergence.

Jatinder wants Asian and Black theater to be part of the mainstream on their artistic merits, rather than being restricted to the political imperative of finding and asserting your own voice – the original impulse that animated the establishment of Tara Arts after the murder of Gurdip Chaggar. Otherwise, he says, what you have is cultural separatism, and Asian and Black theater remains on the fringes of the mainstream.

He tells the story of how he asked a theater reviewer from a broadsheet why he came to see the work of Tara Arts:

> In other words, what I asked him was… does he come because it is this particular company, it's a work he knows, likes the work and so on, or does he come because it is an Asian company, it's a Black company, it's an ethnic minority company… he was… honest enough to admit that actually he comes because it's black work.[29]

The content of Jatinder's art was immaterial to the reviewer; the only thing that was important was "how is it ethnically, and therefore politically". That, says Jatinder, "was a salutary… insight".[30]

But black and minority ethnic (BAME) groups are still marginalized in UK theater. The white middle class still dominate audiences, even in London where the BAME population is now more than 40 percent of the total, and black and Asian actors are still often restricted to "secondary roles as hoods, hoodlums and hookers".[31] The "political imperative" is just – if not more – acute: a problem to which Tara Arts, in its permanent home at the Tara Theatre, seeks to be part of the solution.

Tara Theatre: the building

Tara Arts is the first building in the country dedicated to cross-cultural theater and his institutional legacy. Jatinder captured the new in creating an Asian theater company, and the fact that a building exists, a concrete physical structure, a performative space, is his legacy to the world of British theater.

The building has a nineteenth-century façade concealing a twenty-first-century up-to-date modern theater with seating for one hundred people. The fabric of the building articulates Tara Arts' cross-culturalism. The building contains both Indian and English pargeting and is inscribed with motifs that come from the UK and India. The wood floor can be removed to expose the earth. A raw earth floor is used in many sites across the world for dramatic performance: in India, China, Latin America and Africa. Having created a performative space, with a huge effort to get the building made with money from foundations and charities (but none from wealthy, British Asian entrepreneurs, Jatinder says), Jatinder hopes Tara Arts will continue to innovate. He talks about the notion of collisions and that part of what makes the modern are the collisions – "the more you can push that the more you will gain."

Jatinder has a desire to ensure that the diverse populations of Britain become an asset to theater, "that you are not depending on the Asian show to bring in the Asians – that's fine, they'll come then, but will they come to *Henry VI*? How do you get them to come to *Henry VI*? I think the only way to do it is…" He talks about the importance of mixing casts and producers rather than looking for a particular play which reflects a particular community.

FIGURE 9.2 The Tara Arts Theatre on Garratts Lane, Earlsfield, in south-west London

Source: © Helene Binet

He talks too about Tara Arts' annual pantomime, taking the "known traditions of white theatergoers – the iconic traditions which at Christmas time… have simple stories like Cinderella, Aladdin, and are full of terrible jokes, a simple story which is full of song and dance and full of jokes that are very topical and pick up on whatever is happening in the day". The *Bollywood Jack* panto which I went to see in January 2017 had a mixed audience with older people and younger people and children from all the local communities with a greater number of Indians. It was a mixed audience, which is something Jatinder wants to encourage, and which fitted with his ambition for cross-cultural theater and performances that generate dialogue and connection.

Conclusion

Jatinder's legacy and the inheritance of future generations will be that he was the maker of performative spaces that encode the lives and expertise of both his

FIGURE 9.3 Tara Arts Theatre stage

Source: © Helene Binet

maternal and paternal grandfathers and also their journeys and professions that he sees an affinity with.

Jatinder fuses supremely complex landscapes, a remixer par excellence of multiple languages, styles of thought and performance. Like his grandfather, he has bound together landscapes of movement, location, dislocation and disruption, both dissonant and consonant with the world contemporary and past.

The pioneering role of Tara Arts in nurturing, discovering and incubating new creative and performative talent has been significant. Many talented Asian performers, writers, designers, directors and choreographers, now well known to the world, gained vital experience working with Tara. Tara Arts has performed the role of midwife to a new creative talent pool; many skills, including the general know-how required to run an arts institution, has been learnt in the bosom of Tara Arts.

Jatinder has done performative, transformative work for a lifetime, more than four decades, and in the making of this theater building he has played out another kind of performance – a legacy of making. A journey of exodus from East Africa to Britain and all the achievements and disruption encountered in this journey are encoded in this new theater made from an older Tara building, a circle of settlement completed. From that space new journeys will flow, and within it new collisions and connections will occur. It is a space for the catalyzing of dialogues and cross-cultural flows, for co-constructed and improvised conversations both unexpected and significant, conversations that talk of complex histories and historical moments. It is a space where those who fought for their voices to be heard in the mainstream or even the peripheries of British performative landscapes will be acknowledged, voices that were in the past considered transgressive, now rendered, performed and their stories told and heard.

Notes

1 Jatinder Verma, from an interview with the author, January 16, 2015.
2 FIPAarts, 'Jatinder Verma (British South Asian Theatre Memories)', March 25, 2014; www.youtube.com/watch?v=4WcJux902S8 (accessed August 8, 2019).
3 FIPAarts, 'Jatinder Verma'.
4 Tara Arts, 'Tara history', www.tara-arts.com/about-us/history (accessed August 8, 2019).
5 James Callaghan, Home Secretary in Wilson's government, took his proposals for emergency legislation to a cabinet committee meeting on 13 February – see Mark Lattimer, 'When Labour played the racist card', New Statesman, January 22, 1999. Jatinder arrived on 14 February – www.tara-arts.com/about-us/meet-the-team/jatinder-verma (accessed August 8, 2019).
6 My older sister, who was eighteen years old at the time, and Jatinder's family and many of my relatives living in Kenya were impacted by this legislation and had to leave Kenya in a rush within a three-month period.
7 Jatinder Verma, '"Braids" and Theatre Practice', talk given at the British Braids conference at Brunel University, April 20, 2001; www.brunel.ac.uk/creative-writing/research/entertext/documents/entertext021/Jatinder-Verma-Braids-and-Theatre-Practice.pdf (accessed August 8, 2019).
8 Jatinder Verma, 'Telling political stories', The Socialist Review, June 2016 (414); http://socialistreview.org.uk/414/telling-political-stories (accessed August 8, 2019).
9 SustainedTheatreUK, 'Jatinder Verma Artistic Director (Tara Arts), interviewed by www.sustainedtheatre.org', June 11, 2009 [film]; www.tara-arts.com/whats-on/the-black-album-2009. "In my rebirth, when we migrated to Britain…" (accessed August 8, 2019).
10 From an interview with the author, January 16, 2015.
11 Verma, '"Braids" and Theatre Practice'.
12 See Parminder Bhachu, 'Twice Migrants and Multiple Migrants', in The Wiley Blackwell Encyclopedia on Race, Ethnicity and Nationalism, ed. Professor John Stone, Dennis Rutledge, Anthony Smith and Polly Rizova (Hoboken, NJ: Wiley Smith Publishers, 2015); 'The Invisibility of Diasporic Cultural and Multiple Migrant Creativity', in Mutuality: Anthropology's Changing Engagement, ed. Roger Sanjek (Philadelphia, PA: Penn University Press, 2014); Dangerous Designs: Asian Women Fashion the Diaspora Economies (London: Routledge, 2004); 'Identities Constructed & Reconstructed: Representations of Asian Women in Britain', in Migrant Women: Crossing Boundaries and Changing Identities, ed. Gina Buijs (Oxford, UK and New York: Berg Publishers Limited, 1993); 'East African Sikh Settlers in Britain: Twice versus Direct Migrants', in The Modern Western Diaspora, ed. C. Peach, S. Vertovec and C. Clark (Delhi: Oxford University Press, 1991); Twice Migrants: East African Sikh Settlers in Britain (London: Tavistock Publications, 1984); Ivan Light and Parminder Bhachu, 'California Immigrants in World Perspective', in Immigration and Entrepreneurship: Culture, Capital and Ethnic Networks, ed. Ivan Light and Parminder Bhachu (Piscataway, NJ: Rutgers University, Transactions Press, 1993).

13 This is something to which we were all exposed. I used to hear the drums on a regular basis as we lived on the edge of a compound of Africans in Kampala, Uganda.

14 SustainedTheatreUK, 'Jatinder Verma'. "Ever since coming to this country, race has been a major – er – not just cloud, but is part of the air one breathes."

15 Jatinder Verma, 'What the migrant saw', *The Guardian*, January 10, 2008.

16 Hanif Kureishi, '"Knock knock, it's Enoch". Hanif Kureishi remembers the effect of Enoch Powell', first published in *The Guardian*, December 12, 2014. Copyright © Hanif Kureishi 2014; www.bl.uk/20th-century-literature/articles/knock-knock-its-enoch-hanif-kureishi-remembers-the-effect-of-enoch-powell (accessed August 8, 2019).

17 Verma, 'What the migrant saw'.

18 Verma, 'What the migrant saw'.

19 Kureishi, 'Knock knock, it's Enoch'.

20 Benjamin Bland, 'Gurdip Singh Chaggar, the Southall Youth Movement, and the background to 1979', *Discover Society*, April 3, 2019; https://discoversociety.org/2019/04/03/gurdip-singh-chaggar-the-southall-youth-movement-and-the-background-to-april-1979/ (accessed August 8, 2019).

21 SustainedTheatreUK, 'Jatinder Verma'.

22 Verma, 'What the migrant saw'.

23 The phrase was taken from the title of Amrit Wilson's book, *Finding a Voice: Asian Women in Britain* (London: Virago, 1978).

24 *Civilisation: A Personal View by Kenneth Clark* (1969) [TV series], BBC Two.

25 Verma, 'What the migrant saw'.

26 Verma, 'What the migrant saw'.

27 Peter Brook's version of the Mahabharata was originally performed as a nine-hour stage play in 1985 and then toured the world for four years; a shorter version was filmed in 1989. Jatinder wrote a three-part dramatization of the epic with Claudia Mayer for BBC Radio 4, first broadcast in 2007.

28 Pierre Bourdieu describes the belief-producing role of influential consecrators of art, theater, classical music and other creative products. They are powerful interlocutors who determine the value and prestige of cultural commodities in the field of cultural production, conferring artistic legitimacy upon them. See Pierre Bourdieu 'The Production of Belief: Contributions to an Economy of Symbolic Goods', in *The Field of Cultural Production*, Pierre Bourdieu and ed. Randall Johnson (Cambridge, UK: Polity Press, 1993).

29 Victoria & Albert Museum, 'Interview with Jatinder Verma, artistic director of Deadeye' [film], www.vam.ac.uk/content/videos/i/video-interview-with-jatinder-verma,-artistic-director-of-deadeye/ (accessed August 8, 2019).

30 Victoria & Albert Museum, 'Interview with Jatinder Verma'.

31 Danuta Kean and Mel Larson, *Centre Stage: The Pipelines of BAME Talent* (London: Andrew Lloyd Webber Foundation, 2017).

10

PROFESSOR SIR TEJINDER VIRDEE

Extreme engineering and the quest for
the 'god particle'

…When I asked him where he got his tools made he said he made them himself and laughing added if I had staid for other people to make my tools and things for me, I had never made anything.[1]

Progress in science and progress in technology are inextricably linked and feed off of each other… Novel technologies will be deployed to further enhance the capabilities of CMS, which already is one of the most powerful scientific instruments ever built.[2]

Physicist Tejinder Virdee represents the zenith of diasporic technical capital.

On July 4, 2012, CERN (European Organization for Nuclear Research), a multinational European research center near Geneva, Switzerland, announced, with admirable restraint, "the discovery of a particle consistent with the Higgs boson".[3] Referred to popularly as the "God particle", the Higgs boson[4] was long-sought after, theorized for some forty years as the particle that gives the property of mass to other particles – but only observed for the first time in 2012. Scientists hailed this as the biggest scientific breakthrough of the twenty-first century, a "triumph", and "the coalescing of four decades of intellectual and engineering effort to create a new understanding of the universe's structure".[5] Jim Al-Khalili, professor of physics at the University of Surrey and anchor of BBC Radio 4's *The Life Scientific*, said, "After the hype and speculation, after decades of designing the worlds' most ambitious experiment and months of careful checking of data, today is pay-off day".[6]

Key to this breakthrough was the Large Hadron Collider (LHC), a $5.5 billion particle accelerator which hurtled protons at just below the speed of light around its 27 kilometer circular tunnel underneath the French-Swiss countryside, together with the two particle detectors, ATLAS and CMS, which recorded what happened when the protons collided. The experiment recreated the conditions of the universe when it was created 13.7 billion years ago, or more specifically a fraction of a nanosecond after the Big Bang.[7] To find the Higgs particle, CERN's scientists analyzed more than 1,000 trillion proton collisions: these sometimes create a Higgs boson, which at once decays into more familiar particles; an unusual excess of these appears as a bump in the data – and indicates the hitherto elusive boson.[8] The LHC and its detectors are considered to be the most complex scientific instruments ever made – an exemplar of "extreme engineering"[9] – and the experiment constituted one of the largest international scientific collaborations in history.

Tejinder Virdee, professor of physics at Imperial College, London, was a "founding father" of one of the two detectors – the Compact Muon Solenoid (CMS) detector – the experiment's deputy leader between 1993 and 2006 and then its elected leader (spokesperson) from 2007 for a period of three years.[10] Since 2012 – and even before – he has been inundated with honors and prizes, including the 2017 American Physical Society Panofsky Prize for his pioneering work and outstanding leadership in the making of the CMS experiment and, in 2014, a knighthood from the Queen. He is now leading the work at CERN to upgrade the CMS detector with an even more sophisticated and powerful calorimeter (the instrument which measures the energy emitted by the particles). "Progress in science and progress in technology are inextricably linked and feed off of each other", he says. "Novel technologies will be deployed to further enhance the capabilities of CMS, which already is one of the most powerful scientific instruments ever built".[11] The intellectual and technical capital of the diaspora and its legacies are thus being reproduced in the realms of cutting-edge science.

A competitive start

Born in 1952, Tejinder was raised in Kisumu, a small hub town on the shores of Lake Victoria in Kenya. The Kenya–Uganda railways ended here, and ships took freight and passengers from Kisumu across the Lake to the neighboring countries of Uganda and Tanzania. All these countries were part of the British Empire and decolonized in the early 1960s. Prior to independence, Kisumu had a close-knit Asian community, with the conviviality and collaborative ethos of many pioneering communities in the diaspora.

Tejinder's father had been a star student at his college in the Punjab, an educated man known for his oratory and intellectual skills. There is a photograph of him in this college as the top student of his time and the top student to this day. He worked as the customs officer in the port of Kisumu. I have heard many stories from people who were in his peer group and those who heard him speak in public at the temple and ethnic institutions; they speak of his eloquence and progressive ideals, both for his own children and the community at large. Tejinder sees his father as a critical definer of his life and his sensibilities. "A lot of things I am doing stem from him one way or another", he told me.

Tejinder's mother was born in Nyeri, a small town in the Kenyan white highlands. She was a Girl Guide and educated in the local Asian schools. People took a great deal of pride in doing things well, and all diasporic Asian woman in East Africa were expected to command the skills of craft and domesticity. In this small town, where everyone knew each other, "Nyeri girls" taught and learnt from each other and also competed to outdo each other. I have stories from other Nyeri women of this generation who were fierce learners and competitors in the local economy of home making and craft skill. All of them, including Tejinder's family, were and are accomplished and gifted makers of all kinds, that is, the carpenters, the builders, the metal workers, the brick layers, and so on. The skills of making and crafting and building are and were their milieu, and constitute his inheritance and legacy.

Kisumu High, a government school for Asians, has produced some very successful people in the diaspora. Most were the children of fathers and grandfathers who had worked as administrative and service employees of the institutions controlled by the colonial British. This included the public works department, the post office and communications, as well as the railways and harbors. There were also the children of entrepreneurs, building contractors, farmers with small farms around Kisumu, and retailers. Tejinder and his siblings – two brothers and one sister – always got the highest grades in school. He explained to me that the desire to learn and excel was encoded in the hierarchical ranking system prevalent in schools in colonial British East Africa, as in India and all the British colonies at the time. Students were ranked according to their overall grades; the ranks were made public and students competed to get the best grades. Of course, this hierarchical system also shamed people and there were many negative consequences of coming at the bottom of the class. The stigma attached to not doing well stayed with people for the rest of their lives, as did the positive reinforcement that accrued from achieving high grades. This coded the future in the top-ranking students' favor and encouraged them to do even better.

Kisumu High had a white British headmaster, Mr. J. A. Chubb. As the family prepared to leave for Britain, Tejinder's father asked him to provide letters verifying his children's excellent school performance. In Birmingham, he used them to ensure his children gained places at a grammar school, the King's Norton School. This smoothed their transition from a Kenyan "British commonwealth" education into the British system. The public grammar schools selected their pupils by means of an academic exam and were designed to provide an academic education, as opposed to the vocational education of the non-selective secondary modern schools, or the all-welcoming comprehensive schools being introduced at that time, which aimed to do both. In contrast, most new immigrants who entered the educational system in the 1960s in their teenage years were mostly put into the non-selective schools.

At King's Norton, physics teacher Howard Stockley inspired Tejinder's passion for physics and for understanding the laws of nature. At the Birmingham Science Museum, a cloud chamber fired his imagination and got him interested in studying the substances and structures of matter that constitute the universe. He went on to study nuclear science at Queen Mary's College, University of London, the only place that then taught this subject, but switched to physics. From there, having developed a particular interest in particle physics, he went to Imperial College to do a PhD on "an experiment conducted at the Stanford Linear Accelerator Centre in California" – and then in 1979 he joined CERN as a Fellow in the Experimental Physics division. Working to verify the idea that "quarks" (a type of elementary particle: they combine to form protons, neutrons, etc.) are electrically charged, Tejinder gained his first experience of overseeing a large construction project, as this research also required the development and building of a detector to observe the subatomic particles' behavior. In particular, he developed expertise in calorimetry, inventing new techniques to collect light and thereby measure the energy emitted by the particles.

The CMS and the hunt for Higgs boson

In 1983, scientists at CERN identified the w and z bosons of theoretical physics as physical realities – and the hunt was on to find similar evidence for the Higgs boson.[12] CERN's scientists knew what sort of accelerator to build and how, but at that point they didn't have the technology to build a detector to go with it – an instrument that could measure 1 billion proton–proton interactions per second, manage large particle flows generating 40 terabytes of data per second, and withstand high radiation levels… If you made it out of lead, for example, it wouldn't last more than an hour.

Tejinder meanwhile was continuing his work in calorimetry at CERN and by 1990 he and a few colleagues thought they had found an idea that could work. Their idea – after twenty years of conceptual design, intensive R&D, prototyping, construction and installation and with the involvement of some 3,500 scientists from forty-five countries[13] – was eventually to become the Compact Muon Solenoid (CMS) detector.

He describes its final design in a way that makes it sound simple: the beams of protons enter into a cylindrical "onion" consisting of four principal layers, each of which has a particular function, and which work together to measure the direction, identity and energies of the particles produced by the colliding protons. But its development involved many different disciplines – civil engineering, mechanical engineering, cryogenic engineering, computer software and so on – each of which had to perform at the cutting-edge. Reliability of each and every element was also crucial: once installed in its concrete chamber 100 meters below ground level with the hadron collider hurtling protons through it at the speed of light, it wasn't going to be possible to replace a failed part.

Tejinder had identified a particular type of scintillating crystal for the calorimeter with which to measure the particles' energy: lead tungstate. But it wasn't straightforward: between 1993 and 1998, Tejinder and his team worked to improve the crystals' hardness and their purity and tested them – could they survive the high levels of radiation, for example? Finally they could, but then the problem was that there were only some five or seven such crystals in existence, and the detector required 75,000. Moreover, it took three days to grow just one of them. There was a particular factory in Russia equipped to manufacture them, which ran ten years

FIGURE 10.1 Tejinder Virdee and the Compact Muon Solenoid, CERN, in 2011

Source: Imperial College London

round the clock between 1998 and 2008 – when it was then possible to install them in the CMS calorimeter at CERN.

With similar amounts of hard work and pushing the boundaries of their respective disciplines, scientists from each of the different countries involved built their particular part of the CMS in their laboratories, and then brought it to CERN for the CMS to be assembled. "Fortunately for us", Tejinder says, "everything fitted".[14]

Team work: collective intelligence

The CMS experiment was enormous, in all dimensions. The detector was 21 meters long, 15 meters wide and 15 meters high. It weighed 14,000 tonnes. The cylindrical coil that made up the solenoid magnet consisted of some 50 kilometers of superconducting cable; it generated a field of 4 tesla, about 100,000 times the magnetic field of the Earth.[15] But the experiment was also an immense feat of international scientific collaboration.

For the CMS to succeed, Tejinder had to work productively with a huge team of smart people – some 3,500 particle physicists, engineers, technicians, students and support staff – from diverse backgrounds and nationalities.

The fact that the project needed big investments of talent and finance was recognized early on. One of the early things they had to do was "to match capability of the countries and the scientists in those countries with the requirements of the experiment, which were severe". They had to persuade people and countries to join. He referred to it as the "grand tour", as it took him and his colleagues to Taiwan, China, Russia, and almost forty other countries, talking to ministers and government officials as well as academics; they visited several countries several times. They put in "a huge effort in selecting the right team". Because the results were likely to be significant in scientific terms and "very valuable", everybody would have to cooperate to achieve that goal.

The resulting team of people was good, he told me, the best people in their fields. "Everybody comes from a different trajectory, a different point of view and different strengths. No single individual has all the strengths and knowledge. It is a collective enterprise."

I'm reminded of Chandra Mukerji's description of the construction of the Canal du Midi in the seventeenth century, now a UNESCO World Heritage Site. Cutting across a corner of France between the Atlantic Ocean and the Mediterranean Sea, it was a triumph of "impossible engineering", as Mukerji describes it, drawing on the "collective intelligence" of women and artisans from the Pyrenees who carried past knowledge of Roman methods of hydraulic engineering, as well as personnel from the military and academic realms.[16] No one group working on the canal could have conceived of the whole: similarly, within the CMS no one group of scientists laboring in their national institutes and laboratories could have conceived and constructed alone the detector in its totality.

Bringing together the experiment's participants to work within the one team to create the detector and analyze the data it collected was as big a task as constructing the instrument itself. The CMS was a gargantuan project of collective intelligence. Tejinder's multiply migrant background and biography of movement from Kenya to the UK and then to Geneva, and a familial history of movement from India to Kenya, are conducive to working with a range of ethnicities, to going to different countries to find the appropriate people to work with, and to negotiate or invent new ways of doing things. Reflecting on his father's life, Tejinder talked to me about how multiple-migrants "learn to adapt and change and progress", which is something he himself has done in a very high-profile and inventive way.

He has now lived more years in Geneva than anywhere else, in fact: thirty years there, fifteen in Kenya and only twelve years in the UK. "We get to identify with no particular country. You have to live in a multicultural environment. Geneva is very cosmopolitan…" he told me.

The fact that he does not associate with a particular country is also what helps to make him open to people from many backgrounds and nationalities and ethnicities. He is not bound or committed deeply to one nationality and does not see the world in exclusive terms. As a transnationally orientated citizen, he can bring together and collaborate with a diverse group of people. His biography prepared him for and predisposed him to this kind of work.

Creating consensus was important for him and critical for the project to work. He referred several times in our conversation to the "art of managing people without making people feel upset". He described the process of working with 3,500 brilliant scientists: "They are all individuals… They have big egos – rightly so. People have ideas and they argue forcefully". But the demands of their collective enterprise helped to "flatten egos" because they all wanted "to succeed and do the physics" and knew they could not succeed on their own, only collectively, so they had to understand each others' ideas and test them and compare their performance within the experiment. But even so, it was not always clear what the right next step was. "There has to be clarity of vision", he told me. "You take the input and make the decision" – and then create consensus around that decision. "And almost all the decisions that were the tough ones succeeded", he told me.

This negotiative sensibility of collaborative teamwork is the *modus vivendi* and *modus operandi* of the diaspora. It is the creative sensibility of conducting a life in new settings, trying out solutions, paying heed to other peoples' opinions, not assuming you know the correct way of making and building. Everything is done by trial and error to create the new on the terms of the new. It is the nature of living with doubt and without rejecting other ways of doing and making. It is about being open to the new and of finding a solution through improvisation. There is a certain humility and lack of arrogance integral to the success of migrant makers.

Racism and how he has escaped it: the muting of racism in concrete, proof-based sciences

Tejinder does not feel racism has shaped his life; rather, he says, it gets muted in scientific teams because you must work collectively and you are dealing with facts that can be proved or disproved using criteria that have a defined order of proof making.

He had a job in industry after his undergraduate degree with a physicist who was a production engineer in a company which made boxes close to his parents' house in Birmingham – this was a formative experience. He got bored after three months and decided he did not want to work in industry and instead began his PhD at Imperial. It was at box-making company that he heard some racist comments, he told me: "Here and there – I won't say there was nothing, but it is not something that today I feel has shaped my life".

I gave him examples of cultural producers – among them, Jatinder Verma (see Chapter 9) and Bhajan Hunjan (see Chapter 3) – who had formative experiences of race, notably the epoch-defining Gurdip Chaggar murder in Southall. Such experiences he felt did not apply to science because it is "a more absolute subject". Tejinder told me, "When you work collectively in scientific teams that are good, you have to prove yourself and can do so with concrete proof" – that is to say, racial dynamics do not work in the same way as they do in the more interpretive human-ities and social science fields. Indeed, as spokesperson for the CMS experiment – a collaboration between a huge range of people and countries – he required both diplomatic skills and enormous media savviness.

There were powerful exemplars who had opened these spaces of innovation and creativity in science for people of color. For example, Professor Abdus Salam was in an earlier generation at Imperial College where he played a pioneering role in setting up its physics department and won a Nobel Prize for physics in 1979, the year in which Tejinder gained his PhD there and first went to CERN. Tejinder has been a beneficiary of Abus Salam's groundwork and perhaps this militates against racism. Just as Tejinder stands on the shoulders of the illustrious scientists of color from the past, in generations to come others will benefit from the innovative new paths he has created.

Tolerating dissonance, material daring, episteme and techne

Tejinder has the ability to make new technologies, methods and processes that have not been tried and tested by anyone before. Embarking on the development of the CMS using new technologies and pushing the boundaries of science in every dir-ection over a period of two decades, Tejinder exemplifies superbly the ability of the multiply migrant to deal with extreme dissonance and disequilibrium, in his case high level and long term, operating in the realm of the almost impossible. I asked him if he needed courage and daring in thinking about inventing such a complex instrument as the detector. He replied that when they started work on the making of the CMS, he and his pioneering colleagues – a couple of French men, a couple of German men and Tejinder, who had worked together on a previous project – "were told we must be out of our minds".

But he is comfortable with a very high level of risk – he said they were calculated risks – and confident that he can solve problems by identifying and accepting them. He told me that "knowing that you have a problem is the most difficult thing to do – to recognize that you have a problem and not saying, 'I don't have a problem'." With the right team around him in the CMS project, invariably they found the answers they needed. "There is not a single problem we had to which we didn't find a solution", he told me. "…We had many problems, but we solved them all." For this it was crucial too that he was open to being told that he was wrong. In fact, he said, this shaped the team: "You have to have a set of people for these complex projects who stand up to you and collectively come back".

He refers often to technology being pushed to the limits – the notion of extreme engineering. For example, he told me that at the time when his team was developing the CMS, the radiation-proof electronics that they required existed only within the military and were extremely expensive to replicate. In addition, there was an absolute requirement for the sophisticated technologies to operate without breaking down or error. As it turned out, they were extremely reliable.[17]

I was particularly struck by what he told me about his quest to identify, refine and manufacture the 75,000 lead tungstate crystals required for the detector's calorimeter – a quest which lasted some fifteen years, from 1993 to 2008. It is another version of the material daring displayed by both Bhajan Hunjan (concrete "embroideries") and Jasleen Kaur (marbled plastic) in their artistic domain. Russia had mastered the production of these crystals, but Tejinder had to make some twenty trips there and the manufacturing process took ten years. It was a real struggle. He talked about how this was a difficult stage of the project when a lot of his colleagues were telling him that he was not going to succeed, and he should change course. He refused: "because in the end when you have to make mid-course changes, they end worse and [are] more costly". But it was the earlier theoretical work he'd undertaken with a colleague using CERN's sophisticated simulation software that really determined that decision, he told me: "the physics drove that decision".[18] Once the experiment began in earnest and the scientists were able to analyze the protons colliding in the detector, it was clear he had been right to stand his ground because, as he told me in early 2012, the "channel that is speaking the loudest [about the existence of the Higgs boson] is the one which uses the crystals". The use of these crystals and the technologies developed around them have had other benefits, too, leading to improvements in the medical scanners used to diagnose cancer.

We talked about the late Steve Jobs of Apple and his desire to make both the inside and the surfaces of any object look good.[19] This desire for perfection, and for a job that is well done and works and looks good, is displayed also by Tejinder and the team he led. He said: "The surfaces look nice but the insides do all the work". This desire for perfection is an aspect of good craftsmanship, which his maker ancestors emphasized over and over; they practiced their crafts with care and perfection. For Tejinder, "The beauty lies in the intricacy and in the technologies pushed to the limits and all put to a pattern. They are like a work of art". This level of skill in creating sophisticated, technical, functional objects which are at the same time beautiful and elegant is something that the nineteenth-century British administrators praised in the work of the Punjabi artisans whose artisanal lineage Tejinder Virdee shares – the reputation which enabled the Punjabi artisans to find their way to into diasporic locations in the first place.

What is so striking to me in all of this is the importance of hand and mind knowledge within the experiment, techne as well as episteme. The scientists at CERN were investigating the ideas of fundamental physics and its Standard Model, but what they needed to do this was a huge machine, their immensely sophisticated instrument, their 12,500-ton steel-encased detector (bearing out Davis Baird's argument that "a major epistemological event of the mid-twentieth century has been the recognition by the scientific community of the centrality of instruments to the epistemological project of technology and science"[20]). And to make this a physical reality, again what they needed was boundary-pushing episteme to solve their techne problems: How to record the energy emitted by the colliding protons? How to protect the calorimeter from the electromagnetic field of the solenoid? How to keep the cables cool enough to prevent them from melting? How to store the vast quantities of data amassed? I am reminded of the scientific advances of the Renaissance, made possible by an alliance between the artisans and the theoreticians, as described by historian of science and technology, Pamela Long.[21] But, like Isaac Newton, who ground his own lenses with which to construct his telescope, and the inventive Lunar men of the early Industrial Revolution,[22] Tejinder embodies both theoretician and artisan. He is simultaneously both a thinker and a maker, and both his technical and intellectual abilities are further catalyzed by the cutting-edge thinking and technologies at twenty-first-century CERN on the French-Swiss border – in a manner at once hugely similar to and radically different from his forebears encountering the industrial technologies of the British Empire in the late nineteenth and early twentieth centuries.

Tejinder's advice and guiding motto: navigate uncharted territories

Tejinder urged his audience of young scientists at the 2009 Intel International Science and Engineering Fair "to discover the undiscovered and to navigate uncharted waters".[23] He first told them the story of the CMS and the experiment which gave physical reality to the Higgs boson, before quoting the words attributed to Isaac Newton:

> I do not know what I may appear to the world, but to myself I seem to have been only like a boy playing on the sea shore, and diverting myself in now and then finding a smoother pebble or a prettier shell than ordinary, whilst the great ocean of truth lay all undiscovered before me.[24]

He thus encouraged his listeners to explore the new frontiers of knowledge – which is precisely what the CMS experiment has done, to expand the vista and visions of science and furnish an advance in scientific knowledge. This is what Tejinder himself was part of, and led, a process encompassing so much more than the science itself: seeking out finance, gathering a team – matching talent and locating expertise and funds – and then collaborating with hyper-diverse teams from dispersed geographic locations, while also designing and creating the instrument with which to carry out the experiment. He is a pioneer and a collectively minded problem solver. Like the multiply migrant population that produced him, he has honed his ability to live with and work with extreme dissonance and disequilibrium for many years, that is, extreme risk for more than twenty years. He is a product of the competitive educational and craft economies of learning, sharing and teaching in both Kisumu, Kenya, and his British Midlands grammar school. He is a classic product of his inheritances and legacies rendered in the new technological and scientific domains of the late twentieth and early twenty-first century. He is a new kind of person in the new landscapes of a fluid and liquid twenty-first century who is recommending that we "discover undiscovered things" and who has himself done precisely that which he recommends.

Notes

1 Sir Isaac Newton, scientist, mathematician and physicist, quoted in the John Conduitt, Memorandum, 31 August 1726, Keynes MS 130.10 - www.newtonproject.ox.ac.uk/view/texts/diplomatic/THEM00172 (accessed December 1, 2020).

2 Personal communication, July 30, 2020.

3 CERN, 'CERN experiments observe particle consistent with long-sought Higgs boson', Press release, July 4, 2012.

4 The subatomic particle known as the boson is named after the Bengali physicist Satyendra Nath Bose. Based at the University of Dhaka, in 1924, he sent a paper to Albert Einstein that laid the basis for describing two new classes of subatomic particle as well as a new field of physics, quantum statistics. Einstein ensured the paper was published and Bose subsequently worked in Europe with both Einstein and Marie Curie. It was Paul Dirac, another British physicist, who eventually named the two classes of subatomic particle: bosons, after Satyendra Nath Bose, and fermions, after the Italian physicist Enrico Fermi (Subhro Niyogi, 'Satendra Nath Bose towers over Higgs in the world of physics', *The Times of India*, July 6, 2012). There is a great deal of global media coverage and many accolades for Professor Peter Higgs, the Edinburgh-based theoretical physicist who proposed in the early 1960s that there was an invisible field made of particles by which matter in the universe gained mass, but absolutely no mention of Bose.

5 Robin McKie, 'Higgs boson: A cause for celebration. But will it be our last great discovery?' *The Guardian*, July 8, 2012; www.theguardian.com/commentisfree/2012/jul/08/robin-mckie-higgs-boson-discovery-where-next (accessed August 8, 2019).

6 Quoted in Rob Waugh and Fiona Macrae, 'Professor Higgs wipes a tear from his eye as fellow scientists find his "God particle" on "momentous day for science" – 40 years after he predicted its existence', *Daily Mail*, July 5, 2012.

7 Tejinder Virdee, speaking at Intel ISEF, 2009, stated: "Scientists believe the Higgs-Boson is the particle that gives the property of mass to other particles such as electrons and so on. If we can prove that it exists and that this is the case, we will have taken a big step towards a much fuller understanding of how the universe works, and indeed, what happened in the instants immediately after it was formed… The CMS detector is where protons are 'hit head-on', in fact it's the constituents of the protons that hit head-on, which are quarks and gluons, and they create a sub-set of reactions or events that would have been taking place in the universe one hundredth or one-thousandth of one nanosecond after the Big Bang. So we are going back in time, creating the conditions of the universe at that time, in a controlled way, and looking for what are the particles that existed at that time and what the forces that existed at that time." Taken from: Society for Science, 'Dr Jim Virdee (CERN) speaks at Intel ISEF – Part 2', www.youtube.com/watch?v=zr8Jn31uHP0 (accessed August 8, 2019).

8 Ian Sample, 'Higgs boson: It's unofficial! Scientists at Cern find missing particle', *The Guardian*, July 4, 2012; www.theguardian.com/science/2012/jul/04/higgs-boson-cern-scientists-discover (accessed August 8, 2019).

9 "Extreme engineering" is the expression Tejinder uses during his 2009 address to the International Science and Engineering Fair (Society for Science, 'Dr Jim Virdee (CERN) speaks at Intel ISEF – Part 2', June 24, 2009; www.youtube.com/watch?v=zr8Jn31uHP0)

(accessed August 8, 2019); it is also the title of a TV series about engineering feats on the Discovery Channel which ran between 2003 and 2011.

10 Imperial College, 'Professor Sir Tejinder Singh Virdee FRS', www.imperial.ac.uk/people/t.virdee (accessed August 8, 2019)

11 Personal communication, July 30, 2020. See also Amit Roy, 'Knight toasts "Sir" in glory', *The Telegraph Calcutta*, June 17, 2014.

12 The hunt for the Higgs boson wasn't the only reason for the experiment: the scientists were also studying the Standard Model – the theory developed during the 1970s to explain how fundamental forces and particles (including the Higgs boson) work together; and searching for extra dimensions and particles that could make up dark matter; https://home.cern/science/experiments/cms (accessed August 8, 2019).

13 These are Tejinder's figures (Virdee, 'The Long Road to the Higgs Boson'); the CMS website says 4,300 staff from forty-two countries, https://home.cern/science/experiments/cms (accessed August 8, 2019).

14 Cambridge University Physics Society, 'Prof. Sir Tejinder Virdee: The Long Road to the Higgs Boson', talk given to Cambridge University Physics Society January 13, 2019; www.youtube.com/watch?v=bRFtS7HVmwo (accessed August 8, 2019).

15 'CMS', https://home.cern/science/experiments/cms (accessed August 8, 2019).

16 Chandra Mukerji, *Impossible Engineering: Technology and Territoriality on Canal Du Midi* (Princeton, NJ and Oxford, UK: Princeton University Press, 2009), 221.

17 Cambridge University Physics Society, 'Prof. Sir Tejinder Virdee'.

18 He emphasized this point, too, in Virdee, 'The Long Road to the Higgs Boson'.

19 Steve Jobs said admiringly of his craftsman stepfather: "He loved doing things right. He even cared about the look of the parts you couldn't see." Quoted in: Walter Isaacson, *Steve Jobs* (New York, London and Toronto: Simon & Schuster, 2013), 6.

20 Davis Baird, *Thing Knowledge: A Philosophy of Scientific Instruments* (Berkeley, Los Angeles, CA, and London: University of California Press, 2004), 5.

21 Pamela Long, *Artisan/Practitioners and the Rise of New Sciences 1400–1600* (Corvallis, OR: Oregon State University Press, 2011 and 2014).

22 Jenny Uglow, *Lunar Men: The Friends Who Made the Future 1730–1810* (London: Faber & Faber, 2002).

23 Society for Science, 'Dr. Jim Virdee (CERN) speaks at Intel International Science and Engineering Fair', June 24, 2009; www.youtube.com/watch?v=071f_tU_nzQ (accessed August 8, 2019).

24 As quoted in David Brewster, *Memoirs of the Life, Writings, and Discoveries of Sir Isaac Newton: Volume 2* (1st ed. 1853); available at https://archive.org/stream/memoirslifewrit01brewgoog/memoirslifewrit01brewgoog_djvu.txt

CONCLUSION

The immigrant imperative – sharing and contributing for the common good

Every advance in culture commences, so to speak, with a new period of wandering.
Carl Bucher, 'Industrial Evolution', 1901[1]

...with a new period of migration and movement in populations... 'the cake of custom'
is broken and the individual is freed for new enterprises and for new associations.
Robert Ezra Park, "On Human Migration", 1928[2]

The potency of migration: movement capital catalyzed and creativity unleashed

Migration frees you "from earthly laws"[3] – so said border-crossing architect Zaha Hadid (1950–2016). She was born in Iraq, went to boarding school briefly in England, and studied as an undergraduate at the American University in Beirut, Lebanon. She moved to London for graduate studies at the Architectural Association, and made London her home for the rest of her life. She was also a woman of color. Art critic and curator Achim Borchardt-Hume described Hadid as "a border walker between different cultures from the very beginning".[4] Hadid was adamant about the liberating aspect of displacement though cognizant of its costs. People who have migrated "don't have to live in the past... and can invent the new", she said, and:

> For people who are displaced, that displacement actually gives you enormous freedom,
> but you also pay a price [my emphasis]. People don't know why you are behaving
> in a certain way, because you are nuts, or because you are a woman, or a for-
> eigner or whatever. But it does give you freedom because you don't have to
> abide by certain rules. I find displacement very liberating...[5]

This is a point of view echoed by Noubar Afeyan, celebrated as the CEO and founder of the biotech company involved in the development of the Moderna coronavirus vaccine: that his lived experience as a multiple-migrant itself underpins the ability to innovate:

> Uprooting, re-routing I think is very much at the core of what innovation is about. I have come to think over the last few years that innovation is a form of intellectual immigration… You have to kind of escape the intellectual gravity of expertise and be able to dare to look on the other side and ask if there could be another reality.[6]

The movers and makers on whom this book focuses are, above all, resilient in times of uncertainty and can deal with complexity – and even hyper-complexity – because they have had to make their lives in new terrains of disequilibrium and dislocation each and every time they have moved. But they have gained, not lost, from this disorder: their resilience has much in common with an antifragile sensibility,[7] a way of being which does not seek equilibrium but, rather, thrives in fluid conditions of dissonance.

The creative people that I write about and their forebears have not only survived their multiple movements but each transformation of their lives has added value. Some are explicitly grateful that their great-grandparents, grandparents and parents took the risk to migrate. They say that migration has enhanced their movement capital. They take succor from their movement legacy and attribute their risk-taking capabilities to their forefathers and mothers: if their grandparents showed such courage, then, as their progeny, they can take a higher level of risk in their own creative work.

What we learn from the people I am writing about is that movement can enhance creativity and innovation and catalyze collaboration and sharing of knowledge and resources. This is the story of many people who move to new countries. It has resonances with the making of the United States, whose earlier immigrants, skilled artisans in different domains of work, created the country that has produced more cutting-edge inventions than any other. These immigrants of old instituted new ways of doing and making and crafting, including what Richard Sennett calls "the craft of cooperation". This social skill of cooperation, making and doing things collaboratively in a sharing, dialogic way, engenders the art of negotiating and building dialogue among a diverse group of people.

The people I spoke to are also technically sophisticated and knowledgeable in deep, expansive ways. They are makers whose technical expertise has evolved and advanced with each migration. They are making a big impact in the multifold worlds of science, technology, art, architecture, music, and beyond, as makers who have been able to translate their skills into modern twenty-first-century technical capital.

They combine their technical expertise with a deeply rooted aesthetic of sharing and collaboration with the world at large, a defining feature of their creativity and *modus vivendi* and *modus operandi*. They are in synch with the currents of our times, which are about open-source technology, the Free Souls movement, participative pedagogy and sharism.[8] They are distributors and contributors who give without expectation of reciprocity and pass on the knowledge that they command. They break down knowledge hierarchies and generously share the expertise which they possess, an open-source, free-licensing strategy which has much in common with many digital domains and helps to build a creative commons.

What can be concluded from the case studies I have presented is that immigrants make an enormous contribution to the countries in which they live, which not only benefits local residents, the non-movers, but also benefits the world at large. How foolish, then, how self-defeating, is the venomous discourse of our times about immigration, the politically charged and fear-inducing rhetoric about building walls and policing borders, the anxieties and nervousness about "foreigners and immigrants".

Risk-taking and resilience: the moxie of the multiply migrant

None of the people I write about began life in the mainstream nor have their lives and creativity been undergirded by status quo power. As migrants or the children of migrants, they were all outsiders to the domains in which they now create and work. They possess what I have called "movement capital", in particular an ever-present resilience, a product of the earlier disruption, but which has further evolved into an expertise in dealing with complexity, with deeply liquid terrains of uncertainty in which, as Thomas Friedman reminds us, nothing is given and, "you have to make it on your own… You have to go and earn your place in the world".[9]

The movers and makers I write about have had to rely on their own resources and skills to construct their lives, building their community infrastructure in inclusive and collaborative ways, often from scratch. They possess sophisticated social skills and a cultural dexterity with which they manage their minority status, which have progressively evolved at each stage as they deal with disequilibrium on a quotidian basis. The more they have moved, the better they have been able to hone all their skills – cultural, technical, economic and technological – in dissonant terrains.

Despite the disruption and disorder created through movement, after the absorption of the initial shock, it catalyzes the mover's ability to work, improvising new frames of understanding often in defiance of the categories left behind in older sites. Leaving familiar terrains can be traumatizing but also liberating. Away from a homeland setting bounded by centuries-old caste or class hierarchies of command and establishment power circuits, creativity can flourish in more dynamic ways. Such experiences of disruption facilitate the creation of the new based on the new rather than the old. Singer-songwriter Jay Sean and music producer Rishi Rich's music falls into precisely this category of antifragility – things that gain strength from disorder. Both Jay and Rishi are not just soft tinkerers. They are both hardcore radical experimenters and discoverers of new paths.

Both they and the other creative agents I write about had to make their own paths and to believe in themselves regardless of the terrain because they were doing things previously unknown to them – but they are aggressive, combative combiners of multiple forms, melding and welding the old and new in their own creative fusions. This coalescing and merging of hybrid forms, the need to grow along new paths, is all the time craved and found. This is the creative agents' strength, emerging from struggle and requiring the courage to persist and adhere to their versions and visions of creativity. This is movers' and makers' migration advantage: movement makes the capital they carry with them from their home countries even more elastic and plastic and ever more durable. Traveling new paths facilitates new combinations, organically formed and rendered. Moving away from the sites in which they were initially formed, separated from the soils of familiarity and primary socialization, compels makers to create in sites of disorder, where their classificatory frames of origin are disturbed and disrupted. In a way, disorder is good for the creators because it allows their creativity to flourish in different sites, to breathe fresh air and grow in new directions in unfamiliar – possibly more fertile – terrains. The durability of their capital combined with its supreme adaptability and elasticity in responding to new situations is enhanced further by each new movement where it finds a new life, unleashing a resilient force unrestricted by unchanging, rule-bound networks of power and social capital.

As I was writing this, I heard Sheryl Sandberg, chief operating officer at Facebook, describe her Jewish grandmother's experience of migration from Eastern Europe with her three young children in steerage, with a paucity of possessions and having to beg food and water from upper-class passengers.[10] She said she has studied resilience since her husband died in 2015 and thinks of her grandmother's ability to survive across the ocean journey from Eastern Europe, how this resilience of an earlier generation has been built upon further both individually and collectively by the generations that have followed. This inheritance of resilience and risk-taking with miniscule resources, a way of being in the world, is so resonant with the movers and makers I am writing about.

As I mentioned earlier, the creative agents in this book not only honor and admire their forebears for having migrated, often more than once, with few resources and into domains of complete unfamiliarity, but also take succor from the risk-taking of earlier generations; they explicitly attribute their own daring and courage to the audacity of earlier risk-takers. Jasleen Kaur, the artist, says her great-grandfather is the "flame that burns in her" and which her creativity encodes and renders. Suneet Singh Tuli, the leading educational entrepreneur and co-inventor of the low-cost handheld computer, states explicitly that his globally influential technological invention would not have been possible in India where he was born: his father's migration to Iran first and then to Canada opened the opportunity structures and helped make him a transformative force in bringing computing powers to the billions.

These earlier, often perilous, journeys into new lands by the older generations are the source codes and fonts of the present generation's innovative and creative ventures – all of which have been executed in the face of hostility and antag-onism, and always against the conventions of the status quo. Their risk-taking is translated into technically and technologically sophisticated projects, in fact super-complex scientific endeavors, innovative architecture, arts, music, and much more as I have described throughout the book. The risk-taking inheritance, the moxie of generations past, endures and thrives and generates new modes of resilience and new maker expertise, a reworking of older capital.

Maker skills and aesthetics

The movers and makers I describe, progeny of earlier generations of movers and makers, already had artisanal and craft skills honed and advanced generationally with each movement, entering into more sophisticated technical realms, catalyzed by movement to new sites.

Each generation has benefited the economy into which they have settled while advancing their own skills – as in the case of making canals in the Punjab, constructing railways in East Africa, and the infrastructure of other British colonies in Asia. They had ancient maker skills acquired over many millennia, skills which were then professionalized, as I outlined earlier, in institutions such as Mayo College in Punjab established by nineteenth-century British colonial agent John Kipling for training in traditional arts and crafts.

These ancient technical and maker skills have been taken in new directions in the current generation, for example in the making at CERN of the hugely daring scientific instrument, the Compact Muon Solenoid, by physicist Tejinder Singh Virdee; the translation of traditional Punjabi harvest songs into internation-ally popular dance music by means of Kuljit Bhamra and Rishi Rich's digital sound engineering; the designing of iconic European buildings by Amarjit Kalsi; the making and marketing of a handheld computer affordable by the masses by Suneet Singh Tuli; and in the redefinition of British art by Jasleen Kaur, whose work facilitates border-crossing conversations, the Singh Twins, who rework the Indian miniature tradition to tell contemporary stories about Britain and its place in the world, and Bhajan Hunjan, who has experimented boldly with the use of new materials in public art.

They are an example of talent and expertise from the margins which has flourished, in fact, has been catalyzed within professionalizing institutions of higher education, made possible through movement into more open opportunity structures. Formal study has advanced their epistemic (mind) knowledge in com-bination with their inherited techne (hand) skills and made them thinker/makers, sharing much in common with the makers and technical revolutionaries of the past and also the present. The contemporary generations have thus converted their forebears' craft and maker skills into sophisticated maker capital – technical and technological – of the twenty-first century, capital that is defrayed in many cultural and social zones for the common good.

All of them are also collaborators par excellence and work collectively and collaboratively in complex teams which have a diversity of expertise and people of a range of temperaments, ethnicities and nationalities to render their creativity. They replicate the pioneering, community-crafting aesthetic of their forebears who worked collaboratively to build their community infrastructure, both physical and social, perfectly in tune with the twenty-first-century notion that "creativity is a collaborative process".[11]

Sharing and contributing for the common good

The creative people I write about and the migrant communities that produced them contribute enormously to society with their knowledge and expertise, with all of the movement and maker capital which they share and want the world to benefit from, without expecting a return. They also have highly developed abilities to work and collaborate in complex teams with a range of expertise and diversity of people.

They translate their skills and inheritances into new directions in an open system which is inviting. Kuljit Bhamra represents the sharing and distributive aesthetic supremely well through his use of digital technology, his invention of the world's first electronic tabla and a standardized notation system for music for the tabla so that learning to play the instrument is accessible to all. He and the other creative people I write about are not into reproducing privilege and keeping that privilege for themselves by hoarding their expertise and by patrolling the boundaries of their maker skills to prevent sharing and entry into their domains of knowledge power. They are bridge builders who collaborate and make connections, generating further social and technical capital, a capital they are transferring by digital means, the tools of knowledge distribution of the contemporary period, as well as via traditional channels. They make an impact not to enrich themselves financially or to lead a hedonistic lifestyle, but to influence through their own particular expertise.

By capturing the new as it emerges, they dent knowledge hierarchies and closed systems of knowledge transmission. They make ideas and knowledge accessible to people who are not part of their own group, for the world at large to absorb and learn from; they disseminate and share what they know and what they have. They thus democratize knowledge, sharing it to deepen and extend knowledge domains in an open-source, creative-commons way. They are deeply distributive and contributive in the ways in which they collaborate with others, sharing what they know to make the world a better place for the common good of humanity. In this way, the movers and makers I write about foster precisely that "sense of connectedness"[12] and the "social ties"[13] that commentators such as academics Robert Reich and Robert Putnam identify as missing or weakening in contemporary society. This propensity to collaborate and to share is undergirded by the Sikh religious and cultural ideology which engenders this powerfully – *vand kay shako, sarbhat dha bhalla and kaam sikho tay kaam sikhayo* (share with all, seeking good for all and learn tasks and skills and teach them) – that is to say, give generously of your time, knowledge, skills and resources. Such an outlook is powerfully reminiscent of the ethic of the pioneers of the Northwest Territories as summed up by McCullough towards the end of his account of their lives:

> But then it can be said, too, that those others of the foremost pioneers of [the town of] Marietta had finished their work, each in his or her own way, and no matter the adversities to be faced, propelled as they were by high worthy purpose. They accomplished what they had set out to do not for money, not for possessions or fame, but to advance the quality and opportunities of life – to propel as best as they could the American ideals.[14]

Sharism catalyzes the building of social capital, the defining ethos of the migrant communities and their creative progeny. Pioneering traditions of cooperation, collaboration, and an open and inclusive *modus operandi* are the source codes of the contemporary generation of movers and makers' innovative and distributive creativity, now transnationalized. In the pioneering context, skills and resources had to be shared and distributed through a diasporic creative commons in order to survive in new settings in which the infrastructure was non-existent and had to be established, a sharing that was "mind expanding"[15] and also developed technical skills and the sensibilities of cooperation,[16] embodying Rutger Bregman's beliefs about the goodness of human beings.[17] This is not at all the same capital as that transferred by migrants who are already part of an elite and are supremely influential; the elite's mechanisms of exclusion and monopolized capital endure and have supreme powers of reproduction.[18] However, in the twenty-first century, a new group is also entering their domains of knowledge and power through mindsets and mechanisms that are diametrically opposed to the values of the elite.

The enduring value of immigrants

As the anti-migrant political and popular discourse of the destination countries becomes ever yet more virulent, we learn from Sonia Shah[19] that the "migration instinct" and "life on the move"[20] are not anomalous but "a force of nature, rooted in biology and history along with that of scores of other wild species with whom we share this changing planet".[21] Indeed, the world has been moving continuously since time immemorial despite the misconception of being anchored in an invariant sedentary past. Yet, it is also the case, as recent statistics show, that only a tiny proportion of the world's population – 3.3 per cent – actually leave the locations of their birth to take the risk of migration and move to new sites[22] – thus countering the alarmist and toxic rhetoric about keeping immigrants out, which abounds in political discourse across the world. The majority of the world does not move or want to migrate beyond national borders, even though movement has been continuous historically and biologically. At the same time, economists of differing ideologies and business people are loudly enthusiastic about the benefits of migration, for both individuals and national economies, sending and recipient.[23]

Yet, most people in the world refrain from leaving their countries of birth and thus do not possess the movement capital I have referred to throughout the book. Most people live in terrains of familiarity, locality, kinship, friendship, modes of social interaction conducive to conviviality. They stay put within national borders, often regardless of economic uncertainty and a fragile future, and do not risk migration to a new, unfamiliar site. Most of the world does not want to conduct their lives in economies of unfamiliarity and dissonance which migration into new terrains necessarily entails, contexts in which you must grope to find your way without familiar family networks and in which uncertainty and disruption has to be taken for granted, the only mode of operating.

However, enduring the volatility and disruption of migration catalyzes thinking through new frames as older ones are left behind. I suggest that movement and disorder can facilitate, ignite and catalyze creative powers, in a way that immobility in the site of birth and long-term entrenched settlement does not. In these sites, the same hierarchies reign supreme, as do long-established classificatory frames. This is not to say that there are never changes and volatility in sites where people stay put and few new people arrive, but that the ability to think of and bring in the new can increase exponentially when you are uprooted from everything that is familiar and faced instead with dissonance and disorder. In unfamiliar terrains, the mover is forced to grow because they no longer have the power structures of origin to buttress familial and familiar forces of socialization.

The people I am writing about live fruitfully in an immensely complex world. They are at ease and comfortable with terrains of hyper-complexity; faced with fluid complexity, they move on further, dynamically navigating contending currents as they render themselves visible. As Robert Park, cited above and at the beginning of this book, observed in 1928, every advance in culture commences with movement. My story shows that immigration and migrants can contribute significantly to innovation and change of the recipient country in any domain. It is a message of hope and an argument against some of the prevalent anti-immigrant themes of political discourse.

Movement across international borders is capital-enhancing: it advances the existing collective expertise that has been built up and has endured across the generations. The craft and technical skills of the people I am writing about have advanced with each migration and take on a new lease of life in new directions – as indeed they do for so many immigrant groups. Mobile people add to the cultures and economies which they enter, enhancing them through the expertise they bring, which they further sophisticate and render for the general benefit: movement catalyzes creativity and innovation. This is the point made by Harvard professor Ricardo Hausmann when he says:

> I study how places become good at different things, and how the things that they're good at evolve. And what I find is that they tend to diversify

into things that are somewhat related, but somewhat more complex or more advanced. And in the process of diversifying, they rely enormously on talent *that came from the outside...* [my emphasis] Genius is not really about individuals. It's really about a collective. It's about a community of practice.[24]

The people whose creativity and life narratives I describe are making significant contributions to the world in both large and small ways – in architecture, painting, sculpture, music, science and technology; and through their style of giving and generosity. Their interventions are mostly invisible in a world in which migrants are denigrated, and in especially venomous ways at present. But such people add hugely to the contexts into which they move, and do not subtract from them as the prevailing political discourse would have us believe – a virulent rhetoric that powerful and prominent world leaders are fueling and promoting.[25]

The cosmic fears and anxieties around immigration, abiding discourses around migrants and immigration, gain new valence and viciousness depending on the particular economic and political climate. In fact, such discourses are all politicians can actually control and manipulate for their audiences and voters. They have no control over borderless economies and transnational financial markets in which there are trillion-dollar money transactions and flows every minute, which cannot be controlled by any single head of state or national government. But the discourse of immigration is one that "enfeebled" politicians, in contexts of "untame-able uncertainty" and "liquid" times,[26] fluid terrains that they cannot command, can choose to manipulate. They both promote and exploit the anxiety and nervousness about immigration to the hilt.

Over and above the people I write about in my case studies, the award-winning Nishkam Swat Team (the Sikh Welfare and Awareness Team), who are described as "The Street Food Servants", feed the homeless in more than twenty-one locations across the UK, twenty-eight times a week.[27] The organizers are all volunteers who have full-time jobs and who gather the materials and distribute hot meals, and provide clothes, blankets and other resources. Many of them, including Randeep Lall, who set the charity up in 2012, are from the same multiply migrant backgrounds and share the same migration trajectory as those I write about in my case studies. They share the principle of open and generous reciprocity, without expectation of material returns or rewards; the reward for them is a symbolic one, a nebulous expectation of good deeds that beget goodness for humanity, the common good for the world at large. In 2019, Nishkam Swat launched an additional project, offering support and guidance to anyone suffering from or affected by substance addiction.[28] The group's interventions contribute and distribute mobilized powerful bridge-building capital that connects people regardless of social divisions and hierarchies of race, class, ethnicity and religion, underpinned by their ethos of *vand kay shakho* (share what you have).

Such distributive sensibilities are something the world needs to pay attention to. Migration and migrants are good for every economy of the world they enter creatively, innovatively, dialogically, with generosity, with deeply rooted collaborative and distributive sensibilities that give open-heartedly to the world at large. They do this with openness and a profound acceptance of hyper-diversity and the dialogic ability to navigate liquid worlds of uncertainty, fragility and disequilibrium, the norm for twenty-first-century global landscapes.

My friend Les Back of old, the eminent Professor at Goldsmiths, University of London, said when I started this book almost a decade ago that my story was about the making of "corrugated iron sheet temples by pioneer migrants in late nineteenth-century East Africa". What until then I had thought was simply a further installment in the story of the new cultural producers from the diaspora was in fact about a crowd-sourcing and sharing of expertise and resources, a style of working, making and creating reproduced by the progeny of those temple-builders and which thrives today.

My book, many years later, is now a story about the progeny of these pioneer makers and builders of the past, people who are innovatively creative and have enormous powers of recontextualization and reimagination in rendering their inherited and durable capital. I have interrogated a contemporary rendition of technical and cultural legacies in many domains, a huge diversity of interventions and impacts. It is a powerful creativity that is largely invisible to the world and yet defines many twenty-first-century creative scientific and artistic landscapes.

Notes

1 Carl Bucher, *Industrial Evolution*, 1901, cited in Park, 'Human Migration and the Marginal Man'.
2 Robert Ezra Park, 'Human Migration and the Marginal Man', in *The American Journal of Sociology*, Vol. 33, No. 6 (May 1928): 881–893. Robert Park was the founding sociologist of the Chicago School.
3 Zaha Hadid, in conversation about Suprematism with Achim Borchardt-Hume, head of exhibitions at Tate Modern and curator of the Malevich exhibition, October 30, 2014.
4 Hadid, in conversation.
5 Hadid, in conversation.
6 Noubar Afeyan, interview with Walter Isaacson on *Amanpour & Co.*, November 20, 2020.
7 Nassim Nicholas Taleb, *Antifragile: Things that Gain from Disorder* (USA: Random House, 2012).
8 Isaac Mao, 'Sharism: A Mind Revolution, Freesouls Essays', https://freesouls.cc/essays/07-isaac-mao-sharism.html (accessed August 6, 2019); Howard Rheingold, *Smart Mobs: The Next Social Revolution* (New York: Basic Books, 2003).
9 Thomas Friedman and Michael Mandelbaum, *That Used To Be Us: What Went Wrong with America* (New York: Picador, 2012).
10 PBS, ' Season 5, Episode 4: Dreaming of a New Land', February 2, 2019; www.pbs.org/weta/finding-your-roots/about/meet-guests/sherylsandberg/ (accessed August 8, 2019).
11 Walter Isaacson, *The Innovators: How a Group of Hackers, Geniuses, and Geeks Created the Digital Revolution* (New York, London and Toronto: Simon & Schuster, 2014), 479.
12 Robert Reich, *The Common Good* (New York: Alfred A. Knopf, 2018), 4.
13 Robert D. Putnam, *Bowling Alone: The Collapse and Revival of American Community* (New York: Simon & Schuster, 2000), 19.

14 David McCullough, *The Pioneers: The Heroic Story of the Settlers Who Brought the American Ideal West* (New York: Simon & Schuster, 2019), 258.

15 Rheingold, *Smart Mobs*.

16 Richard Sennett, *Together: The Rituals, Pleasures and Politics of Cooperation* (New Haven and London: Yale University Press, 2012).

17 Rutger Bregman, *Humankind: A Hopeful History* (New York, Boston, MA and London: Little, Brown and Company, 2020). Being generous and collaborative, giving to the world, Bregman says: "That's a truth as old as time. Because, like all the best things in life, the more you give, the more you have", p. 378.

18 For an account of one such elite, see Ajantha Subramaniam, 'Recovering Caste Privilege: The Politics of Meritocracy at the Indian Institutes of Technology in New Subaltern Politics', in *New Subaltern Politics: Reconceptualizing Hegemony and Resistance in Contemporary India*, ed. Alf Gunvald Nilsen and Srila Roy (Oxford Scholarship Online, 2015); 'Making Merit: The Indian Institutes of Technology and the Social Life of Caste', *Comparative Study of Society and History* (2015), 291–322.

19 Sonia Shah, *The Next Great Migration: The Beauty and Terror of Life on the Move* (New York: Bloomsbury Publishing, 2020).

20 Shah, *The Next Great Migration*, 30.

21 Shah, *The Next Great Migration*, 282.

22 Phillip Connor, 'International migration: Key findings from the U.S., Europe and the world', *Pew Research Center*, December 15, 2016: "Overall, international migrants make up to 3.3% of the world's population today." www.pewresearch.org/fact-tank/2016/12/15/international-migration-key-findings-from-the-u-s-europe-and-the-world/ (accessed August 8, 2019).

23 Jonathan Woetzel et al., 'Global migration's impact and opportunity', *McKinsey Global Institute Report*, November 2016: "… migrants make up just 3.4 percent of the world's population, but MGI's research finds that they contribute nearly 10 percent of global GDP. They contributed roughly $6.7 trillion to global GDP in 2015—some $3 trillion more than they would have produced in their origin countries. Developed nations realize more than 90 percent of this effect." www.mckinsey.com/featured-insights/employment-and-growth/global-migrations-impact-and-opportunity (accessed August 8, 2019); Devon Van Houten Maldonado, 'Why migrants are good for the Global economy', *The Daily Dose*, April 13, 2018: "Populists, nationalists and xenophobes have it all wrong when it comes to immigration… decades of research show that more immigration, not less, creates prosperity for wealthy nationals and that that plus side of people flow extends to non-immigrants… immigrants are catalysts for innovation, resulting in more patents per capita." www.ozy.com/acumen/why-migrants-are-good-for-the-global-economy/86064 (accessed August 8, 2019); Tim Cook, CEO of Apple, interviewed by Christiane Amanpour, said that the United States needs immigrants to discover "the next big thing that creates more jobs" and that "…the US needs large immigration to continue to grow…. there are lots of people with significant skills coming into this country that add to GDP – and not only from a humanity point of view, which I feel deeply – but from a sheer business point of view, immigration is adding to the GDP"; www.psbs.org/video/apple-ceo-tim-cook-8bi76d/ (accessed August 8, 2019). Cf William R. Kerr, Professor of Business Administration at Harvard Business School: "…immigrants are reshaping the geography of innovation in America – one in every eleven US patents is developed today by a Chinese or Indian inventor living in the San Franciso Bay area", *The Gift of Global Talent* (Stanford, CA: Stanford Business School, 2018), 8.

24 Ricardo Hausmann, in discussion with Paul Solman and Eric Weiner, January 2016, www.pbs.org/newshour/show/hotbeds-of-genius-and-innovation-depend-on-these-key-ingredients#transcript (accessed August 6, 2019).

25 See, for example, Stuart Anderson, 'Trump immigration plan may throw 4 million people off immigrant waiting lists', *Forbes*, May 16, 2019; www.forbes.com/sites/stuartanderson/2019/05/16/trump-immigration-plan-may-throw-4-million-people-off-immigrant-waiting-lists/#7537db8b6943 (accessed August 6, 2019); Matthew d'Ancona, 'Let's be honest about what's really driving Brexit: Bigotry', *The Guardian*, December 2, 2018; www.theguardian.com/commentisfree/2018/dec/02/honest-brexit-bigotry-ugly-chapter-history (accessed August 8, 2019).

26 Zygmunt Bauman, *A Chronicle of Crisis: 2011–2016* (Falkensee, Germany: Social Europe Edition, 2017).

27 Tim Adams, 'OFM Awards 2018: Outstanding achievement – Nishkam Swat', *The Guardian*, October 22, 2018.

28 Nishkam Swat, 'About our projects', http://swatlondon.com/projects.html (accessed August 8, 2019).

BIBLIOGRAPHY

Aiyar, Sana. *Indians in Kenya: The Politics of the Diaspora*. Cambridge, MA: Harvard University Press, 2015.

Anderson, Chris. *Makers: The New Industrial Revolution*. New York: Crown Business, 2012.

Architectural Association. *Spirit and Invention*. London: London Architectural Association, 1982.

Ata-Ullah, Naazish. 'Stylistic Hybridity and Colonial Art and Design Education: A Wooden Carved Screen by Ram Singh'. In *Colonialism and the Object: Empire, Material Culture and the Museum*, ed. Tim Barringer and Tom Flynn. London: Routledge, 1998.

Baird, Davis. *Thing Knowledge: A Philosophy of Scientific Instruments*. Berkeley, CA, Los Angeles, and London: University of California Press, 2004.

Bauman, Zygmunt. *A Chronicle of Crisis 2011–2016*. Falkensee, Germany: Social Europe Edition, 2017.

Bauman, Zygmunt. *Strangers at Our Door*. Cambridge, UK: Polity, 2016.

Bauman, Zygmunt. *Liquid Times: Living in an Age of Uncertainty*. Cambridge, UK: Polity, 2007.

Bauman, Zygmunt. *Liquid Modernity*. Cambridge, UK: Polity, 2000.

Benkler, Yochai. 'The Wealth of Networks: How Social Production Transforms Markets and Freedom'. In *Journal of Media Economics*, Vol. 20, No. 2 (May 2007): 161–165.

Bernstein, Basil. *Pedagogy, Symbolic Control and Identity: Theory, Research and Critique*. Lanham, MD and Oxford, UK: Rowman and Littlefield Publishers Inc, 1996, 2000.

Bhachu, Parminder. 'Twice Migrants and Multiple Migrants'. In *The Wiley Blackwell Encyclopedia on Race, Ethnicity and Nationalism*, ed. Professor John Stone, Dennis Rutledge, Anthony Smith, and Polly Rizova. Hoboken, NJ: Wiley Smith Publishers, 2015.

Bhachu, Parminder. 'The Invisibility of Diasporic Cultural and Multiple Migrant Creativity'. In *Mutuality: Anthropology's Changing Engagement*, ed. Roger Sanjek. Philadelphia, PA: Penn University Press, 2014.

Bhachu, Parminder. *Dangerous Designs: Asian Women Fashion the Diaspora Economies*. London: Routledge, 2004.

Bhachu, Parminder. 'Identities Constructed & Reconstructed: Representations of Asian Women in Britain'. In *Migrant Women: Crossing Boundaries and Changing Identities*, ed. Gina Buijs. Oxford, UK and New York: Berg Publishers Limited, 1993.

Bhachu, Parminder. 'East African Sikh Settlers in Britain. Twice versus Direct Migrants'. In *The Modern Western Diaspora*, ed. Ceri Peach, Steve Vertovec, and Colin Clarke. Delhi: Oxford University Press, 1991.

Bhachu, Parminder. *Twice Migrants: East African Sikh Settlers in Britain*. London: Tavistock Publications, 1984.

Blixen, Karen. *Out of Africa*. 1937. International edition. Middlesex: Penguin Modern Classics, 1985.

Bourdieu, Pierre. 'The Forms of Capital'. In *Handbook of Theory of Research for the Sociology of Education*, ed. John G. Richardson. Westport, CT: Greenwood, 1986.

Bourdieu, Pierre. 'The Production of Belief: Contributions to an Economy of Symbolic Goods'. In *The Field of Cultural Production*, Pierre Bourdieu and ed. Randal Richardson. Westport, CT: Greenwood, 1986.

Bregman, Rutger. *Humankind: A Hopeful History*. New York, Boston, MA and London: Little, Brown and Company, 2020.

Byatt, A. S. *Peacock & Vine: On William Morris and Mariano Fortuny*. New York: Knopf Publishing Group, 2016.

Cashin, Sheryll. *Loving: Interracial Intimacy in America and the Threat to White Supremacy*. Boston, MA: Beacon Press, 2017.

Chandra, Vikram. *Geek Sublime: The Beauty of Code and the Code of Beauty*. Minneapolis, MN: Graywolf Press, 2014.

Conduitt, John. Memorandum, 31 August 1726, Keynes MS 130.10. www.newtonproject. ox.ac.uk/view/texts/diplomatic/THEM00172 (accessed December 1, 2020).

Durrani, Nazmi, *Liberating Minds, Restoring Kenyan History: Anti-Imperialist Resistance by Progressive South Asian Kenyans 1884–1965*. Nairobi: Vita Books, 2017.

Feingold, Henry. 'Investing in Themselves: The Harvard Case and the Origins of the Third American-Jewish Commercial Elite'. In *American Journal of Jewish History*, Vol. 77, No. 4 (June 1988): 530–553.

Florida, Richard. 'America's Looming Creativity Crisis'. In *Harvard Business Review*, October 1, 2004.

Friedman, Thomas and Mandelbaum, Michael. *That Used To Be Us: What Went Wrong with America*. New York: Picador, 2012.

Gladwell, Malcolm. *The Outliers: The Story of Success*. New York: Little, Brown and Company, 2008.

Guest, Robert. *Borderless Economics: Chinese Sea Turtles, Indian Fridges and the New Fruits of Global Capitalism*. New York: Palgrave Macmillan, 2013.

Hannerz, Ulf. 'Cosmopolitans and Locals in World Culture'. In *Global Culture: Nationalism, Globalization and Modernity'*, ed. Mike Featherstone. London, Thousand Oaks, CA and Delhi: Sage Publications, 1990.

Hochschild, Arlie Russell. *Strangers in Their Own Land: Anger and Mourning on the American Right*. New York: The New Press, 2016.

Isaacson, Walter. *The Innovators: How a Group of Hackers, Geniuses, and Geeks Created the Digital Revolution*. New York, London and Toronto: Simon & Schuster, 2014.

Isaacson, Walter. *Steve Jobs*. New York, London and Toronto: Simon & Schuster, 2013.

Katz, Lawrence. 'Get a Liberal Arts B.A., Not a Business B.A., for the Coming Artisan Economy'. *PBS Newshour Making Sen$e*. July 14, 2014; www.pbs.org/newshour/nation/get-a-liberal-arts-b-a-not-a-business-b-a-for-the-coming-artisan-economy (accessed August 8, 2019).

Kean, Danuta and Larson, Mel. *Centre Stage: The Pipelines of BAME Talent*. London: Andrew Lloyd Webber Foundation, 2017; http://blacktheatrelive.co.uk/media/files/centre-stage-the-pipeline-of-bame-talent%281%29.pdf (accessed 1 December 2020).

Kerr, William R. *The Gift of Global Talent: How Migration Shapes Business, Economy and Society*. Stanford, CA: Stanford Business Books, 2018.

Korn, Peter. *Why We Make Things and Why It Matters: The Education of a Craftsman*. Dorking, UK: Square Peg, 2013.

Kureishi, Hanif. *The Word and the Bomb*. London: Faber & Faber, 2005.

Lessig, Lawrence. *Free Culture: The Nature and Future of Creativity*. New York: Penguin Books, 2005.

Lévi-Strauss, Claude. *The Savage Mind*. Chicago, IL: University of Chicago Press, 1962.

Light, Ivan and Bhachu, Parminder. 'California Immigrants in World Perspective'. In *Immigration and Entrepreneurship: Culture, Capital and Ethnic Networks*, ed. Ivan Light and Parminder Bhachu. Piscataway, NJ, Rutgers University: Transactions Press, 1993.

Long, Pamela. *Artisan/Practitioners and the Rise of New Sciences 1400–1600*. Corvallis, OR: Oregon State University Press, 2011 and 2014.

MacCarthy, Fiona. *Gropius: The Man who Built the Bauhaus.* Cambridge, MA: The Belknap Press of Harvard University Press, 2019.

Mao, Isaac. 'Sharism: A Mind Revolution, Freesouls Essays'. https://freesouls.cc/essays/07-isaac-mao-sharism.html (accessed August 9, 2019).

Mathur, Saloni. 'Diasporic Body Double: The Art of the Singh Twins'. In *The Art Journal*, Vol. 65, No. 2 (2006): 34–57.

McCullough, David. *The Pioneers: The Heroic Story of the Settlers Who Brought the American Ideal West*. New York: Simon & Schuster, 2019.

Mukerji, Chandra. *Impossible Engineering: Technology and Territoriality on Canal Du Midi* Princeton. Princeton, NJ and Oxford, UK: Princeton University Press, 2009.

O'Reilly, Tim. *WTF: What's The Future and Why It's Up To Us.* London: Random House Business, 2017.

Obama, Michelle. *Becoming*. New York: Penguin UK, 2018.

Park, Robert Ezra. 'Human Migration and the Marginal Man'. In *The American Journal of Sociology*, Vol. 33, No. 6 (May 1928): 881–893.

Putnam, Robert D. *Bowling Alone: The Collapse and Revival of American Community*. New York: Simon & Schuster, 2000.

Radjou, Navi, Prabhu, Jaideep and Ahuja, Simone. *Jugaad Innovation: Think Frugal, Be Flexible, Generate Breakthrough Growth*. San Francisco, CA: Jossey-Bass, 2012.

Reich, Robert B. *The Common Good*. New York: Alfred A. Knopf, 2018.

Rheingold, Howard. *Smart Mobs: The Next Social Revolution*. New York: Basic Books, 2003.

Roy, Kaushik. *War, Culture and Society in Early Modern South Asia 1740–1849*. London: Routledge, 2011.

Rusbridger, Alan. *Play It Again: An Amateur Against the Impossible*. New York: Farrar, Straus and Giroux, 2013.

Saberwal, Satish. *Mobile Men: Limits to Social Change in Urban Punjab*. 1976. Revised ed. New Delhi: Institute of Advanced Study, Shimla, in association with Manohar Publications, 1990.

Schama, Simon. *The Face of Britain: The Nation Through Its Portraits*. New York: Viking, 2015.

Schor, Juliet B. et al. 'Paradoxes of Openness and Distinction in the Sharing Economy'. In *Poetics* Vol. 54 (February 2016): 66–81.

Sennett, Richard. *Together: The Rituals, Pleasures and Politics of Cooperation*. New Haven, CT and London: Yale University Press, 2012.

Sennett, Richard. *The Craftsman*. New York: Penguin Books, 2008.

Shah, Sonia. *The Next Great Migration: The Beauty and Terror of Life on the Move*. New York: Bloomsbury Publishing, 2020.

Sharma, Harish C. *Artisans of the Punjab: A Study of Social Change in Historical Perspective 1849–1947*. New Delhi: Manohar Publishers and Distributors, 1996.

Singh Twins, The. *The Making of Liverpool: Portraits of a City by the Singh Twins*. Liverpool: Twin Studio, 2010.

Steinberg, Stephen. *The Ethnic Myth: Race, Ethnicity and Class in America*. New York: Atheneum, 1981.

Subramaniam, Ajantha. 'Making Merit: The Indian Institutes of Technology and the Social Life of Caste'. In *Comparative Study of Society and History*, Vol. 57, No. 2 (April 2015): 291–322.

Subramaniam, Ajantha. 'Recovering Caste Privilege: The Politics of Meritocracy at the Indian Institutes of Technology in New Subaltern Politics'. In *New Subaltern Politics: Reconceptualizing Hegemony and Resistance in Contemporary India*. Oxford Scholarship Online, 2015. doi:10.1093/acprof:oso/9780199457557.001.0001.

Supple, Barry. 'A Business Elite: German-Jewish Financiers in Nineteenth Century New York'. In *The Business History Review*, Vol. 31, No. 2 (Summer 1957): 143–178.

Swallow, Deborah. 'John Lockwood Kipling: A Post-Postcolonial Perspective'. In *John Lockwood Kipling: Arts and Crafts of the Punjab and London*, ed. Julius Bryant and Susan Weber. New Haven, CT and London: Yale University Press, 2017.

Taleb, Nassim Nicholas. *Antifragile: Things That Gain from Disorder*. New York: Random House: 2012.

Taleb, Nassim Nicholas. *The Black Swan*. New York and London: Random House, 2007.

Turkle, Sherry. *Life on the Screen: Identity in the Age of the Internet*. New York: Simon & Schuster, 1997.

Uglow, Jenny. *Lunar Men: The Friends Who Made the Future 1730–1810*. London: Faber & Faber, 2002.

Van Hensbergen, Gijs. *Gaudi: A Biography*. New York: Perennial, 2001.

Waitz, Theodore. *Introduction to Anthropology*. London: Longman, 1863.

Weiner, Eric. *The Geography of Genius*. New York: Simon & Schuster, 2016.

Wilson, Amrit. *Finding a Voice: Asian Women in Britain*. London: Virago, 1978.

Woetzel, Jonathan et al. 'Global Migration's Impact and Opportunity'. *McKinsey Global Institute Report*, November 2016; www.mckinsey.com/featured-insights/employment-and-growth/global-migrations-impact-and-opportunity (accessed August 8, 2019).

Zolli, Andrew and Healy, Ann Marie. *Resilience: Why Things Bounce Back*. New York: Free Press, 2012.

INDEX

Note: Page numbers in *italic* indicate figures, end of chapter notes are indicated by a letter n between page number and note number.